MINNESOTA
fish and fishing

MINNESOTA
fish and fishing

by KIT BERGH

A Practical and Tested Guide for Successful Fishing in the Land of Lakes with Complete How, When, and Where Suggestions by an Expert Fisherman.

Publishers

T. S. DENISON & COMPANY

Minneapolis

PRINTED IN THE U.S.A.
BY THE BRINGS PRESS

Library of Congress Catalog Card Number: 58-10937

TO PAT

By the lake he sat and pondered,
By the still transparent water;
Saw the sturgeon, Nehma, leaping,
Scattering drops like beads of wampum,
Saw the yellow perch, the Sahwa,
Like a sunbeam in the water,
Saw the pike, the Maskenozha,
And the herring, Okahahwis . . .

—LONGFELLOW

Contents

Introduction

It was too early for anyone but the birds and the fish to know that morning had come.

The chorus began feebly as a nuthatch and a bluejay began a short duet and a crack of half light in the east invited others to join. They awoke a squirrel far off in the hardwoods and the fisherman heard the faint chatter as he made his way through the dripping brush and sawgrass toward a sandy beach. Dangly-legged mosquitoes crowded him with their humming as he felt his way in the semi-darkness and his booted feet made a squishing in the clay.

In the shallow sandy-bottomed bay where the fisherman was bound, minnows collected just offshore and began feeding on tiny cells that pulsated in suspension like a microscopic milky way, swelling the water imperceptibly as they surged erratically along a few feet of beach, fed, and moved on. Small silver-sided fish, olive on top with fine-rayed, opaque and delicately tinted fins of yellow cream, ate with ravenous abandon as all small fish with small stomachs must feed to exist.

Mealtime was disturbed and the fisherman now on the shore heard the splash! At once he knew a hungry smallmouth was running these blackeyed minnows onto the beach. SCHOOSH! The water parted as the snout of a top-heavy fish throttled through a shower of bait-fish, driving them to refuge up on the sand again and into the air like scattering straws in a wild wind.

This the fisherman had seen before and hoped to see again. Upon watching the play he became shaken and unsure and this, too, he had known before. Quickly he searched for a feather popper and snapped it to his line. Alone in the twilight of a new day he cast to an explosion at his left. In midair he changed his mind as another bass surfaced at his feet. But the lure settled quietly and sent out rings to overtake those the first fish had made. The bass spent a scant fraction of a second studying the lure and then glided toward the pearl underside of the popper. He catapulted from the fiery water in the pink dawn and charged away, making the reel give line grudgingly with a bitter rasping sound. The fish jumped again—throwing rubies into the air. At last it was nearly done and the angler, with thumb and forefinger, hefted the heavy fish in the yellowing light and the three were silent together for a moment—the fisherman, the bass and the Minnesota morning.

As he stood marveling at the living thing he held between his fingers the nostalgia of other fish and places came to him: the bitter cold mornings by the Knife River when steelheads ran in the early spring runoff, the frenzied run of his first big trout heading downstream, the sudden slack line and queer feeling of losing a strong steelhead as he tried to follow it over jagged rocks in the frigid water. There was the giant largemouth that gleamed like a jewel in the morning sun at Minnetonka, bright against the shiny wet reeds, towering in the summer sky before shaking itself free.

Now he held a great amber-green pike by the eyes and it was midday among a hundred islands of Lac La Croix. These were memories of days a few summers past, but they were not his early recollections.

He recalled that he had fished Minnesota waters for several years before he'd learned to find different species, how to catch some of them and something about the best tackle designed for the job. But he knew that man, in his limited time on earth, devotes a very small part of his short span at fishing; there wasn't time to find the answers to every phase of fishing by himself. A man cannot acquire, in a lifetime of spaced trips to the water, sufficient knowledge to overcome the advantages of evolution and interrelating factors of aquatic partnerships between fish and their environment. He must combine forces and form a partnership with fishermen who have kept an honest record of their successes and failures; compared notes and tried to answer questions prompted by both. There had been other anglers that he had shared experiences with on the dock and by the evening fire—vacation and native anglers whose failures and successes on the water added up to his own.

He walked up the gentle bank with the mottled fish and laid it carefully on a hummock of sawgrass, as carefully as a mother would lay an infant in its cradle, because this fish was the brainchild born of his efforts to learn exact fishing. He was pleased with the result of his study.

Fishermen have groped for better ways to take fish for many years. At times they learned from others, but more often they mimeographed the same answers and stacked them away. The angler goes as far as his limited time permits, gleaning a few crumbs from fellow fishermen but invariably dead-ending within a stone's throw of the others.

This book has been written in the hope that it will help the average weekend angler who, in spite of his love of fishing, must devote time to his job and family, mow the lawn and paint the house, when he'd like to be out fishing. It's for fishermen who come from Kansas, Tennessee and Illinois to fish Minnesota's thousands of lakes and hundreds of streams and rivers. It has been written for those who want to get to the fish and the fishing without a lot of wasted time and expense. Assuming that he has acquired average skill with his tackle, this book should help him find the fish he prefers to catch, show him how to catch them, adding little suggestions that often spell the difference between a successful fishing jaunt and a dismal sorté from the point of view of fish caught. There is a great difference in fishing for snook among the Mangrove Islands of Florida and angling for largemouth bass among the submerged crags of Elephant Butte Lake in New Mexico. A fisherman who has fished Atlantic salmon in Nova Scotia may be in for a tricky time outwitting the golden trout of the Sierras of California. Little differences in technique are often the hallmark of angler success and at times seem to be perceived only by the fish and the individual lucky fisherman. Even in Minnesota's fishing valhalla of endless first-class fishing lakes, where Lake Superior laps her agate coast for 150 miles and great rivers hem the angler in on three sides, fish can be choosey and sophisticated, favoring one retrieve or lure one day and something entirely new the next. An angler must learn to read signs and decipher the invisible causes that make a fisherman choose right more often than he chooses wrong.

These chapters are dedicated to this premise and I believe the methods outlined here will add enjoyment to your fishing and fish to your stringer.

Because Minnesota is situated smack on top of three watersheds we have fish peculiar to all three and something like forty species that can be taken on hook and line. Many of them, considered game fish in less fortunate states, are referred to as rough fish and have no possession limits. Others, such as pan fish, have generous limits and are open the year around with a trend to longer seasons and more liberal limits on other species as well. Emphasis has long been given to walleye propagation because of the ease with which they can be reared, but fish such as muskies are getting more attention now and recent grayling introductions and trout lake reclamations attest to forward-looking fisheries' management.

While it is true a few Southern states boast year-around fishing, fish catching and fishing are not necessarily synonymous. States that have open water twelve months of the year, harbor warm water species that refuse to bite during the winter months. In Minnesota, all preferred species continue to bite well throughout the year. In fact, winter angling provides some of the best walleye and crappie action often equal to the best summer splurges.

Within the scope of my experience and that of my fishing friends who have provided helpful information and encouragement, I've tried to supply a guide that, while imperfect, gives an angler a framework within which he can begin catching fish. The major fish treated can be taken consistently in Minnesota waters and are available to every angler. They can be found in various areas and in some cases in waters of the entire state. Rare species like the paddlefish, so uncommon that odds of catching one are at least a million to one, are omitted.

I want to express my gratitude for advice by Dr. Moyle, Supervisor, Bureau of Research and Planning for the Division of Game and Fish, Minnesota Conservation Department, to biologist, John Dobbie, for photographs and technical assistance, to fisheries' biologist, Bob Schumacher, for access to files, and particular thanks to Chuck Burrows, Fisheries Research Supervisor, for proof-reading and advice, and to my friends and fellow writers who have offered encouragement, released pictures, and helped in countless other ways.

And now it would be better to let you get closer to the fishing that you, too, may someday hold a smallmouth high in the morning light and look back on fond memories of fish caught and fish lost, of battles with great pike and of trout and walleyes that will be remembered for their savor in the pan as much as for the account they gave of themselves on the end of your line.

CHAPTER I

Basic Tackle

Minnesota has a wide variety of fish species of vastly different habits and habitat. For example, brook trout search the stream bed at one time of year and feed at the surface at other times. Often they are found feeding in the middle water between, taking nymphs as they rise to the surface. During the day they haunt what is known as a hold, behind a rock or submerged snag, feeding only on what comes to them in the current. They eat caddis nymphs and grasshoppers, angleworms, minnows, small lizards and midges. Northern pike prowl by the hour in search of sucker minnows, frogs, ducklings, small turtles, mice and each other. They feed at all levels at once. Anything that is small enough to be eaten is potential fare on a northern's menu.

Microscopic plants and animals feed shad and whitefish. Insect larvae help sustain trout, sunfish, crappies and bass. Small minnows provide meals for crappies, walleyes, trout and others. Larger forage minnows, suckers, mooneyes, shad, shiners and smelt fall prey to northern pike, muskies, walleyes, lake trout and bass.

With so many kinds of forage in the lakes and streams, and different feeding habits characteristic of the fish that pursue each of them, it becomes apparent why a variety of lures and tackle suitable for taking these fish has developed. At one time the multiplying reel was virtually the only weapon raised against all fish but gradually seeds from a small stand of fly-fishermen began to fall on the fertile panfish country until fly-fishing for sunfish and crappies has become an accepted method. While fly-fishing was invading the canepoler's domain, spinning got its delicate foot in the door and in recent summers spinning has gained ground with fishermen who had long been unwilling to make the transition to a new way of fishing. The spinning barrier has come down with a crash, falling with miraculous gentleness on the hearts of those who were its boldest enemies.

Each kind of tackle has a place in Minnesota fishing where it works better than any other. Occasionally these areas of efficiency overlap, but each has its limitations beyond which its usefulness is rapidly replaced by other tackle. This in no way implies that every angler who fishes in Minnesota must lay out a couple hundred bucks for equipment. Fishermen who are content to catch crappies on minnows with no intention of ever fishing trout would have no foreseeable need for a fly rod in most cases. The plug caster who hunts bass or probes for walleyes may well be satisfied with a good casting outfit.

Generally fishermen who go in for plugging like to use a rod with enough power and backbone to cast lures from 3/8 to 5/8 of an ounce. There are many good rods of this description available, five to six footers that are suitable for casting and trolling for pike and walleyes and for bass casting. Many pan-fishermen use an identical rod changing only the terminal by fitting a light leader and a bobber to the business end. If you intend to fish with casting tackle, first make up your mind what you'll be fishing for. You won't like an extremely stiff rod to cast or troll light lures for walleyes. On the other hand, if you're after the big guns of the pike family, casting fatigue is a factor if your rod is too light, and you should consider some of the two-fisted musky rods designed for tossing 2-ounce spoons and plugs. There's nothing more tiring than trying to toss heavy plugs or bucktailed spinners hour after hour with a rod too light for the job. I know no better way to grow old before your time than using a boy's toy to do a man's work. My experience in musky fishing is limited to lighter tackle. But my friend, Ray Ostrom, who has hung several dozen tiger muskies, uses a two-fisted and a standard Pflueger Supreme reel. He considers light rods pure murder and something to be avoided like atomic radiation.

Pike fishermen can make good use of South Bend's Model 2720 solid glass casting rod with self-seating reel clip and cushioned butt.

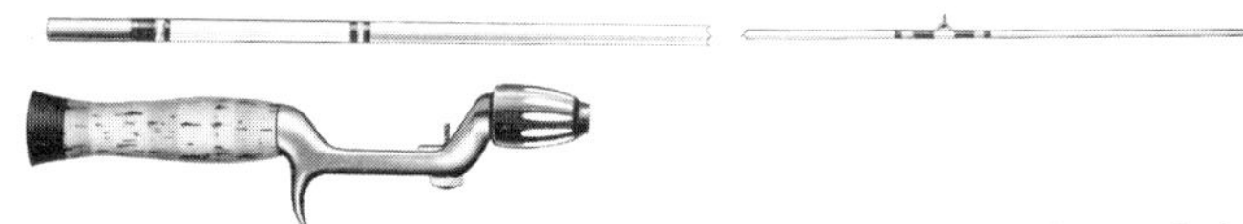

Heddons "Pal Spook" solid glass riptide casting rod, designed for musky fishing is perfect for casting for large northern pike.

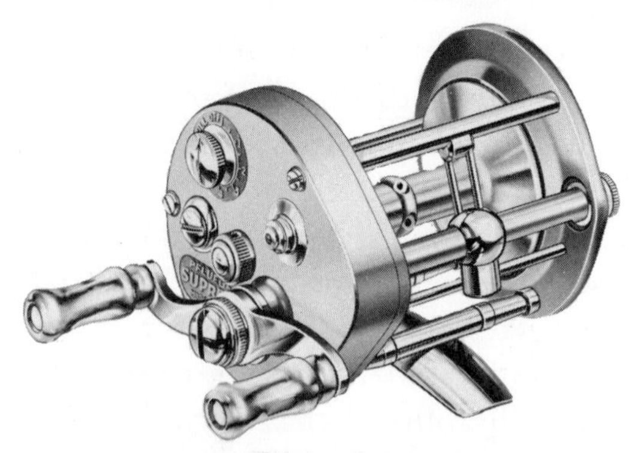

The Pflueger Supreme reel is built to toss heavy spoons and plugs hour after hour. A good choice for musky and pike hunters.

Langley Mod. 310 Streamlite.

Two first rate casting reels, the Langley Mod. 500 Reelcast and the Mod. 310 Streamlite.

Fishing over weed beds where heavy pike lie, provides some of the fastest and most fascinating fishing an angler can imagine. Most of the fish taken there run between five to fifteen pounds and can be handled nicely with a medium action 5½-foot rod and standard capacity reel. Langley makes a reel that is hard to beat for this kind of casting—a light-spooled, trouble-free reel with adequate line capacity, ideally suited for bass and pike fishermen. I'd hesitate to suggest a reel for this tackle-punishing fishing unless I owned one and put it to the test. Slugging it out with heavy pike brings out the weaknesses in tackle for they have to be turned and snubbed on their initial runs if you expect to boat a fair percentage of those you hook. The heavy spoons used and the constant action they must be given through jerking and slacking demand a lot from the tackle. You may be sure that a reel that will stand up to it year after year has been well made.

There is a growing optimism among those who have gravitated to spinning tackle that a spinning rod will do anything that can be done with heavier tackle. While I have yet to find a job it can't do, my largest fish taken by spinning was only fourteen pounds. There will undoubtedly come a day when a lunker will shatter my smugness, but since average fish run much smaller than those I've already caught, I see no reason to use tackle that will handle only one fish in a thousand. The accent in spinning is rather on the light touch than the occasional giant. While it may put the odds so ridiculously in favor of the fish that any spectator might be inclined to call the man in the white coat, the light line that makes spinning such a gamble is adequate for average fish.

There seems to be no limit to the number of game species that are attracted to small lures. I've taken twenty different kinds of fresh-water fish on spinning gear since I was introduced to a spin-stick. No doubt other species will prove to be suckers for this method. One reason spinning is so versatile lies in the fact that it will cast lures as light as 1/16-ounce and will handle 3/8-plug casting lures as well. With small compact lures, and a line that has very little water resistance, fishermen can dredge the deep holes, seeking out bottom-feeding fish that show no interest in lures that pass even a few feet above them. But the spin angler is not restricted to small lures. He can use a saltwater spinning rod and, by changing spools on his reel, can fish speckled trout in a beaver pond at daylight and be trolling for lake trout or casting for northerns with baitcasting lures before lunch. The full impact of this method was not felt until fishermen began toying with spinning, suiting it to their preconceived ideas of what fishing tackle should do. They didn't change their fishing style but simply adapted spinning to their way of fishing. As a result, walleye fishermen began trolling spinning lures on Mille Lacs, were seen panfishing with spinning tackle on Pelican Lake, and began to harvest the state's bass surplus from Clearwater, Miltona and many others, with their new equipment. Spinning has begun to fill a gap that once existed between fussy fish and determined fishermen, tipping the balance a little more in favor of the angler. A nearly invisible spinning line, coupled with tiny lures, often spells dinner to fish that would pass up larger lures. Small spoons and bucktails are very effective on crappies and trout, while bass and northerns have been faced with a whole new set of problems posed by spinning.

I had no idea how important spinning was to become the first time I used a spinning rig. In fact, I was a little disappointed in the results because I'd been led to believe in this new deadly fishing method. It was the snowy first of May when Ralph Thorp and I drove to St. Cloud to fish one of the quarry holes for rainbows. Ralph painted pretty pictures of the efficiency of spinning tackle as we drove up to the granite quarry. Numbed and shivering fishermen ringed the snowy pond, standing on the rock overhangs and along the rock slides, purple noses protruding from their parkas like so many crocuses pushing out of their winter beds. We perched ourselves on some large boulders where the water dropped off a little less abruptly than the rest of the hole. Ralph was rigged and fishing before I could work the combination to my new spinning reel.

"Here's how it's done!" The wind carried his words by me and I shielded my eyes from the blinding snow to watch him land a 10-inch trout. I was impressed. By the time I had a line in the pond his salmon eggs found a new fish.

"What's the matter, boy?" he plagued. "You might as well sit in the car and keep warm if you're not going to fish."

It was too cold to argue and I had my hands full already. This seemed like a miserable way to fish and

I was beginning to resent my partner's cockiness when I was having such a difficult time. The combination of cold and unfamiliar gear caused me to miss one fish after another. I was still working on my fourth fish by the time Ralph was ready to pick up his limit and go home.

"Well," Ralph asked, "see what spinning can do?"

"Yes, I see," I said, burning a little, "looks like you've finally found a way to outfish me, doesn't it?"

Before I began spinning, my trout-fishing experience was confined to use of flies, streamers and natural baits. While I caught a reasonable number of trout on fly-rod tackle it wasn't until I began spinning that I discovered how many trout existed below the fly-fishing level in lakes and ponds. While small spoons have not replaced streamer flies they have certainly added acres of new water where trout can be caught. Spinning has put many fat stream trout in the skillet and has made the reclaimed trout lakes, that recently were only bait-fishing territory, the specialty of spin-anglers. They no longer have to wait for the big square-tails while they nurse a gob of night crawlers or a minnow. Spinning allows good water coverage in a short time, presenting small tempting lures to a number of good fish in a few casts. Anglers now stand on the shore of some of our lakes and catch lakers and rainbows without moving from the spot; something unheard of a few years back.

Spinning tackle is at its best in river fishing. River fish seem to have a weakness for small spoons and bucktails. There were a number of times last summer when I caught four or five different species on spinning lures in the course of an hour's fishing in the St. Croix. One of the best lures for river work is a small bucktail jig. Fished right downstairs, on the bottom in most cases, a bucktail jig will normally generate some lively walleye and bass action as it bounces purposefully along in a straight line.

It would be hard to forget the time I introduced Minneapolis Tribune outdoor's writer, Jim Peterson, and tackle shop owner, Ray Ostrom, to the little salt-water bucktail. I'd been telling Jim about how we were knocking off big walleyes with little jigs and encouraged him to come and see for himself. Like most outdoor writers who are subjected to brainstorming by everyone that has revived an old fishing idea he smiled slyly when I told him. Finally I got under his skin and he called me one day. "How about hitting the river today and see what those bugs of yours are good for?" he asked.

"Fine!" I agreed.

"O.K.," he said, "I'll pick up the boat and be right over."

When he arrived, I saw two in the car. Jim explained that Ray Ostrom had decided to come along and see how the jigs would produce.

We launched our boat across from Point Douglas and came back to the Minnesota shore where the current of the St. Croix eddies with the muddy water of the Mississippi. We dropped the hook and began casting. I was using a small white bucktail but I could see right away that my friends weren't a bit impressed and far from convinced that what I told them about the little jig was true. After about half an hour of fruitless casting Ray asked, "Didn't you say there were some fish down here?"

"Yeah," Jim joined in, "I thought that bug of yours was supposed to be good", he grinned and made a half-hearted cast downstream.

"Stick around," I repeated, "just stick around."

"Two bits on the first, most and biggest," Jim offered. "That ought to make it more interesting," he added.

"Swell," Ray agreed.

"O.K. with me too," I answered and made a quartering cast against the deceptive current. I let the bucktail get down to the bottom and began to jump it toward the boat by reeling very slowly and imparting a whip to the rod tip for each turn of the handle. Then the lure stopped and a pulse followed the rod to my hand. I set the hook and a heavy walleye began to peel line and pound the bottom rapping the rod solidly on the gunwales of the boat. Already Ray and Jim were changing lures.

"Well, I'll be doggoned," Jim said, and a trace of excitement merged with the look of pleasure and disbelief on his face.

"Now, maybe I'll get some help around here," I joked. "Never saw such quick converts in my life."

In the next hour and a half we caught eighteen walleyes, most of them going from two to three pounds. Several times we all had a fish on at once.

My experience with little bucktails dates back to salt-water fishing where fishermen have used them for years. Starting with a couple of Upperman bucktails given to me by a Florida outdoors' writer, I soon learned that Minnesota fresh-water species, silver bass, walleyes and small mouth especially, can't resist the minnow-like behavior of this lure. Fished slowly on the bottom, it does things to river fish that only the fish themselves can explain.

In spite of a lot of popular opinion to the contrary, fish of considerable size can be landed with the very lightest spinning gear. I've finished off dozens of northern pike running to ten pounds using a light-action South Bend rod without noticeable strain on the tackle. Even in fairly heavy currents big fish can be beaten with surprising speed. Occasionally where obstructions were present and I was using four and six pound-line, I'd lose heavy fish in the weeds and snags but even with the cards stacked against me I've landed many more than I've lost. I began spinning with heavy eight-pound line and then shifted to six but I was reluctant for a long time to go to lighter stuff. Now, since using four-pound monofiliment line in most fishing situations, I've gradually forsaken heavier line and still lose fish only occasionally. It's pretty hard for a fish to break a four-pound line if there are no weak spots in it. After a few runs against an adjusted drag, big fish can be worked in close to the angler by pumping the rod. To pump a fish to your boat simply wait until he's stopped running; then raise the rod, starting the fish in your direction. Now begin reeling as you lower the rod and repeat the procedure. This will take the wind out of fish in a hurry. After being pumped to the boat and running against your drag tension a few times, it's a spunky fish that doesn't roll over beside the boat in a state of exhaustion.

Probably the most important single factor in spinning enjoyment is choosing the right reel. The reel used in spinning differs from the anti-backlash casting reel in the way the line comes off the reel. While the spool on a bait-casting reel revolves as the lure speeds to the target, the spinning reel spool is stationary during the cast. The bail, or spooling mechanism, on a spinning reel is lifted away from the line which is controlled by the first finger. As the cast is made the line is released and the weight of the lure takes the line from the stationary spool. As a result backlashes are impossible in spinning. But other difficulties, while uncommon, can put your spinning reel out of commission. The most frequent trouble in spinning comes from having your reel spool either too full of line or not full enough. If filled to more than an eighth of an inch of the spool lip, double loops or loops-out-of-sequence may result in a snarl that will end in line loss. If not full enough, no casting distance can be achieved since the line binds on the lip of the spool.

More fishermen have soured on spin-fishing because of faulty low-priced reels than for any other reason. My own bitter experience with poorly built reels leads me to this conclusion. Light lines used in spinning will snap if the compensating relief of the clutch or drag tension is set too tightly or if it tightens while playing a fish. A smooth clutch is the criterion of a good reel and extremely important to satisfactory reel operation. Most fishermen fish for pleasure so it's foolish to buy an undependable reel. Besides, the loss of lures gets to be expensive and losing fish through malfunctions is exasperating. The choice of full bail or manual pickup on a spinning reel is a matter of personal preference and not a subject of frustrating self-debate. I know anglers who swear by a manual bail, where you guide the line into the pickup position with your index finger. It has the advantage of a fool-proof nature and rugged construction but the automatic is preferred by most fishermen in spite of these alleged advantages. Some reels, made especially for salt-water spinning, are corrosion proof, but any reel you buy will resist rust in fresh water. A spinning reel should have a stainless or carboloy bail and pickup roller to resist wear from hard monofiliment. One outstanding spinning reel that deserves mention here is the Ted Williams "400", a light-weight compact reel designed for salt-water use, it holds 200 yards of eight-pound line, enough for any fresh-water fish. Another one, the Record, which has the unique feature of a rear clutch control, is a slightly heavier reel with a smooth drag and good line retrieve ratio.

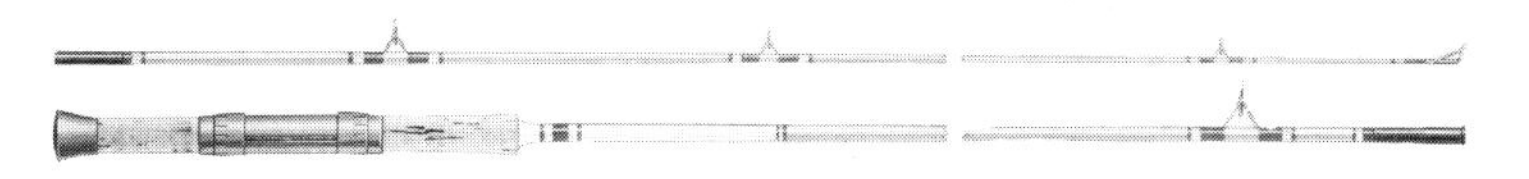

A best buy for spin anglers is South Bend Model 4269 with "Fast-Lock" reel seat of plastic material. A comfortable cold weather rod.

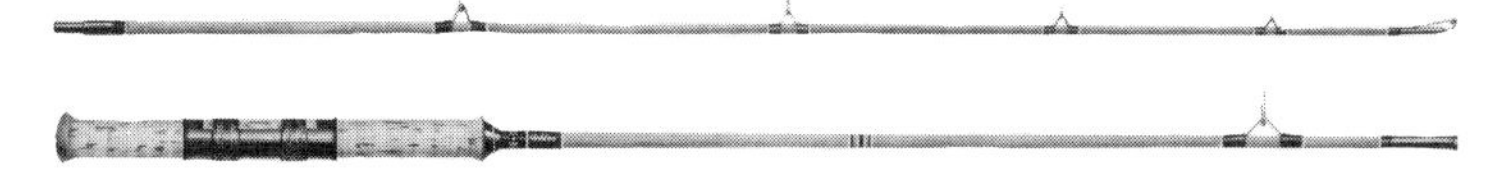

Light, well made rods like Heddon's No. 175 Black Beauty "Pal" are ideal for tossing light spoons for trout and will handle the deadly midget walleye plugs and bass poppers.

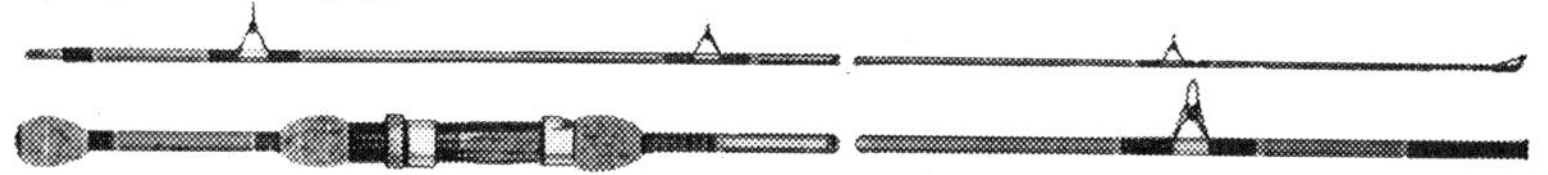

The Ted Williams 503XL is an extra light rod ideal for tossing 1/10 and 1/4 ounce bucktail jigs into a school of feeding walleyes.

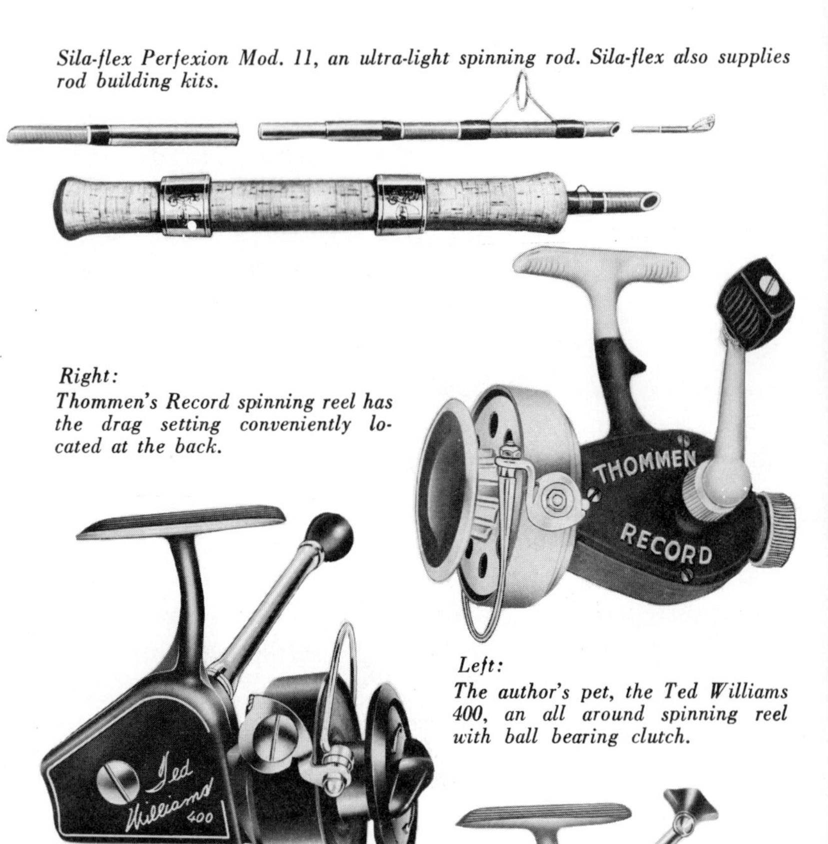

Sila-flex Perfexion Mod. 11, an ultra-light spinning rod. Sila-flex also supplies rod building kits.

Right:
Thommen's Record spinning reel has the drag setting conveniently located at the back.

Left:
The author's pet, the Ted Williams 400, an all around spinning reel with ball bearing clutch.

Right:
Pike, lake trout and musky anglers could use a light weight large capacity heavy duty saltwater spinning reel like this Ted Williams 500.

Above:
The Langley de Luxe is a well-made spinning reel of moderate price. Available in left or right hand styles. Wt. 8 ounces.

Below:
Langley's Spindrift is a rugged big fish spinning reel with a capacity of 250 yards of 10-pound line.

My choice of spinning rods is a six and a half or seven-foot hollow glass rod with just enough backbone in the butt section to set the hook in heavy hard-mouthed fish. The tip should have a fast action in order to do a good job of casting light lures and the midsection should have a stiffish action. Many rods of light action feel mushy from butt to tip and lack the speed in the tip to handle small lures properly. Some anglers favor reel-seat construction in preference to rings. They contend that rings tend to slip while playing big fish. While the seat type is more rigid, I prefer rings for a reason that is obvious to old hands at cold-weather fishing. When temperatures hang around forty or fifty degrees, a thermal range common during the course of a Minnesota fishing season, a metal reel-seat becomes painfully cold, even to the point of weakening the caster's wrist until he has difficulty holding the rod in his hands. I've experienced this even with the ring type of reel holders and with a solid metal seat holding the rod becomes impossible. One manufacturer has marketed a plastic lock-type reel seat that may be unintentionally designed for early season anglers, but it's ideally suited to northern latitudes. When you buy a rod be sure to get one that has a handle long enough to allow positioning your reel in a comfortably balanced position.

Picking fly-fishing tackle always seems to be a big problem for beginners. Terms like dry-fly action, steelhead and wet-fly action are at best only conditional descriptions given to various rods as a guide to assist beginners. Each has characteristics of action peculiar to itself, but is often confusing to a beginning angler who pictures a rod in his mind as something different than what it really is. His idea of a dry-fly rod seldom agrees with that of the manufacturer and many manufacturers disagree on what a given action is. Rods of identical weight and length don't necessarily have the same action nor does it follow that a long, stiff-action rod will be much heavier than the lightest dry-fly rod. While some stream fishermen prefer a short stick of 7½ or 8-feet, I prefer one with more authority, between eight and nine feet long. The longer rod will often be within an ounce of the 7½-footer since the finished rod weight depends on insignificant things such as the number of guides used, density of cork in the grip, type of reel seat and even the thickness of the laminations in the case of hollow rods. A dry-fly rod of eight and a half feet with a fast tip is hard to beat. It will cover stream and lake fishing in all situations the angler normally encounters including bass-bugging and wet-fly fishing. I've used a long dry-fly rod for streamer fishing and dry-fly work and for casting poppers. But if bass were my only target I'd like a little slower and more powerful rod.

Settling for a fly reel, that merely serves to hold line for the fly-fisherman, is another area where debate rages long and hard. There are only two basic types to choose from: single action where you wind line on by hand and automatic where the line is spring wound. The automatic reel has some advantages under certain conditions. When fly fishing from a boat or canoe an automatic will keep your line off the deck where it could get tangled around your feet or other gear at the critical time that a hooked fish decides to run. I use a Bristol single-action reel for most of my fly fishing. It holds thirty yards of fly line and enough backing to handle any fish during long runs. There are other good single-action fly reels on the market such as the

The Fli Tosser by Thommen enables the flyfisherman to flyfish with spin tackle.

A flyrod like the South Bend Model 3150 nine-footer shown here will handle all flyfishing situations you'll meet in Minnesota from panfish to steelhead with plenty to spare.

For the big fish specialist South Bend's 5½-ounce nine-foot Model 3370 flyrod is a good choice.

An automatic flyreel like South Bends Model 1130-1140 helps keep your feet out of the line when flyfishing from a boat.

A stout, all steel single action reel like the Bronson No. 16000 is priced under $2.00.

The upright nine-ounce Bronson Royal-Matic flyreel is silent and free stripping, can be taken down without tools.

Cortland 333 line is a non-sinkable flyline that needs no dressing.

Bronsons No. 370 Royalist holds 30 yards of HCH line plus 50 yards of 15-pound test backing.

Pflueger Gem and Bronson Royalist that sell for under six dollars and skeleton type reels can be had for less than two. Automatics like the South Bend No. 1140 and Heddons No. 87 cost less than twelve dollars.

Fly fishing is beginning to appeal to more people every day probably because all the easy-to-catch and abundant species of Minnesota will hit a fly presented in one way or another. Bass, panfish and trout are constant targets of the thousands of fly-fishermen and a few fish for lake trout and northerns with fly tackle. Fly fishing has more followers than spinning among pan fishermen and bass specialists. Even anglers who have never laid a fly on the water prefer fly rods when bait-fishing for sunfish and crappies or drift-fishing for walleyes and crappies. With the new nonsinkable lines fishermen can avoid the fuss of line dressing and their lines will stay up all day long. Lines no longer cost staggering prices either and floaters like Cortland 333 and Miller's Hollow are priced from a couple of bucks for level lines to about ten for bug-tapers. Most fishermen use a level line of a size recommended by the manufacturer of the rod, although as a rule, the maker has no way of knowing what line you'll be using. A hollow floating line of a given size is larger than the same designated size in a normal line and weighted line is smaller in diameter. An 8½-foot, 5-ounce rod fitted with a level line should require a size C, but if a floating line were used a size smaller than normal is called for. The best way to fit a line to your rod is to borrow one from a friend and try it on your own rod. Most fly-fishermen own several lines and if none of them work on your rod at least you've eliminated one or two line sizes. For the average fly rod of five ounces in 8½-feet the proper double taper line would likely be an HDH or HCH. Double tapers are important to a fisherman especially when fishing quiet water because it is in effect a continuation of your leader and isn't as apt to scare spooky fish. But a double-taper line has some limiting factors often overlooked by the beginner although experienced fly-fishermen will be quick to recognize them. Because the weight of a fly line is what bends the rod tip and casts the fly, a double-taper used with a long fine leader will pile up on short casts. It requires a number of false casts to get a double-taper out where the level belly of the line goes to work. Anglers who fish where extremely short casts are the rule often cut most of the taper away to overcome this weakness. Remember when looking at fly lines that size A is a heavier line than size B and AA is heavier than A and so on. Size I, for example, calibrates .022 of an inch while 5A is .080 of an inch in diameter.

In my earliest days of fly-fishing I believed that I should use at least a 12-foot leader to get any results

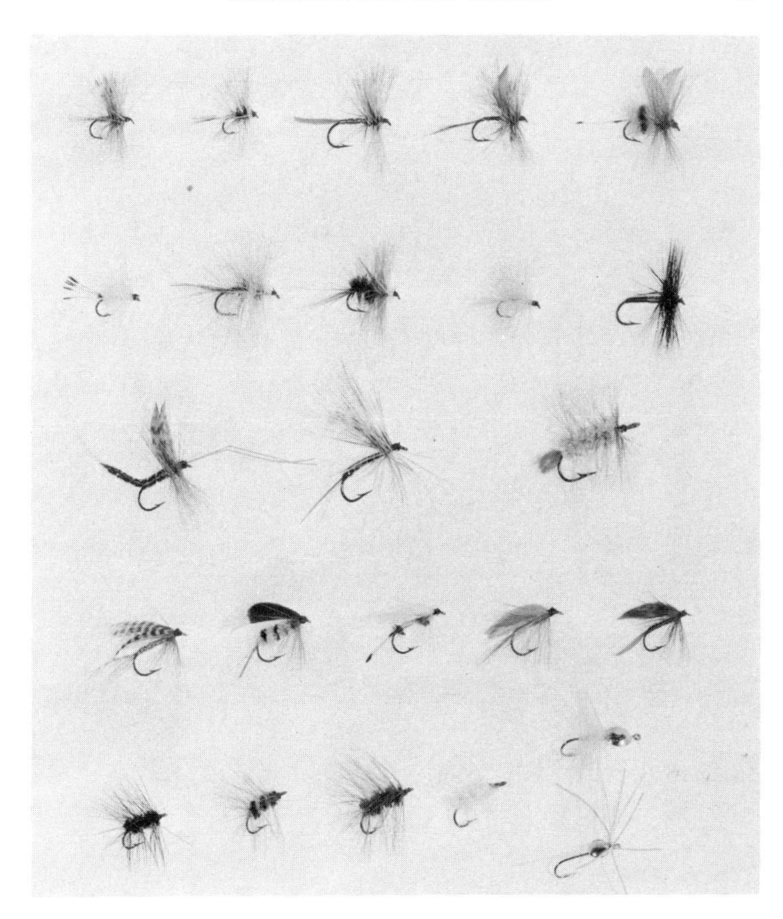

Top Two Rows *show dry flies including bivisibles that can be seen as well by the angler as the fish. Large dry flies imitate mayflies and other large insects, smaller dries like the No. 14 Adams at upper left are best for streams and late fishing on lakes. These patterns will also take panfish.*

Row Three Left to Right: *Natural looking mayfly imitations like this one by Weber, fool even smartest trout. Slim Jim Wet, and Western Wooly Worm.*

Row Four: *List of deadly wet fly combinations starting at left are: Light Cahill, McGinty, California Coachman, Dark Caddis, Montreal.*

Row Five: *Popular wet flies for panfish: L. to R. Black Gnat, McGinty, Brown Heckle Peacock, White Miller. Last two flies are: top, Hackle Dunker ice fly, Spider Dunker ice fly.*

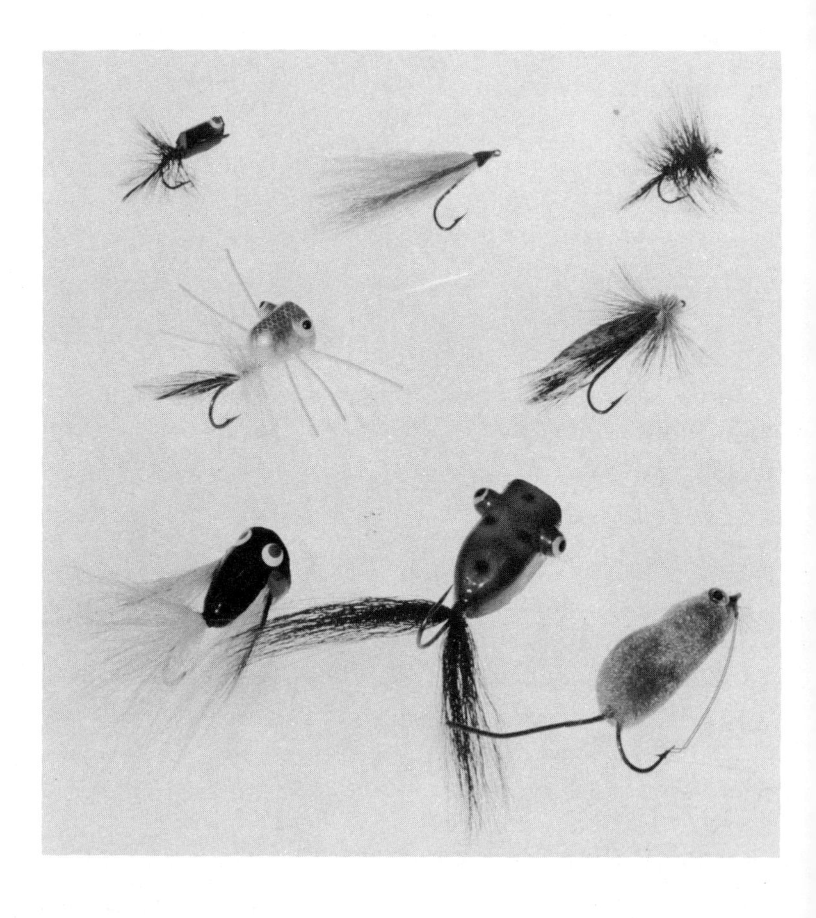

Flies and poppers that catch bass, panfish and trout in Minn. waters.

Top Row L. to R.: *Size 10 Weber Nitwit, for sunfish, crappies. No. 6 Mickey Finn streamer, for bass, northerns. Large dry bivisible for fishing bass topside.*

Second Row L. to R.: *Size 4 Weber's Scaly Popper made of dylite, has rubber legs, natural for bass, large crappies. No. 4 Muddler Minnow, deadly on both trout and bass.*

Third Row L. to R.: *Size 2 Weber Super Duper bass bug, Weber dylite frog with inverted No. 10 hook, Weber Mouse, weedless, body of flocked dylite.*

with trout. As my casting style developed, it worked fine until I tried bass-bugging. Then I found that a light leader wouldn't cast the heavy, wind-resistant lures I used. The leader would hold a bass all right but the problem was one of delivery. Snagging on pads was a little rough on light leaders too, so I developed something more suitable to the fishing at hand. I now use a bass bug-taper of about seven feet but the taper isn't preferred by most anglers. I still use fine tapers when clear water demands them and to get exactly what I want in a tapered-leader I make them myself. I try to match a long butt section of leader within a few hundreths of the line size I'm using and graduate the taper to a fine tipet for small flies. I increase the leader diameter to go with the larger flies and also where wind resistance is a problem.

Most flies and lures designed for fly fishing were made to imitate some form of insect or animal life in the area where it originated. When a fisherman had a need for a new fly he filled it himself. This is true even today for new flies are born every season by anglers who believe they can improve on nature and on the work of other tyers. Many flies, like mosquitos, gnats and mayflies, are universal insects and those tied to represent frogs and minnows are all as common and familiar to Minnesota as if they had been first tied by natives. Some patterns work better than others but there are times when an exotic creation will outfish the stand-bys. Three fly-rod lures that have produced for me consistently under all conditions include a cork bass bug of any color, an imitation bee wet-fly pattern for panfish, a white streamer for walleyes and crappies and an outsized mayfly and small bivisible for lake and stream trout.

This basic tackle is the departure point for Minnesota fishing. Some anglers own and use all the equipment described here but he's the rare angler indeed.

Some favorite lures for Minnesota walleyes.

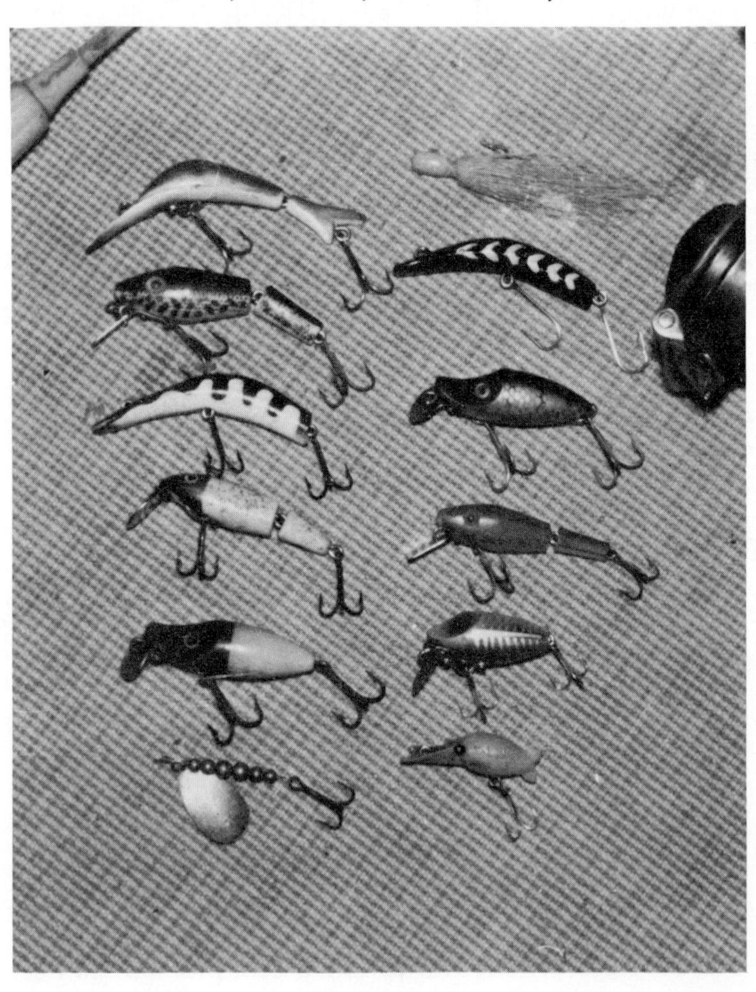

This section is devoted to giving fishermen insight into the scope of fishing the North Star State offers native and visiting anglers. With any of the three basic types of tackle the beginning or experienced fisherman will catch a majority of the fish discussed in the following chapters. But spinning is the real key to fishing success for most of today's hurried anglers. Fishermen with imagination will find it has fewer limitations than any other method. For example, quarter-ounce lengths of fly line available from Gladding and Thommen allow him to handle dry- and wet-flies or bass-bugs. A heavier rod will let him toss large lures and there are new spinning lures coming out every day. It looks like the accent will be on spinning for some time to come.

Tom McCutchan displays two-pound Lake Miltona crappie.

CHAPTER II

Northern Pike Come Big

Did you ever watch a big northern jump high and wide the moment he felt the hook or see one throw a great shower of spray and lathery foam while coming out of the water straight and true before smashing back? That's when your heart will crowd your teeth because a ten or fifteen-pound northern in full view on the end of your line looks like a whale and you gape in disbelief. The first magnificent jump of a heavy northern pike will scar your memory and frighten you silly. Like a typhoon on a calm sea, the sight of a big pike in full flight during his initial burst into the air is an unbelievable show of power! I've had them jump completely across the boat landing in the water on the other side without even touching. I remember one little northern that jumped right over a log, sliding on his belly as if he were going off a ski jump.

One June day in 1955, Danny Sams and I were fishing one of the shallow river bottom lakes along the Minnesota River. Danny had never had any experience with big jumping pike and he didn't know what to expect from them. We drifted into range and began casting one of the spring creeks that empty into the lake.

Rushes and cattails grew in profusion on both sides of the creek and except for the delta of silt at the creek mouth the whole place was choked. Snags and tree limbs cluttered the opening. I lobbed my spinning spoon within a foot of a half-submerged log that lay in the creek itself. Before I turned the reel handle an elongated form that looked only a little smaller than the log hurled headlong from the water, gysering spray like a tin fish released from a torpedo bomber. My reel moaned pathetically and I turned down the tension control in an effort to stop his run. The fish never even faltered. He cut a swath into the rushes and proceeded to mow hay with my line. A frantic commotion followed as smaller fish swam in all directions. Finally, in a paroxysm of terrible gyrations he left my line neatly woven among the cattails and my lure hung in a mass of decaying vegetation.

"Holy Moses, what was that?" Danny asked.

I set my rod down and began paddling toward my lure. "That, I think, was a northern pike, and a pretty good one," I admitted. I shoved the canoe into the tangle of rushes and lifted dead stems from my line.

"Do they all do that," Danny asked, "or just the big ones?" he demanded.

"The big ones?" I teased. "Gosh, Danny, wait until you *see* a big one!"

We resumed fishing and Dan hooked the next fish: a fat, determined northern that alternately cartwheeled and clawed the silty bottom for a foothold against the relentless, bending rod. Finally he brought the spotted green-backed fish to the boat. But this is when a pike usually begins to fight and this one used the standard procedure of showering us with water. His broad tail lashed water into the canoe and he smoked away on a new run. Twice more Dan brought the fish in close and at last the fish was done in. I lifted him from the water, carefully avoiding the hooks and the fish's sharp teeth.

"Wow," Dan exploded, "what makes these guys act so big?" He looked at the eight-pound pike I held. "Man, did you see him jump?"

"Yes," I said, "now let's see if we can get a big one, now that we've warmed up on the small fry."

Danny gave me a look of sympathy, then shook his head and began to cast since I'd lost my mind anyway. The fish we were catching were good ones and he knew I was aware of it.

After landing two more eight-pounders and losing a couple my spinning line wouldn't hold, Danny caught one of about ten pounds that snagged and unsnagged itself twice before coming to the boat. As I made what was to be my last cast I tied into a jumping lulu that made the mistake of heading into the relatively open water of the creek mouth. I screwed down the drag one more notch, as tight as I dared, and before he'd gone thirty yards the fish slanted off and I reefed back on the rod to turn him.

"That's the one I want," I told my partner.

"I suppose you do," Danny philosophized, "but you can say you lost a good one anyway. Maybe you'll learn to use something that will handle a big fish some day if you lose enough of them."

"I'll get him, don't worry," I pretended, with a confidence I didn't feel. After the pike made several effortless, tornadic jumps and I managed a couple of

Pike are not normally good jumpers but they sometimes have a very short fuse!

unexplained rescues from hazards, I strained and pumped the big fish to the canoe.

I could see he was tiring but there was still a chance that I'd lose him. Finally he admitted he was whipped and my confidence returned. "As I said," I beamed, "don't worry," and I lifted 13½ pounds of spotted northern into the boat.

Pike are not normally considered to be jumpers but a big one is usually good for one thrilling show of aerial acrobatics, especially when you apply heavy pressure and don't give line unless he literally takes it. When a heavy northern hits a fast-traveling surface lure he has no sympathy for cardiac anglers. Many fishermen have lost a good one because they froze to the reel handle when a big mouth engulfed their lure right in front of their eyes. Northerns are good infighters and more than one angler knows that a big pike will sometimes play possum until you face him with a net or gaff. Then he turns into a green-eyed monster that snaps 30-pound lines and tears landing nets to shreds. Or he runs under the boat and takes the end of your rod with him.

The northern pike is one of five members of the pike family found in the United States, and is one of the two pike species found in the state. He's a sharp-nosed broad-tailed set of canine teeth, a malignant-eyed cream-spotted king of game fish who rules most of Minnesota's lakes and rivers. He's found from the farm lakes of southern Minnesota to the Mississippi headwater country, and in both the Great Lakes and Arctic drainage. Pike reside in shallow weedy lakes or clear lake trout and walleye waters, and they thrive in rivers as well. The statewide distribution and exceptional game qualities of these fish coupled with their ability to reproduce in the face of heavy fishing pressure make them our most valuable game species. Their extreme importance as a balance species is recognized by fisheries' men, another factor assuring continued efforts to maintain their abundance, for in lakes that lack northerns, panfish populations are stunted from overcrowding. Fish-management practices designed to preserve and restore spawning habitat and set limits based on fishing for sport, have been established to keep this key species in balance. Where possible, fisheries' crews rescue oxygen-starved fish from shallow lakes. Lake channel improvement has in some cases made it possible for some fish to return to deep water during the winter. Fisheries' men and fishermen alike have come to consider the pike a number one game fish. They have learned to respect his value as a predator, but more important, as a package of fused dynamite that has the endearing phobia of blowing up right in the angler's face!

Pike feed on other fish, such as perch, suckers, shiners, or in fact anything that swims. I opened the gullet of a northern two summers ago that had eaten an adult kingfisher! They'll eat muskrats, ducklings, frogs and even turtles. They'll even eat each other. From the time they're a few days old they chew on each other's tails if there is nothing better to eat. There have been cases in the past few years of pike choking on beer cans tossed overboard by anglers. Cannibalism among pike is not unusual. I've caught five-pound northerns that have had deep teeth marks and gashes where larger

The northern pike, King of Minneota waters. Here is a fish that looks like a stick of cord wood and acts like a stick of dynamite!

fish have missed a dinner. More than one large fish I've examined has had a 14-inch brother under his button. Even in the hatchery young pike will devour each other if the keeper loses the kitchen key and they have to wait for the locksmith.

Northern pike and muskies frequent the same waters in Minnesota and often anglers catching a large northern will talk about the muskie they caught. I think it's often a case of a fisherman refusing to admit to himself that the fish he's caught is really a northern. I can't see much sense in kidding yourself about a thing like that because in my book a big pike has as much appeal as a musky any day. Now and then a pike mutation, known as a silver muskie or silver pike, will really confuse fishermen. This mutant northern, while not uncommon, is apparently restricted to a few lakes in the Nevis area where a number have been caught in recent years.*

The author plays frisky pike in river bottom lake of South Central Minnesota. Northerns taken on light spinning tackle nearly always sky-rocket.

*Northern Fishes, Surber and Eddy

Where muskies and pike are confused they can be distinguished best by counting the mandibular pores, small holes arranged in rows on each side, on the under-part of the fish's jaw. Northerns have five or less of these holes and muskies have more than five.

Tiger musky

Usually where the two species share the same water, muskies tend to be crowded out by the northerns. Northerns spawn earlier than muskies and have such size advantage over the musky fry that they are able to prey heavily on them. As a result Minnesota has very little true musky range and the pursuit of muskellunge in Minnesota is not the average man's fishing. A program of artificial propagation currently in progress is going to have other states looking to their laurels in the future. Wider distribution and maximum muskie populations are the goal of the present fisheries' administrators, but emphasis will always be on giving fishermen a lot of average fish rather than only a few big ones. When Minnesota fishermen demand more sport from their musky population and call for an end to spearing and set up separate big game fishing rules for them as a few states have already done, anglers will catch muskies by design rather than by accident and fishing for them will have more appeal.

Pike anglers have no illusions about the musky shortage but it doesn't mean much because they know a big northern is pound for pound as game as any fish that inhabits fresh water—the real king of Minnesota fish. The appeal of pike fishing becomes clear after you've tangled with a good one. No fish is easier to incite into a rage of anger, and hunger is his middle name. No fish displays more courage and stamina accented with gymnastic prowess than the northern pike. Many fishermen have hung ravenous pike while reeling in a fair-sized walleye or a big sunfish. The largest pike I've ever seen followed a three-pound fish to the boat in less than three feet of water. He looked to be about forty pounds and was probably larger!

Pike inhabit many different kinds of water but prefer certain parts of the lake for feeding, usually where food, cover and oxygen conditions are just right. A good place to start is a sparse growth of curled-leaf pond weed growing in from five to eight feet of water. If the water is deeper, you can usually forget it. These weeds seem to be good oxygenators and baitfish are attracted to them because of the presence of insects on which they feed. This is often the corner restaurant to mossybacked old northerns who need a half dozen perch for breakfast each morning and feed on foot-long suckers for lunch. Here is where heavy-weight spin-fishermen and baitcasters who want to learn something about northerns should begin. If you're looking for a snaggle-toothed pike of trophy size, you'll find him here.

It's difficult to think about fishing pike in the weed beds without recalling a time a few years ago when Arnie Lyndall introduced me to a new kind of pike fishing.

We were drifting across a small bay of Lac La Croix in the June twilight, plug-casting the weed beds. I was using a red and white spoon while Arnie cast a ridiculous behaving prostituted Heddon lure. It looked ridiculous but it was catching fish while the spoon I used drew blanks. Finally when he caught and released his third fish and missed a couple of others I began to want a closer look at the lure he was using.

"Let's see that thing," I asked casually, not wanting to show too much interest. Arnie obligingly held it out in front of my nose for inspection.

"Look closely at the bill of the plug," he suggested. "See how it's bent, sort of twisted to one side?" he asked.

As I scrutinized the scarred, green plastic minnow, I noticed that the scoop was canted considerably.

I had to know more. "Now where'd you get that idea?" I asked as I began looking in my tackle trays for a facsimile.

"It was an accident," Arnie said, and I studied his serious face for a sign of a gag. "I banged the lure on the boat one time while making a backcast and on the retrieve the lure began behaving in a strange way, like it's doing now and . . . " A wide jaw full of teeth slashed at the lure. He missed and lined up again for another shot at it.

I found a lure that looked right and was snapping it onto my leader when something hit the boat. Arnie's fourth fish had crashed into the bottom of the canoe in a successful effort to take his crazy lure and now was trying to rip the guides off of Arnie's rod.

I bent the bill of the lure and when Arnie landed and released his fish I held the plug up for his inspection. He just frowned. I gave it a little more English.

"That's better," he nodded and I lobbed a cast and began reeling in at a moderate rate, raising the rod every few feet as he was doing to bring the lure to the top. But instead of splashing, it rolled lazily on its side and dove again.

"Speed it up, granny," Arnie cracked. "Make it look alive. They don't want last week's hamburger," he needled.

My next cast drew fire. As the lure blurped for the first time, a pike had it full in his jaws.

"You're right, boy. They do want it hot," I tossed back.

The fish slanted out of the water, belly flopping in a storm of spray, then arching around the bow of the canoe, he jumped, bore away, reversed his field and jumped again near the boat.

"A four-pounder," I announced, lifting the fish aboard.

"Peanuts," Arnie stated.

"Eatin' size," I corrected.

This is really fishing weed beds at its best, the real thrill of pike fishing once you try it. The wonder of this particular brand of topwater pike fishing is the awe-inspiring way northerns will hit your lure. At times they'll slash at the plug four or five times before nailing it right next to the boat. Sometimes they'll run under it to avoid a collision.

When fishing the weed beds with this type of lure, keep your rod down while you reel at a pretty fast clip. Every few feet raise the rod tip sharply at a diagonal. This causes the lure to keel over, skittering and ploping along the surface for several feet before submerging again. As the lure comes to the top I reel very fast, taking up the slack that develops as the lure skips and hops along. At this critical point be sure your line is tight because a trailing pike will paste your lure on the fly or on the way down. Experience will soon tell you how much to adjust the bill and how fast to retrieve in order to get the lure surfacing every five or six feet.

Other surface lures work well too. I've taken dozens of northerns on paddle-type plugs and crippled minnow, "fore-and-aft" propellered lures, the same ones I use for bass fishing. But the technique employed in bass fishing won't work effectively on pike. The slow deliberate retrieve that teases a finicky largemouth into striking won't even get a vacant stare from a hungry pike. They want their dinner on the hoof. Once in awhile you can catch bass fishing a steadily moving bait, but you'll rarely if ever catch a northern on a plug lying motionless or twitched on the water.

Compiled percentages may favor the man with the spoon where big pike are concerned,* but I think the figures fail to reveal how few fishermen specialize in the sport of beguiling northerns in plain sight. But if the records are of any account it might be well, just for

*McClane, Field and Stream Magazine

something to shoot at, to mention that the present world's record northern pike, a 46-pound 2-ouncer, was banked by a top-water artist.

The real plums, the choice places to fish for northerns, are passed up by trolling fishermen and you can have them to yourself almost every day of the week on many lakes. When you locate a sparse weed patch over a bar or in a bay in about six or eight feet of water you're in big pike country, brother! Here's where the tribal heavies are found day in and day out throughout most of the summer. Fat and lazy, they wait for dinner to wander by in any form and when it looks sick and scared so much the better.

The best time to beat the pike with this combination is from mid-June until early September. Fish late evenings and on overcast or misty days to get the best results with surface lures. When the sun won't reflect brightly on a spoon, it's a good idea to stow the underwater gear and fish on top. It really works! !

Just as the thirty-thirty is the standby of deer hunters with an enviable record, red and white spoons have a reputation for taking more northerns than any other single artificial. Like the thirty calibre its success owes much to its popularity and its popularity in turn is responsible for its success. Pike that won't look at a plug trolled right by their noses, lose any caution they have acquired or have been born with when you wave a red and white spoon in their faces. As a little boy that sees the flag go by, he has to join the parade. At times a spoon presented in any way at all will interest pike but to catch them consistently you have to fish the lure. You have to give it action that will appeal to northerns. Most fishermen know that a spoon is engineered to resemble a live minnow and the egg-shaped red and white spoons turned out by Eppinger, Nebco and Seneca, wobble in a convincing minnow-like way when retrieved at a slow steady pace. Their manufacturers make them in dozens of colors and finishes suitable to all water conditions in weights from 1/8-ounce and less to more than an ounce.

My favorite way of working a weed patch is to cast a ½-ounce spinning-size spoon into an opening in the weed bed and let it flutter down for a five count before starting my retrieve. Your spoon might travel only a foot or two before picking up a haystack or it might fall into the open mouth of a fish. If you're lucky and get through without any weeds, reef the spoon by an upward surge of the rod and then slack off, lowering your rod in time with the settling lure. Don't lower your rod too fast or you may miss a strike, but just fast enough to let the spoon wobble freely toward the bottom. Give a three or four count and reef the spoon upward again. This procedure is repeated until the cast is worked out. It's a standard retrieve that will work most of the time, but keep in mind that the retrieve can be speeded up or slowed down and the count changed. Sometimes a less violent surge of the lure makes a great difference and at other times you can't work the lure fast enough. There were times when I've caught pike with this retrieve only when I turned the reel handle at an impossible speed causing the spoon to bulge the water as I raised the rod.

Armed with this single technique anglers will catch pike most of the time. At times other tricks can be employed that will coax northerns to strike in spite of themselves. One that will get fish is to allow the spoon to settle completely to the bottom. Wait ten or fifteen seconds then start the retrieve with a violent upthrust of the rod and continue to retrieve rapidly until the lure snags in weeds or the cast is fished out. This is sometimes deadly when fish are off their feed and you want to be ready for a hit the minute you start the lure from the bottom because a watching fish can be counted on to sock your spoon at the first sign of life. One lure especially designed for this kind of fishing is the ½-ounce spinning size Weedmaster, a conventional red and white spoon that is as weedless as the name implies.

If the first two retrieves fail to produce some action, I make a long cast and begin retrieving immediately at a fairly fast pace to keep the lure just above the weed tops. If I don't get a hit, I speed up the retrieve until the spoon fairly flies. You can try mixing up all three retrieves and add some more manipulations of your own. You'll probably think of some that will work better than those I've described if you let your imagination go where it will. There is nearly always something that will stir a northern to anger if you can't appeal to his appetite. Don't give up until you've tried everything you can think of, no matter how ridiculous.

It's a good idea when fishing northerns to use a short steel or heavy nylon leader as defense against a pike's shearing teeth. I use a 30-pound leader with loop on one end and a No. 5 barrel snap-swivel or a No. 1 ballbearing snap-swivel at the other. A short leader of eight inches is long enough to prevent your light spinning line from being cut by the pike's teeth and just right for easy casting.

You don't have to roll out of bed at the first sign of daylight to catch big northerns, although they feed early in the morning as well as throughout the day. If you fish between ten in the morning until one in the afternoon, you've fished the best hours of the day. That's when big pike hit spoons best and it's a toss up between fishing spoons during the late morning and fishing topside at twilight. I've taken my best fish during these two periods. Early morning fishing seems to produce much smaller northerns than during midday and evening fishing periods. Many pike fishermen know this and often fish walleyes or bass during the early part of the day and move into weed beds for pike when the walleye or bass action drops off.

In some of Minnesota's lakes, northerns spend the entire summer in their weedy homes moving to deeper water only for the night, and returning to the weed beds during the day to feed. In lakes where shallow water reaches intolerable summer temperatures pike move into deeper water until early September or later. Or they may return to feed until darkness breaks up their dinner. Most of the Minnesota-Ontario border lakes, plus Lake Vermilion, Leach Lake and Big Winnie hold part of their northern population in the weed beds all summer although some fish may move into deeper water for various reasons. Pike that have moved to deeper water will be found off weedy points and along rock and gravel shore lines where the water drops off abruptly. Here they can rise to pick off small fish and minnows as they drift over their position. This is why anglers who troll over points and along rocky shores usually catch northerns when other parts of the lake fail to turn up fish.

I like to anchor on the edge of a sand or rock bar and cast to the deeper water for pike, letting a heavy spoon settle to the count of five before beginning my retrieve. Small, compact, heavy-gauge spoons that get down fast work best. Reel just fast enough to keep from getting snagged continually. If you feel the spoon bump bottom now and then, you know you're getting down where the fish are. If not, count longer or vary the speed of your retrieve. If you pick up a fish, you're almost sure to get more by fishing subsequent casts at the same speed and depth. The count system will keep your lure at the depth where the fish are feeding.

Early in the summer, when northerns are still in two or three feet of water they often hang around stands of eel grass or water celery as it's sometimes called. Work the bays and pockets, where eel grass grows, during the early part of the season. Between the May opener and late June I've snaffled some good fish from under their long floating stems. Some shallow lakes are choked with the stuff and fish have nowhere else to live.

One evening in mid-May, Rod Bell and his wife and I were spinning for walleyes in Lake Sissabagama, east of Aitkin. We couldn't find the walleyes, but in trying to locate them we stumbled onto a gang of starved two and three-pound northerns in several acres of water celery. For about an hour we had a three-ring circus going with fish on all the time. We cast spoons and surface lures and they hit both so readily it provided some of the fastest pike action you could hope for.

When August rolls around and pike are falsely accused of having sore gums and of shedding their teeth, even some experienced fishermen will decide no one can catch them. Certainly anyone will admit that "dog day" fishing doesn't provide the fast action that can be expected at other times of the year. No one with any fishing experience under his suspenders expects fishing in August to be as it was in June. The bloom that blankets many lakes makes it hard to put a lure where a fish can see it. The minnow crop has grown and is still abundant and fish in many lakes have moved to cooler water. But if any fish has a hollow fin during dog days it'll be a northern. Pike are hungry all the time, but during late summer your problem is one of locating the fish. The best way I know to locate pike during dog days is trolling the deep edges of bars and dropoffs out from weed beds. Pike follow baitfish into the deep water because sometimes the fish they feed on are more intolerant of warm water than the northerns themselves. They may seek out spring holes that well from under water banks and by trolling along the drop-offs you'll cross the cooler area where the fish are. To get the attention of northerns during late summer you've got to get your lure right down to them so they can see it. You should troll very slowly giving a fish plenty of time to see and take the lure. Work the plug or spoon occasionally by taking in a few feet of line rapidly or letting out twenty feet of line at one time. Some fishermen make the mistake of just holding a rod when trolling, never checking for weeds or changing pace. Trolling may not have the thrills of spinning but there are many fishermen that enjoy it as a relaxing way to fish. At times it seems to be the only way to pick up any northerns at all when they're out of reach with ordinary casting tackle.

The question of what color fish prefer and whether they're color blind or not seems to me a moot one, but I don't see that it has any relation to practical fishing. Fish react to colors and some colors get better response at one time than others. Basically this is all a fisherman has to know to make use of the various colored lures on the market. Most anglers who troll plugs for northerns begin with a red and white lure or one with a "pikie" finish. One of the best northern plugs I've ever used is a pike-finish L & S Bassmaster, a jointed plastic lure that has exceptional action. I know fishermen who like Creek Chub's Pikie Minnow and I've seen them take fish when nothing else would do. One advantage of a wooden plug like the jointed Pikie lies in the great buoyancy of wood which allows it to begin swimming at a slower trolling speed than any of the plastic models. This is especially true of one of the famous walleye lures that produces so well for Minnesota anglers.

If a red-headed or pikie finish plug doesn't get results, you can change lures again or try different water and sometimes you have to do both. But a change in color and action is more often the answer and if you're sure you're over the hot spot and your redhead doesn't work, switch to a yellow or orange plug. If these don't pay off, try perch and frog finish lures. Change your trolling pace and get to the bottom even if it means getting hung up often. Hanging lures on bottom snags is just part of the price you have to be willing to pay to get some action.

Strangely enough, northerns usually prefer dark-colored lures on dark days and lighter colors on bright sunny days. This fact is backed by my own fishing experiments and the experience of other fishermen. Try trolling a dark-colored lure on a dismal rainy day or

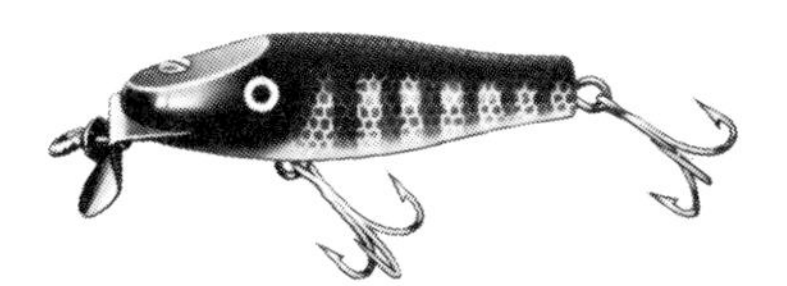

Spin fishermen find a lot of use for the Spinning Pikie in Minnesota waters.

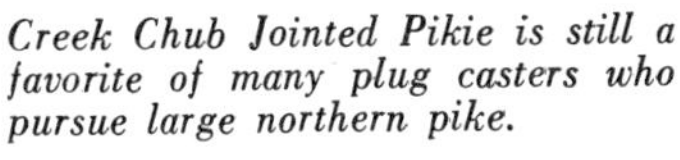

Creek Chub Jointed Pikie is still a favorite of many plug casters who pursue large northern pike.

An old time favorite diving and resting lure for northerns and muskies, the Heddon "Vamp Spook" is the current choice of many anglers.

just before darkness falls and you'll improve your catch. While it very seldom serves as more than another way of delaying defeat, an all-black plug is worth a try during the brightest part of the day. It's a long shot that has paid off occasionally when all else failed.

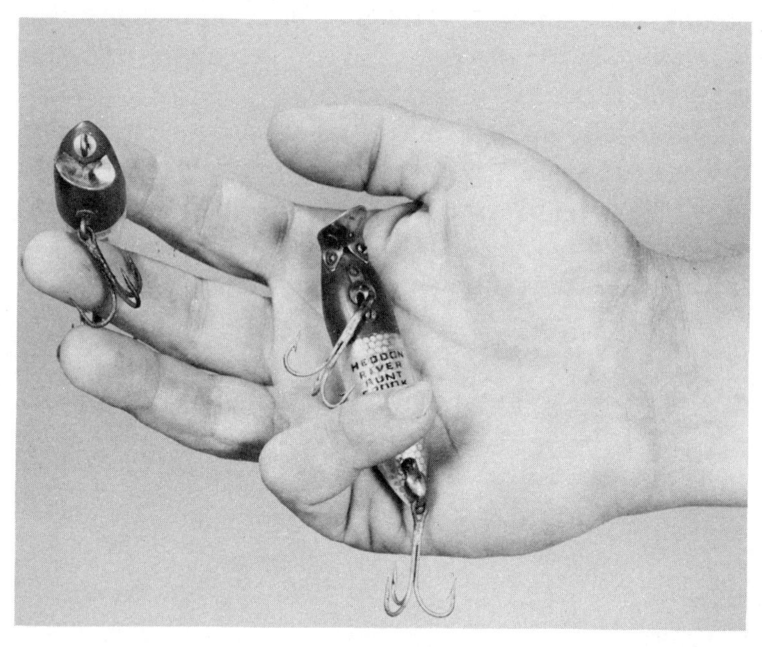

Author's favorite topwater lures for northern pike fishing. Note the way the lip of plug is bent to give lure peculiar crippled action so attractive to northerns.

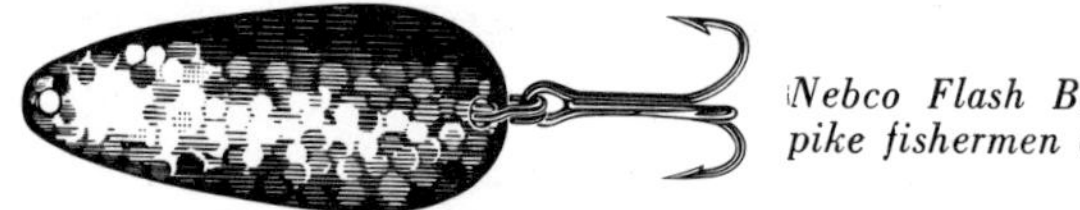

Nebco Flash Bait, a lure northern pike fishermen call the old standby.

Sometimes the biggest fish are real fools for extremely small lures. They'll strike a 1/16-ounce spoon when they won't look at anything else. A tiny spoon trolled very slowly near the bottom or cast and retrieved just fast enough to give it action will sometimes take heavy fish when everything else in the book has failed and other fishermen are saying the lake is fished out. Here is where spin tackle fits like a glove. What looked like a dainty dessert for a big fish has led more than one pike to wind up in the hands of the cook. Big fish just don't always feed on the biggest minnows in the lake. In fact, at times they seem to prefer smaller fare for reasons known better to the fish than the fishermen.

When pike are feeding on small minnows in shallow water a crappie streamer will provide some real sport for fly-fishermen. Almost every time I come across a situation like this, my fly rod is in the car at the other end of the lake, but several times I've been lucky enough to toss a streamer into a bunch of two and three-pound cannibals and enjoy some fast action.

Trolling minnows by means of a strip-on type-spinner combination is a method that some anglers make pay off pretty well. This is a method where a needle-looped wire, spinner-shaft is inserted in a minnow's mouth coming out near the tail. Then a double hook is slipped through the loop. The flash of the spinner blade attracts pike to the bait, usually a three or four-inch sucker or chub minnow, and the central location of the hook catches even short strikers.

Still fishing is a method of pike fishing that appeals to a lot of native anglers. Some fishermen like to relax in a boat or on a shore and give free swimming lessons to a 10 or 12-inch sucker minnow by the hour. These anglers are armed with standard bait casting tackle and 25 to 40-pound line. Terminal tackle consists of a short steel leader or a length of heavy nylon leader material, often 40-pound test. It takes a three-inch bobber to keep track of your minnow if he's a big one. Some fishermen use a smaller bobber and let the minnow have his freedom. Hooks with a lot of gap between the point and shaft are preferred so the point will be exposed to a striking fish. A No. 6/0 forged gripper or claw-type hook or a No. 2/0 Big Bend style are most popular. It's exciting business watching an expert minnow operator at work. It's an exact science that has several schools of thought, the difference lying in when to set the hook to a striking fish. Some anglers strike when the fish begins to run with the bait, maintaining that a pike nearly always hits his prey at dead center, where the hook is located in the muscle of the back beneath the dorsal fin. I'm inclined to favor this train of thought after seeing a few pike grab perch that have trailed my lures. But old hands at this kind of fishing who have had much more experience with this phase of angling than I have, will allow a northern up to half an hour to swallow the bait. This is strictly a gambler's waiting game, one where the fisherman has to control the ever present urge to "see if he's still there," once he decides on the course of action he's going to follow. This method is reminiscent of the early Indian methods of catching pike by using a gorge, a simple device made from bone that was baited with fish or other meat. The fish swallowed the bait and when the angler put on the pressure the bone lodged crosswise in the fish's stomach and the fishermen had fish for dinner.

Northerns will eat anything that moves through their environment. A common visitor to the pike's domain is the spotted leopard frog. In water where frogs are abundant, northerns expect to see them. But even where they're not expected they seem to be accepted without question. I can still see Ernie Swanson, an institutional bass fisherman on Crooked Lake, as he rowed up to the dock one day explaining in Swedish-English how he "whooked a beeg mosky" on a frog. How the "mosky" straightened his hook and nearly wrecked his 20-foot bamboo pole.

When fishing with a frog a lot of anglers have trouble with the darned thing climbing the hook and trying generally to look as unfroglike as possible. Hooked through the lips they just don't behave like a frog. One way to avoid this is by running the hook through the thigh muscles of one leg. Hooked this way a frog will always be off balance, and in the act of trying to right himself he'll present a moving spread-eagle target that pike need to stimulate their murderous hearts. If he swims to the top, he'll kick and fuss until any fish watching will accept the invitation.

Because most fishermen use motors in their fishing they've either forgotten or chosen to ignore the fact that a quiet approach is vital to catching big pike. Unfortunately for boat anglers, who have the advantage of covering more water than shore fishermen, a boat is pregnant with noises that can ruin their chances of getting any good fish. This isn't a revolutionary discovery nor a criticism of modern boat builders. It's simply the restatement of an old axiom that even some anglers who have fished a long time either have forgotten or refuse to believe. There are times when you can make noise and still catch fish but at other times northerns seem as sensitive to the sound of grating oar locks and closing tackle boxes, as bass or trout. This is

The quiet approach is vital to catching big pike.

a self-evident truth but still seems to need constant repetition to be absorbed by even a few serious fishermen. I like to have my tackle pre-arranged before reaching the area I intend to fish. This avoids any chance of notifying the fish of my presence.

Unfortunately most of us have seldom tangled horns with a lunker pike. As a result an angler expects to lose a big fish and he does things that he'd never do with an average northern. The only way a fishermen can develop the skill of handling big fish is by constant practice when playing average-sized ones. If you handle small fish as if they were big ones, you'll be prepared for the day you hook a trophy. Try to remember never to horse a fish, play small ones quickly but avoid heaving them over your shoulder or jerking them from the water. This technique has caused fishermen to cry over a lot of lost fish. You don't want to be intimidated by some "hammer handle" pike and you can play small ones quickly.

When you hook a big northern on bait-casting equipment hold the rod butt against your belly and cup both hands around the reel, applying pressure on the spool with both thumbs. Put on all the pressure your tackle will stand, and incidentally, it will take a lot more than you thought it would. When he stops running pump the fish toward you. When you think you've got him licked, then watch out for a double cross because a subdued-looking northern faced with a landing net or the moving form of an angler will nearly always swap ends and streak off. If you've got too much pressure on him, he'll take some of your gear with him. Or he might bolt out of the water high as your head and shake his spots all over your boat, leaving the lure hanging from your left ear. Don't be in a big hurry to net a heavy northern, unless you like the prospect of nothing more than a fish story and a handful of broken tackle to take home. Let him run each time he puts on a flurry, slowing him down with both thumbs. A big pike is always good for one or two long runs and three or four shorter ones before he's willing to be netted. When netting your fish hold the net still and lead the fish to the net. A moving net will spook him but a fish can be led into a stationary net without much trouble. As the rim of the net passes over the fish, slack your line and bring the net up briskly so the fish won't have a chance to change his mind when you've got him half way in.

When you have a big pike on spin-gear, set the drag tension below the breaking strength of your line and you'll be surprised how quickly even a heavy fish will bow to the constant weight exerted against him. I've whipped pike that weighed ten pounds in less than three minutes on six-pound line and a medium action spinstick. Your real danger of losing big northerns when you're spinning is not by line breakage but rather from snags and weeds. Sometimes you have to decide between stopping a fish at the risk of breaking your line or losing him to snags. This is one of the things that makes spinning for pike a fascinating game. You can buy heavy rods and use stronger line and perhaps boat more fish, but light tackle is what makes fishing the fun it is. The only time I use a heavy rod is when I'm casting lures that are too big for a lighter one. A medium-action rod of six and a half or seven feet has enough backbone to handle ½ and 3/8-ounce standard bait-casting lures and lighter spinning lures as well. A light-action rod is just a little too soft to handle pike in the face of the snag hazards that fill most pike water, but it will easily handle big fish in open water.

I don't like a gaff for landing northerns because a fish lost after a gaff has torn his gill area is a wasted fish. Nets are much better although few fishermen carry one of a size that will handle even a 15-pound pike, the point where he really begins to need one. Fish you plan to return to the water should always be landed with a net and not allowed to bounce around in the bottom of the boat. Some anglers use a "wooden priest," a short length of lead pipe or a stout hardwood club with which they deliver the *coup-de-grace* once they get the fish next to the boat. Used right it works better than a net or gaff although trophy fish handled in this way can be badly marked up and spoiled for mounting.

The author returns young pike to lake—northerns hit along with walleyes in early winter.

If you use one, bring your exhausted pike to the boat and get him in position for the blow. Raise your arm to deliver the strike and if the fish has any spunk left he'll take off. If he's quiet, slack your line by lowering your rod and at the same time you or your partner can pop the pike between, and just back of, the eyes. The trouble with this method is that you have a dead fish on your hands, and if the day is warm and you're a long way from the ice house he might spoil.

Man has been endowed with tools to handle big fish that have adaptability found in no other instrument. To land a big northern with your hands, slip your thumb and forefinger into the pike's eye sockets and lift the paralyzed fish from the water. Once you get him by the eyes don't release him until you've removed your lure from his mouth or placed him on a stringer. Once you turn him loose you'll be picking up lures and loose paraphernalia all over the boat. Sometimes your fish will have a face full of treble hooks and you have to be very careful to avoid getting hooks in your fingers. But if the fish is completely played out as he should be, and you avoid sudden grabs, you won't have any trouble.

Minnesota has more good northern pike water than any other state and you don't have to go far to find a place to fish for them. Any lake in northern and central Minnesota harbors mantle-sized northerns. If you were to draw a line from Warroad on the west end of Lake of the Woods to Fergus Falls, from there to Alexandria, and from Alexandria to Wabasha on the lower end of Lake Pepin, you'd take in the main pike range in Minnesota where big fish can be caught. You'd also take in over three quarters of the area of the state. The border lakes from Lake of the Woods to Pigeon River, are noted for huge pike but lunkers come even from the Twin City lakes each year! Every lake and river harbors some bruisers, although two to four-pounders probably make up most of the northern population. There's nothing much to catching northerns if you want to go looking for them. It's really only a matter of doing something about it!

CHAPTER III

The Minnesota Largemouth

Hal Walters took his nine-foot bamboo fly rod from its rack above the double window overlooking the lake. He tied a cork-bodied hair minnow to the leader and I followed him out the door. His wife, Marge, carried the oars to his boat because she was the one who was going to use them.

Hal had been talking about how easy it was to catch bass on a fly rod.

"Come on," he said, "I'll show you."

Marge rowed him out over the weed bed and I stood off in deeper water, sculling an oar now and then to keep abreast of them but mostly just watching. Hal began false casting to get out some working line and dropped the bug among the emerging weed tips. Then he lit a cigaret. He twitched the yellow minnow slightly. Satisfied then that no strike was forthcoming he picked up smoothly and cast again. A fish took the popper but Hal missed and Marge ribbed him a little. He kept working the cork gently as his wife covered a hundred yards with the oars. Then a good bass took a square chop at his cork and he didn't even have to set the hook. The fish flew from the water and somersaulted through space as Hal applied the nine-foot spring against the fish. Finally he lifted an exhausted largemouth from the water for me to see.

"See how simple it is?" Hal asked and the question echoed across the quiet water in the evening stillness.

It turned out that he was right. Bass-bugging is one of the easiest bass-catching techniques to learn. An angler and the fish keep no secrets and are in plain sight of each other when they meet. The fisherman can see the spots best suited to bass-bugging and he can learn how to handle his lures by constant observation. He'll discover the best ways to control a lure and find the most effective way to fish it so bass will respond.

While there are better ways to catch big bass than with a flyrod, statistics published in the past indicate that an angler waving the magic wand will take more fish in the middle-sized set on light tackle. This in no way precludes the chance of catching a heavy large-mouth on bugs but the practice is not run-of-the-mill-pond.

In my early bass-bugging days I was inclined to favor cork bugs in green and yellow. But somewhere along the trail all anglers must travel toward better understanding. I simplified my selection to light and dark bugs. I still use yellow for daylight fishing but I have no disagreement with those who say red-and-white bugs are best. I've become attached to black poppers for early morning and evening fishing because it appears that fish see a black lure more readily when silhouetted against the lighter sky. When picking a bug selection an angler should give more attention to getting lures of little wind resistance and forget about color. Some of the deeply-cupped popper types are unwieldy and make smooth casting difficult with any flyrod. The Wilder-Dilge, minnow-type bug, shaped like a popper in reverse, is one of the easiest to cast. It's pleasant to cast and is well suited to quiet water conditions. This is especially true where a fast but quiet retrieve is desired.

Most anglers will find that concave poppers cast like a chimney brick are too noisy for use under many conditions. A little rod motion can generate a lot of disturbance and a bass that has approached a lure for observation is often spooked by the gurgle of a hollow cork bug. Popping bugs with a flat diagonal face are better casting and they can be popped and gurgled noisily if an angler feels the need of a noisy retrieve. And there are others, the deer hair imitation frogs and mice, some of which cast quite smoothly in spite of their bulk. There are of course some real lemons on the market that are hard to handle. Try to remember that bass-bugging will slow up your whole casting procedure. The pickup is slower and it takes longer for the back-cast to straighten, necessitating a longer pause before the forward cast is made.

Contrary to popular belief bugging for largemouth isn't restricted to just early morning and late evening hours. Perhaps in some states where bass bear the load of fishing pressure they become quite discerning and will discover indelicate presentations for phonies under the hot light of midday. But I have long ago discovered Minnesota bass are not predisposed to pass up a meal even when it dents the pads at noon under a bright sun. Of course some fish seek deep water during the bright hours but there are always some fish that will tolerate extreme temperatures for the succulent larvae they can collect in the shade of the lily leaves.

One of the reasons anglers catch few fish inshore during the day is because few fishermen fish specifically for bass in Minnesota at all. Bass anglers are in such minority that the total poundage of largemouth taken from 12-creel census lakes in one season amounted to about 4%. Percentage wise they make up a little better than one per cent of fish caught compared to 29 percent walleyes or 19 percent crappies. In view of the fact that bass are rated as the nation's top game species it might seem odd that few Minnesota anglers pay much attention to them. The truth is there are so many schooling species that are more popular that the challenge of largemouth fishing has gone unanswered. But bass are abundant enough in Minnesota that fishermen who bother to seek them have no trouble locating bass water. So the fact that few people tap our bass resources is something of a mystery. It's peculiar that a fish with the fighting heart of a largemouth is shunted to the background, but this status in no way belies his sporting qualities nor his willingness to share experiences with those willing to avail themselves.

Where you catch both large and smallmouth bass in lakes such as White Bear, the angler might become confused. Environmental conditions may make both fish look alike. But the two can be easily identified by the construction of their mouths. The upper jaw margin of a largemouth bass extends beyond the rear margin of the eye while that of the smallmouth does not. Chances of catching both kinds in the same water are slim anyway because even in the few places their range

Mr. Bigmouth. Bass make up less than five per cent of the catch in Minnesota. With the accent on other species bass buggers and spin artists have miles of choice bass water to themselves.

overlap large and smallmouth bass prefer different habitats. Where smallmouth are more at home in rivers and along rocky bars and shore lines and around pilings and in fast water, largemouth bass prefer mud-bottomed, lily-padded bays where the water is normally uncomfortably warm for smallmouth. Largemouth bass are more likely to feed on sand and mud bars and thrive in water of a few degrees higher temperature than that frequented by their cousins. Young largemouth have a very pronounced lateral line stripe running along their sides. But this is usually indistinct in adults and seldom helps in identification on older fish. Range of the largemouth in Minnesota covers a wide variety of water. They thrive in the grayish-green lakes of the prairie counties and the crystal lakes in the Mississippi headwater region. Largemouth bass live in the coffee-colored iron range ponds and lakes of all shades in between. Fish caught from one may be nearly black, while fish from another lake might be silver green in color. But if you never know the difference between large and smallmouth bass it won't matter much as long as the limit for one or both species remains the same. Knowing the two apart just adds a little more fun to fishing.

Bass-buggers will find fish in shallow weedy bays which most plug casters hesitate to invade. As a result you can expect to cover fish that have seen few of the lures that make up everyday traffic in other parts of a good bass lake. Here a patient fly rodder can work undisturbed over two to eight feet of water. Bass will rise a considerable distance to smack a bug, something I was slow to learn.

I've discovered along with the majority of fishermen that largemouth bass fall most often to a slow, nearly lifeless retrieve. The trick here is to lay the bug in a pocket among the pads or weeds and stall around for a strike. While sometimes they're not long in coming, at times patience becomes exceedingly virtuous. Still the bug tosser who drops his guard discovers he's *had* a strike! For all his bulky look a largemouth bass can hit and eject a popper with dazzling speed! This is especially true of hard-bodied bugs and accounts to some degree for the rebirth of primitive deer-hair bodied bugs. Anglers, long wise to the ways of bass, know that they habitually swim off with bait before swallowing it. Deer-hair lures have a life-like feel and cagy fish aren't as quick to drop them as when they smack a cork. Usually they munch on hair bugs long enough for you to set the hook.

Try taking lots of time fishing a small area, giving your fish time to study your lure and make up his mind. In spite of the emphasis on slow, careful fishing, anglers are almost always inclined to see how much water they can cover rather than covering a little water well. Take your time!

Try dropping a bug on the pads and hop it off into the water for a real workable change of pace. Work your bug close to down timber, as close as you can get. Make it look like a beetle that tumbled into the drink from his path to the well. Knocking poppers against rocks and stumps or other obstructions is always a good bet and a religious bass angler will take sulky bass by stumpknocking when nothing else works.

It becomes obvious that bass-bugging demands a lot from your tackle and requires a stout rod. Many bass fishermen lean toward slow-action bass poles of 8½ to 9-feet that weigh from five to six ounces. A rod that will provide the power needed during long bugging sessions, one that handles large dry flies and streamers as well as poppers and bugs. The current trend toward light rods may misguide a would-be bass-bugger to a rod that makes bugging all work and no play. But a heavier stick is easier to use, and if not too heavy, is less fatiguing than some of the wands that pass for bass rods.

When you buy a fly line for bass fishing maybe you'll want one you can use for trout and panfish as well. If so, you might be pleased with a level line. But if you intend to specialize or expect to have several lines, a torpedo or bug taper is what you want. Shy away from double tapers for bass work. Double tapers were designed primarily for dry flies and will cause a bass fisherman nothing but grief. It should be pointed out to beginners that fly-line sizes recommended by rod manufacturers will not always fit your rod and it's best to try a line or two on a rod, if possible, before laying out cash for an expensive weight forward line. As a guide, the average nine-foot fly rod has the power to handle a GBF bug line very well. This line should have about six feet of level G line at the business end, tapering from G to B. This is followed by fifteen feet of heavier B line to provide the forward weight that gives this line its name and makes it work so well. The line slims to F in the next ten feet and is followed by eighty feet of level line. The heavy B section carries the lighter F with it much as a plug carries line out for long effortless casts. Bug-tapers take a lot of the work out of casting wind-resistant lures and are well worth a few extra sheckles to a serious bass fisherman.

Flies take bass too, and there have been times during the summer when I've had a great time pecking away at fish with large dry flies. Big bushy palmers, flies hackled the length of the hook shank, or hairwing mayflies like the Slim Jim, seem to have universal bass appeal. Black and brown palmers tied on No. 6 or No. 8 hooks are my favorites but other colors are okay too. But forget lunker bass! Dry-flied fish will average no more than a pound and a half but they'll be every inch bass! And you'll still be reaching the huddled masses of bassdom since most of our bass population is under three pounds. Bass hooked on flies jump all over the lake and support the theory that bass are the gamest fish that swim.

Occasionally I have worked inshore waters with streamers and lifted a few largemouths, but this is a neglected area of Minnesota fishing and few anglers have explored its possibilities. I've had the best luck with a Mickey Finn, a red and yellow streamer, but I know fishermen who make white crappie streamers produce. The field is wide open. Streamers are probably best suited to early and late summer fishing but this is more theory than fact, supported best by the scarcity of minnows at these periods, especially in early spring. As the minnow crop hatches and minnows become more common, streamers become somewhat less effective.

The real workhorse of Minnesota bass fishing is standard baitcasting gear. Where fishermen pound the heavy pad growths, bait casting has features that appeal to many anglers. The greatest advantage lies in a plug caster's ability to free his lures from obstructions and weeds and power to keep heavy bass from gaining refuge in underwater jungles.

For a fisherman who rolls up his sleeves and dredges the spadderdock fields with pork rind or a weedless spoon, bait casting holds the golden key. A weedless spoon is one successful way to remove some basket-jawed oldtimers from the briers. A weedless silver spoon is a meat hook in the hands of a sober-minded angler and a respectable fish getter in the paws of any beginner. Fitted with pork rind, chamoise or rubber skirts this lure has jarred the molars of many a mossback. I prefer rubber skirts because they come in mixed colors, can be changed swiftly from one lure to the other, and don't get hard or have to be returned to a jar after use. A killing combination is a silver spoon fitted with black and white rubber tails. Another is a black spoon with a black and yellow tail, which is particularly deadly during late evening hours.

One June night Dewayn Shoberg and I took big bass far into the night while rattling black spoons on the gravel of a small bay on Prior Lake. This is no news to many fishermen who will tell you that fish see much better at night than people suspect. These bass certainly had no trouble locating our black spoons and we had big largemouths sky writing to the light of the moon for a couple of hours.

Try a gold spoon with a black and yellow skirt on a dull day and a silver one during average sunny weather. These combinations take deep-feeding bass as well as any lure and better than most.

Shore casters like to toss a long cast, let their weedless spoon settle to the bottom, and retrieve it slowly. This lure has a peculiar side-to-side action that gives the tail a cute little wiggle a bass finds hard to resist. The faster the retrieve the more erratic becomes the tail action. These lures are heavy enough to stay deep even when retrieved rather fast, and are almost snagfree and completely weedless.

Plug casting has always produced a lot of bass and where bass receive as little attention as they do in Minnesota the picture isn't likely to change for a long time. Big fish have big mouths and so the Bass-Oreno, while not quite as popular as it was a decade ago, has lost little of its effectiveness.

When bass fishing first got into my blood there wasn't a morning during midsummer that I slept past daylight. Sleep was shucked off like the husk of a molting miller and the pre-dawn casting hour would begin. During one of these semi-nocturnal affairs the biggest largemouth I've ever had a looking acquaintance with expelled itself from the lake with a friend's red and white Bass-Oreno attached to his coal scoop, a sobering and exciting show that left its stamp of association between big bass and big lures tattooed in my mind.

These big shallow traveling lures are fished slowly and have a wagging action characteristic of the swimming motion of suckers and other large baitfish. They're particularly effective in shallow open water or when fishing over early season weed beds that haven't yet blossomed to the surface.

Deep-running lures are used effectively for largemouth in open water or channels and are very effective for trolling. Use the fast sinking deep runners for deep-water casting and trolling. They get down fast and stay there and if you troll or retrieve at a moderate rate they have good action. Unfortunately heavy-bodied deep-running lures are poor actors when retrieved slowly. They just don't have the buoyancy needed for action at slow speeds, but where a deep moderate action lure is desired they're unsurpassed. When I want a lure that can be retrieved very slowly I use a wooden diving lure. Wooden plugs, because of their buoyancy, start very slowly and at times will take fish when they don't seem to be hitting at all. Probably no deep runner has taken more fish than an all-wood lure with a couple of spilt shot added to the leader to make it run deep.

But what about color? Well, there is no cut-and-dried measure against which a fisherman can gauge what colors fish prefer all the time. But the rule of light lures on bright days and in clear water and dark plugs at night and in dark water has a basis in fact. If you use this idea as a guide and work the scale from light to dark lures on a bright day, or dark to light on a dull day, you'll save a little time arriving at the right color.

When top-water lures enter the scene the color remains more the choice of the angler than the fish. I've taken enough bass topside to have no fear of missing my dinner no matter what color I used. You can buy surface lures in every color but the bass seem to remain unimpressed.

Fishing top-water lures is mostly a matter of technique. To get the fish-eye from largemouth bass you have to retrieve your plug to suggest a struggling creature, an animal or small fish in distress. At times a surface lure can be worked very rapidly and take bass effectively. A fore-and-aft lure fitted with propellers that set up a churning noise is good bass medicine under these conditions. When the water is broken by a good chop I catch bass with a snappy stop-and-go retrieve with this lure. The idea is to reel steadily for a few feet and whip the rod, causing a commotion on the water. With intermittent wave-jumping the lure will make itself known to bass above the tumult of the water. Any bass that resists this retrieve will sometimes fall to

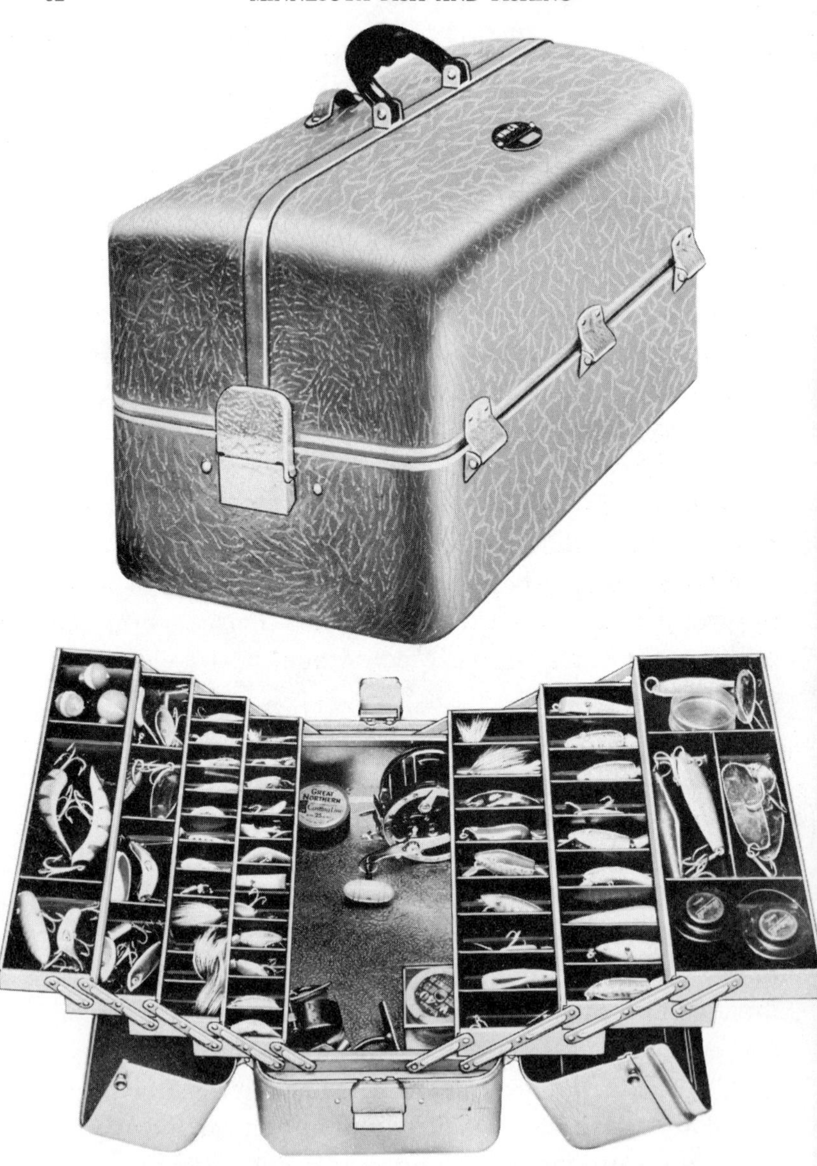

New aluminum 6½ pound combination tackle and spin box with four spin lure compartments and three trays for larger bait casting plugs. All 53 compartments have 18 x 9 x 9½. UMCO MODEL 1000. Hip Roof Box.

another rough water technique involving a gray floating mouse, a boxy little plug fished either on or below the surface. Cast the lure out yonder and let it bob momentarily. If no strike occurs at this point, begin bringing the lure home. If this lure is retrieved slowly with a wave-climbing action it behaves like a half-drowned mouse. This is a good calm-water trick as well, but it pays additional dividends when the wind is getting control of things.

Probably the most reliable retrieve is a straight top-water tactic that is very simple to execute. After your cast is made, fish your lure dead for awhile. Count to 60. Watch the clouds with one eye or listen to your heartbeats. BUT WATCH THAT LURE! Then give it a twitch and grit your teeth! If you don't get a strike, retrieve it a few turns and rest it again. This is a painfully apprehensive kind of fishing but it's the best for bass. When you've tried the slowest possible retrieve, taking several long minutes for a single cast, begin to gradually increase your tempo before you assume all the bass have moved to deeper water.

Bass fishing is quite often an all-day proposition. I can name a half a dozen good fishermen who take bass in the middle of hot August afternoons when most people are drinking lemonade in the shade and waiting for the coolness of evening to bring bass inshore. Many afternoons I've cast the shoreline of a bass lake and caught nice fish from beneath fallen trees that had grown on what was dry land during low water days. Generally fishermen are unaware that bass can be coaxed to the top even during hot sunny days in midsummer. I might have long remained ignorant of the fact too, except that it was a hot sunny day and I had time to go fishing. My good fortune to have fishing time and an unquenchable thirst for fishing have resulted in a lot of crazy experimenting. The outcome is normally less startling than I'd like to admit and catching bass in the heat of the day is a rare success in my fishing log book where failures are numerous.

A much more reliable and even less popular fishing period is passed up by a lot of largemouth men. I'm talking about fishing during a rain, the soft, easy all-day kind. Whenever a general rain is falling unaccompanied by thunder and lightning, bass fishing especially, has an unaccountable upsurge. This knowledge has appeared in print so often that anyone who has any bass hours to his credit has tried it. There are various theories about why fish bite better during a downpour than at other times but the reasons will not alter the fact that BASS FISHING DURING A RAIN IS TOPS! But be sure to carry rain gear. Inadequate rain clothing or failure to carry it is the main reason anglers fail to reap the dewey results of a rainy day. The light rain wear on the market now should be as much a part of your fishing equipment as your tackle box. Few fishermen are willing to get a soaking to see if the rain fishing idea is really true.

Next to bass-bugging spinning provides more bass fishing thrills than any other method. Spin anglers will find Minnesota bass just the right size to handle on ultra-light spinning tackle. You can't expect to drag all the giants from the pickerel weed but you can predict success where conditions are favorable. What appeals both to the spin fisherman and the bass are the miniature plug-casting lures that resemble in size some of the abundant forage bass see every day. Spinning is a welcome fill-in, a middle-sized bass outfit, ideal for in-between situations. Where bass-bugging and plug-casting can't quite clasp hands we apply spinning tackle and catch bass by a new subterfuge.

Spinning has been slow to gain headway in the minds of midwestern bass fishermen primarily because most anglers have had nightmarish experiences with plug casting gear where big bass are concerned. Bass of five or six pounds are rare enough in these waters that anglers are disposed to consider themselves lucky to get one in the trophy class in a fishing lifetime. As a result they either scoff or laugh depending on their sensitivity or the number of big fish they've lost. Still, in spite of the hecklers, there are times that spinning lures will capture the attention of hungry bass in open water and it's there that it does its best work. Like a fine thoroughbred freed from the junk cart, spinning when given half a chance, will outrun its competition without half trying.

During midsummer, when abundant feed and unsavory water temperatures have driven bass into schizaphranic seclusion they will tolerate almost any lure that goes by. But their Jeckyl and Hyde character can be tipped off balance by spinning lures, resulting in a reversion to spring's pugnacious bent.

The hot spots for midsummer bass are sometimes pretty hard to find. But they're not quite a needle in a haystack proposition. Often these places are fairly close to shore, just off a point or a sand bar where the water shelves off abruptly. This is a good place to start fish-

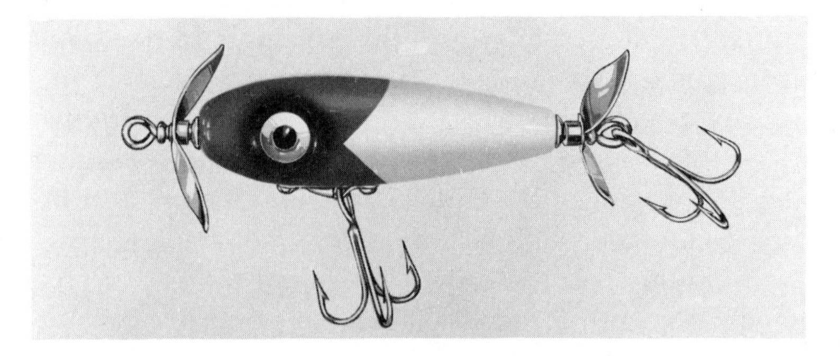

South Bend's Spin-I-Deddee is good bass, musky and northern pike spinning lure for top water work.

Miniature member of the Bass-Oreno family is South Bend's 1/5-ounce Spin-Oreno, a good bet for cruising bass.

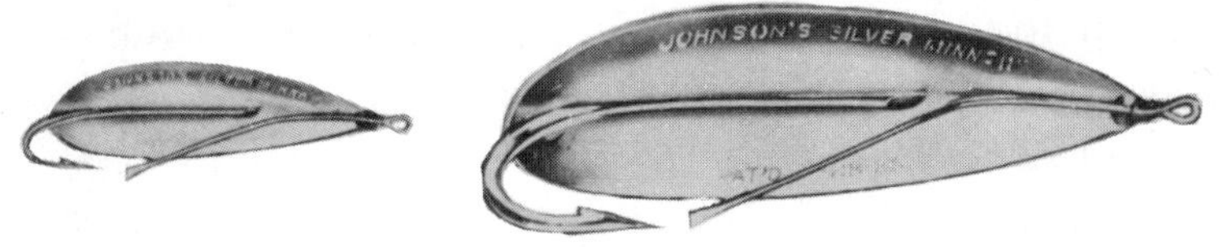

The Johnson Silver Minnow is a most effective weedless lure when applied to a weedy bass lake.

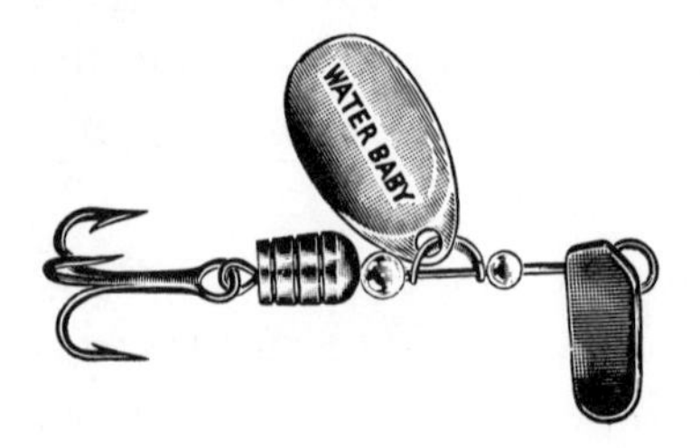

Seneca Water Baby or Mepps Spinner will catch bass that won't look at a top water lure.

ing. Another might be a deep hole outside of a deep weed bed or along the edge of a bar. These spots are nearly always best fished from a boat, for as largemouth fishermen will quickly tell you, bass always feed facing the lake—pointed away from the shoreline. But a largemouth will sometimes follow a shorebound lure and my fattest bass hit a lure so close to my feet I had to count my toes. This was not typical largemouth behavior nor was it during the hot part of the summer when most of the big ones are deep.

Success in the bass fishing game becomes more of an established practice among boat anglers and it is singularly peculiar that a good number of heavy bass are taken by solitary anglers. Next to getting a small spinning lure mixed with a largemouth's next mouthful, freedom from commotion commands your straight-faced attention. Lone anglers are not normally by themselves because they have no friends, although the bass they sometimes bring home cause their fishing friends considerable discomfort. But since one's mental picture of a friendly soul is hardly that of figure standing in an attitude of loneliness in a skiff at twilight, they appear as friendless. In reality they are only doing what is necessary to catch a string of big bass.

Both light or medium action rods are suited well to bass spinning and will handle Minnesota bass well. Choose your rod according to the weight of the lures you like to use. An extra light rod is designed to handle two to four-pound line and lures from 1/16 to 1/4-ounce. If you want to use lighter bait-casting plugs in the 3/8-ounce class a medium rod can be relied on to handle them better than a light outfit. Medium rods

Minnesota bass are perfectly suited to flyfishing. Here the writer plays a scrapper in small lake in the Twin City area.

have fast tip action coupled with the right amount of backbone to spring lures from 1/8-ounce to the lighter bait-casting stuff and they're less critical of line-weight balance than are lighter rods. A medium rod will perform satisfactorily with anything from a four to eight-pound line, either braided or single strand, without a hitch. If you pitch standard plug-casting lures, better use at least 6-pound test monofiliment line on your spool. Lighter line just doesn't stand the shock of a heavy lure and you'll make 300-foot casts with 200-feet of line on your reel. If you cast both light and heavy lures, you can easily carry an extra reel spool with heavier line. With heavier line on one you can be ready to change whenever occasion demands more line strength. There are times when you'll want to fish several situations in one day afloat and the extra spool is extra line at the very least and a change of pace at the most.

Many new lures have been designed for spinning, some of them lightweight copies of casting plugs. So choosing bass lures for spinning is often a matter of selecting pint-sized editions of the lures you now use for bass fishing. The small plunkers, crippled minnows, weedless spoons and deep-running plugs designed for spinning will catch fish even better than their heavier parents.

One lure that is proving its worth as a bass getter in Minnesota is a spinning bucktail jig. Where bass are feeding on clean bars and bays a white bucktail will draw a lot of fire. The bucktail jig is extra deadly during the early part of the season although subsequent experiments are proving them valuable throughout the summer. Bucktail jigs have to be worked by the angler for maximum results. An angler willing to fish them right, will catch bass on them and other fish that feed with bass as well.

When you fish a bucktail remember to let it sink to the bottom before you begin to retrieve. If you're in weedy water, let it sink to just above the weed tops. Then raise your rod and lower it, taking up slack as you go. Raise it again and so on until the cast is fished out. There are a dozen variations of this retrieve and at times some of them will catch fish when the standard retrieve gets nothing. So experiment and play with it. Try things that you know bass don't go for. Some times these are the retrieves that work best.

Spinning is perfect for live-bait fishing. Many Minnesotans do a brisk business each summer with deep-snoozing bass with night crawlers and frogs. A gob of crawlers lowered into the green-light zone during midsummer can be a thorn in the side of a learned fish. As trout anglers know, night crawlers live well on a hook. Even though they're not an item in the natural diet of most bass there are few fish that can ignore a squirming night crawler for long. Make your presentation on a single hook with just enough weight, a shot of lead or two, to hold the bait down. Some mighty big bass have fallen to this combination and it's a comfortable way to fish. When you get a strike on a crawler don't wait around to set the hook! A bass will take a night crawler quickly and when you clip him he'll be hooked.

Another good natural bait for bass is a little green leopard frog. Bass and frogs go together and every kid that ever fished bass knows they're good bait!

You can buy harnesses that are engineered to keep your frog behaving properly when casting or trolling but they don't work well for still fishing. In a harness the frog will be lifeless and unattractive to bass. But hooked in the conventional way through both lips isn't much better. Hooked in the mouth a frog spends all his time chinning himself on your leader knot instead of seducing bass. It's best to hook them through the thigh of one leg. Hooked this way your frog will try to swim to the surface and present a natural, inviting target.

One of the easiest ways to locate bass in strange water is to drift just outside of the weed beds. Or you can get right into the weeds if you use a cane pole. The cane pole is still a favorite with a lot of local anglers when it comes to fishing bass with frogs. In the hands of an experienced cane-pole fisherman it can be a devastating instrument.

There was an old duffer who fished a lake where we spent the summer a few years ago that kept the township in bass. He used to dab a kicking frog in among the lily pads and truck out bass like a stevedore, taking many more fish than I caught on bugs. He enjoyed a great reputation among local fishermen. Fishing frogs was an art with him and several of his bass that I saw went well over five pounds. Proof that frogs in the hands of an expert are deadly indeed!

There have been times when I've had good luck with largemouth while using grasshoppers for bait. In early summer, when the first adult hoppers appear on the warm south side of buildings and feed in the lake is yet undeveloped, large grasshoppers are prime bass bait. I've taken some very respectable fish by spincasting with grasshoppers for bait. I hang the hopper on a No. 6 wire hook by slipping the barb through the insect's midsection. Effortless casting afforded by fine line is the number one bait saver here since even grasshoppers can be cast a respectable distance on a four-pound line. For added distance when tossing live bait keep your reel spool well filled but not more than an eighth of an inch from the lip of the spool. And to avoid killing delicate bait use an underhand cast. If the bait is too light add a split shot, or, if you want it to float, add a light plastic bubble about eighteen inches above the bait.

Bass are often lying along some weedy alley watching for whatever may come by and remind him he hasn't eaten for five minutes, for at times bass seem to feed steadily. When the water is at optimum temperature and feed is scarce, largemouth will have difficulty maintaining a satisfactory balance between hunger pangs and available food. He seldom questions the providence that may have placed a meal in his path at such times. In fact, he shows very little disposition at all until the point of your hook tips him off and he performs the second act of Swan Lake for his appreciative audience. But there are other times when water temperatures and feed supply keep largemouth on a starvation diet and he will refuse everything offered him. Studies conducted to shed light on when bass feed best, revealed they refused to feed at all when the water was 39 degrees. And even at fifty they don't feed readily. The experiments showed that largemouth fed best when water temperatures were between 71 and 93 degrees, taking minnows then as fast as they were introduced to the water. It was noted the rate of metabolism is much greater in small bass than large bass especially at high and low temperatures, one reason why you catch more small bass than large ones. The study revealed bass don't take food readily unless their stomachs are empty, another possible reason why bass don't bite when food is plentiful.*

When fishing live bait from shore with spinning tackle you have to whip your fish quickly. Weeds and light line require an angler to play first fiddle and master his fish in short order. An average fish will bow to constant drag tension if the angler is willing to do his part and gives no ground. But in spite of all you can do, some fish will gain refuge in the spinach. When this happens there is no better cure than to completely slack your line and give his stubborn highness a chance to back out. After a minute or two wait, you will either have a fish coming toward you or a slack line.

Veteran bass anglers seldom carry a net because bass can be handled so easily without one. But if you use a net, remember to lead the fish to the net and not the net to the fish. All fish shy at the movement of a landing net and bass are no exception. Keep in mind, too, that a tired, completely played-out fish is much easier to net than one that is taken green the first time up to the boat. If you prefer, you can land your fish by placing your thumb against the inside of a fish's toothless lower jaw and applying a half bent index finger to the under side. This places your bass in embarrassing paralysis and he will humble himself while you remove your hooks. Although an exhausted fish is rather tolerant be a little careful where you put your fingers if your bass is hooked in the lower jaw. A hook in the hand is no joke! If you don't plan to keep the fish, bass handled this way can be turned back unharmed much smarter for the lesson you taught them. Undersized

*Markus, Transaction of American Fisheries Society, Vol. 62.

bass that have been allowed to bounce around on the boat bottom have little chance of survival even though well-meaning anglers throw them back.

Miles of bass water afford bass anglers a choice of fishing from ponds of only a few acres to huge lakes. In most of them bass are abundant enough to provide better than average success. Anglers who fool around Minnesota bass lakes awhile can expect to reap more fun per hour and more pleasure per fish than when following more popular but less productive lines of angling endeavor. And competition is keen only between you and the bass, most of which have never seen a white man.

The author holds largemouth bass that bit blue bucktail jig.

CHAPTER IV

Chasing Rainbows

One June day several years ago Tom McCutchan and I were returning from an uneventful speckled trout expedition in the Finland area above Duluth. As we headed south toward home we swung off highway 23 near Holyoke to have a gander at the Blackhoof River. We stopped at one of the little wooden bridges that cross the stream and stood looking into the smoky-colored water, both dog tired but thinking exactly the same thing.

"Think we should try it?" I asked Tom, knowing he was about to ask me the same question.

"Might as well," he answered and he started out for the car. "I'll get the rods," he added.

"Up or down?" Tom asked, when he returned.

"I'll go upstream," I answered and slid down the red clay bank just above the cribbing placed under the bridge by a state stream improvement crew.

"Try to be back in a few minutes. My wife expects me to be home for supper!" Tom called and disappeared around a clump of tag alders.

The stream was still high from recent rains upstream and I figured a few fat browns would be on the prowl under cover of the dark water. I baited up with a small red angleworm. Thirty feet above the first bend I dropped an upstream cast into a deep run. The fast water carried the bait swiftly for about ten feet. Then my line stopped. I thought I was snagged and I tugged a little to free the hook. The snag erupted from the stream in the form of a great steelhead rainbow! In a blaze of crimson fire he threw water on both banks of the river, and nearly touching the overhanging alders that met above it. Then he headed downstream. I applied all the pressure I dared, hoping to keep him out of the fast chute below. Then I hollered for Tom! I succeeded in holding the big rainbow and he tore off upstream like a cat in a stovepipe, jumped and headed down again! I stood there looking at the big hatchet-faced steelhead, shaking with fear of losing him and yet not knowing what to do next. I began hollering for Tom again hoping that he'd get the landing net from the car in time to save my fish. Then the big rainbow caught his second wind and streaked into the current again. In midstream he broke water once more in a high, colorful jump and my line went slack—the giant fish was gone! I stared at the end of my leader and saw that the No. 16 light wire hook had been poor equipment to lick a steelhead. The hook had broken at the bend!

I was mumbling to myself and trying to thread a worm on my leader when Tom sauntered up.

"Ready to—what's wrong with you, see a ghost?"

"No," I answered, "but I just lost the biggest rainbow I've ever seen! Where were you when I screamed my head off for a net?" I demanded, irritated now that he should show up minutes after my fish had gotten free.

Tom looked at me sympathetically. "I met two guys headed upstream and I thought it was them. I was going to come but I was sure you couldn't make all that noise by yourself!" he answered.

Many members of the trout and salmon family have been introduced into Minnesota waters in the past 75 years with the thought of adding their exotic names to the game fish list of the state. Atlantic, landlocked and king salmon; brown, cutthroat, rainbow trout and grayling were planted from time to time. Some like the brown and the rainbow found conditions and food supply favorable and made a home in a considerable part of the state. The others, except the newly introduced grayling which shows signs of thriving, are now only memories.

Rainbows were originally planted in brook trout streams that had suffered from deforestation and pollution, streams that were no longer able to support native speckled trout populations. Rainbows were released in the streams in the Red Wing, Wabasha, and Winona area. They were introduced into the headwaters of many fast streams of the Lake Superior drainage where most of them found their way into the cold tempting waters of the big lake. Stocking these north shore streams is now a thing of the past because fish could not be kept in the water above the falls and barriers. Now natural reproduction of rainbows takes place below these falls and rapids, where huge steelhead rainbows ascend many of these rivers to spawn. They come in such great numbers that a special spring steelhead season has been drawing anglers from all over the mid-west. A number of cold lakes were experimentally stocked with shasta and steelhead rainbow stock. Some of these lakes responded, others yielded nothing. At present new lake reclamation methods along with fact-finding research is expanding the rainbow range each year.

The Minnesota rainbow is a foreigner who has successfully migrated for a thousand miles—a fish that has the character required to adapt to a new environment and thrive there. And small cold lakes in northeast and north central Minnesota are providing new fishing thrills for vacation and weekend anglers who are coming to know the rainbow trout as a top game fish.

There are even small trout creeks within fifteen miles of the Twin Cities, stocked with "put and take" rainbows and there is good trout fishing to be found less than two hours driving time from Minneapolis. There are rainbow trout in Grindstone Lake near Hinckley just west of US highway 61, in the granite quarries at St. Cloud on US 10 and the streams around Red Wing along the Mississippi. Rainbow water is scattered statewide but the best trout country stretches from isolated Clearwater River west of Bemidji, across the trackless wilderness of Superior National Forest. There are Loon, Ram, and Duncan lakes reached by portages. But some lakes, such as Bluewater, Echo, Bogus, Trout, Greenwood and Grindstone, have roads to their primitive shores. Streams such as the Knife, Split Rock, Silver and Blackhoof, reached from main highways and secondary roads, are the best in the state.

The steelhead strain of rainbow, now found in Minnesota, is considered to be the same as any other rainbow strain, except for its seagoing character. Long ago the shasta and other inland types were cut off from the sea. This seems to be the basis of any difference between other strains and the steelhead. Rainbows are blue-green deep-bodied fish profusely marked with black spots on the upper part of the body, fins and tail. They wear a brilliant lateral stripe of silvery scarlet from stem to stern. This stripe is very pronounced and striking in spawning males. Some of the lively spotted scrappers that move into the mouths and pools of North Shore streams during the summer, however, are nearly solid silver. Rainbows of inland lakes are a little brighter with olive backs and pinkish stripes on their sides.

But to describe the rainbow in this way belies the fish itself. Certainly no native species offers more horse power per ounce than the trim, athletic rainbow.

While there is a lot of water for the searching angler to investigate, perhaps the greatest amount of pleasure for most of us who follow the clean rise of a feeding rainbow comes during the season's climatic flood of insects that rise from the blue eyes of the wilderness. The rock-bound pools chipped from the face of the Minnesota arrowhead country are the closest thing to a natural rainbow trout setting, where fishermen find good trout fishing combined with surroundings strangely reminiscent of native rainbow lakes of the west.

After the opening weekend, when live bait fishing with eggs and worms gives way to other fishing pursuits, most anglers forsake trout fishing. By the time mayflies begin to appear on the trout lakes and streams all but a handful of anglers have forgotten rainbows completely. But now trout that have been grubbing and tailing for nymphs among the weed stems and rocks will begin to turn their attention toward the sky and a very few, a token of force, of fly-fishermen will mysteriously know what has come about and return to the trout lakes.

Some who fly fish these waters for the first time may be confused by the new conditions they face. But if they will but observe, we will direct their watchful eyes toward the fish.

Rainbows are found in the shelf area of a lake during fly hatches in water from a few feet to possibly ten feet deep. This is where water insects are compelled to live out their lives on weeds or rock and gravel bars. It's best to forget the deeper parts of the lake in most cases unless there is a good wind blowing, pouring terrestrial insects onto the ponds. A wind will also scatter mayfly drakes as they emerge and spiral into a lake-bound breeze. At such times it's not unusual to see the lake boil with feeding trout, and an angler can move at will catching trout everywhere.

Unlike stream fishing where wading is practiced and practical, the angler will soon learn that the wading lake-fishermen is bogged down with woes and difficulties out of all proportion to his meager harvest of realized benefits. In spite of the fact that trout feed facing shore a boat is essential in this type of fishing. Unless the shore is free of trees for backcasting or the angler can wade far enough to avoid shore growths he

Rainbows like this are found in the shelf areas of a lake during fly hatches in water from three to ten feet deep.

will need a boat to achieve any degree of success. Most Minnesota trout lakes drop into deeper water a few feet from shore or are so boggy near their margins that an angler cannot hope to wade them. During the spring rush bait anglers, bolstered by spin gear, can operate from shore, but fly-fishermen are up against disappointment if they go out unprepared to fish from a boat or a canoe.

The author on the shores of small wilderness trout lake. Lakes like these are being reclaimed and stocked with trout each year.

I recall a trip into a bright jewel of a lake called Ram Lake partly because we had to climb a mountain to get in but particularly because four and five-pound rainbows were working out in the lake far beyond our casting range from shore. With steep walls of rock and trees behind us, we could only watch the trout frolic like porpoises, and while the sight of big trout is reward in itself for a difficult caper we would have been at least treated to a closer view if we had carried in a boat or canoe.

Trout like those in Ram Lake are accustomed to feeding on minnows most of the time. Big mayflies and stoneflies add substantially to their diet when present in numbers. It's interesting to note that fishing success seems to be at times related to the type of insects trout are eating. Trout feeding on hard-bodied insects that resist digestion are less apt to be hungry the following day than when they feed on soft-bodied insects or minnows.

Because trout feed on heavy-bodied insects in most lakes during midsummer, the No. 14 and No. 16 bivisibles should be replaced by No. 6 and No. 8 creations that simulate fat drakes. I know anglers that use cork-bodied flies and poppers when a mayfly hatch is on with good results. While many honest fly-fishermen may feel offended by this truth, it would seem that in most cases exact imitations are not required when trout are feeding on large insects. At the peak of a good hatch anything that resembles a green drake will get strikes. I've been fishing out of Bud Kratoska's place on Trout Lake, just out of Grand Marais, many times when fishermen were using flies, that except for size, were each dressed differently and of all shades from yellow to brown. Yet when a rainbrow bent on filling his basket came by it would charge any fly in its path with an honest naivete and without hesitation. As long as the fly stayed afloat or in the surface film it would draw fire from passing trout.

There are smaller hatches too. The angler who pursues rainbows in Minnesota should have black flies tied on hooks ranging from No. 10 to No. 16, black spiders and gnats for daylight fishing and palmer-tied bivisibles in these same sizes for late evening fishing.

When you buy flies for trout it's best to buy them locally because people in the tackle business usually try hard to sell only flies that produce to keep you coming back. To give you an idea of the kind of flies I use during the July mayfly hatches for lake fishing, here are some I consider my favorites: Slim Jim, Ratface McDougal, Muddler Minnow, Adams, Irresistable, a rubber-legged nymphs created by Johnny Pietso, and an original creation of mine called a Shaving Brush. This last is tied with an extra long hair wing to suggest a mayfly emerging from its opening case.

Other than these grasshopper-mayfly imitations I carry several sizes and colors of palmer-tied bivisible flies for stream rainbow fishing. These range from large No. 6 to No. 20, predominantly in yellow, white, brown, grizzly and black. However, I seldom use the larger flies on streams. Here conditions normally call for flies in sizes between a No. 10 and No. 16.

There is usually very little activity on the surface of a trout lake except in the early morning and from late afternoon until darkness. You might see scattered rises during the day and an angler can pick up a fish or two during the bright part of midday if he works hard and long. On windy days sometimes there is local activity on the lee side of a pond, especially along the edge of the ripples that occur out from shore. Here fish feed on insects carried to them by the wind, unafraid in the protection of the broken water above them. Midday is a time for wet-flies. I've sometimes taken rainbows by trolling a fly, usually a black one, with a spinning rod. I learned this technique fishing a Montana reservoir with my fishing friend, Ralph Thorp, a trout specialist. In Minnesota this technique works best in lakes like Echo Lake near Finland, where scattered hatches are most likely to occur. When stone-fly hatches come off, the western Wooly Worm fished just below the surface takes trout when all else fails. Ned Kailing of our town has taken some very respectable trout from Kimball Lake fishing a Wooly Worm. He fishes the fly with a rod-tip jiggle, while retrieving it an inch or so below the surface.

Remember when fishing trout in a lake or pond that more patience is required than in stream fishing. The angler who dabs about will leave many fish with vacant stares on their piscatorial mugs. As a rule a fisherman can rest his fly on the water for some time before a fish will show. Rainbows can be much slower than bass so take your time! I like to leave a fly motionless for at least a full minute, work it slightly and rest it again. I've had fish sock my fly after it's been motionless for several minutes. And since your flies will be on the water almost constantly they must be buoyant and well dressed to stay afloat. Kapok, cork, plastic and deer-hair bodied flies will float a long time without getting water-logged after fish have taken them.

If there is a strong wind blowing I like to drop anchor on the shore side of a weed bed with just enough room between my canoe and shore to allow for a back-cast. But when a mild breeze fans the water you can cover more water by drifting parallel to the shoreline. Wind causes a ripple that helps disguise your leader. This is a factor in favor of the angler when fishing Minnesota's clear water lakes. Most big flies are highly visible and easy to watch even when the water is rough. Short casts are the rule in this type of fishing and when trout are treated to a full-blown hatch they will take flies within inches of a boat. I've watched fishermen who couldn't shoot ten feet of line, get hits a rod's length away.

In Minnesota the best trout fishing occurs during the month of July when big flies are on the water. Hatches of small insects in Minnesota are limited to late summer and warden Charlie Ott, of Grand Marais, tells me he's had good luck on rainbows during late summer trips. But the evening hatch in early July is where opportunity lies. By the time mosquitoes are at their worst, in late evening, rainbows begin to feed carelessly. As the mosquito attack dies off the hatch goes too.

At times trout will feed long after moonrise and there is widespread belief among trout anglers that a full moon affects their catch. Proof of their theory is documented in scientific publications. But it is doubtful that any one factor can be held responsible for good or poor trout fishing. Type of food, lake currents, air

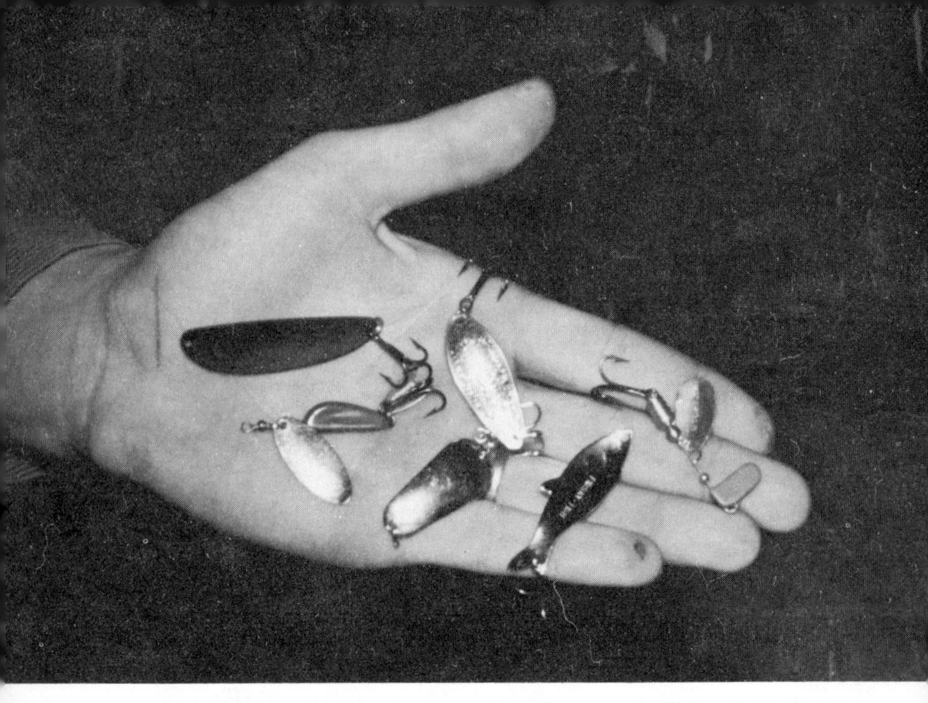

Compact spoons and French spinners like these are the hallmark of Minnesota rainbow anglers. Rainbows are suckers for shiny hardware.

Three-pound rainbow trout landed by the author while fishing Trout Lake north of Grand Marais.

Bud Kratoska weighs in some Trout Lake rainbow while Johnny Peitso re-examines his big brown, as Doc Soderberg looks on with admiration.

pressure, time of year and many more factors go together to affect the reaction of trout. A full moon while an obvious factor is only one of many that affect trout behavior.

Most any fly rod can be used for trout but I find a rod with some backbone is a worthy weapon for my particular brand of inexpert fly-fishing. For unless an angler is alone and standing in his boat it takes a meaty rod to keep the line moving smoothly when reaching out to long rises. This is particularly true with wading anglers who often appear as no more than stumps in the water. With a fly rod of nine feet a wading or seated fisherman can control line much better than he could with a short stick. It doesn't always follow that a sturdy rod must weigh six ounces. Some top-quality, muscular rods weigh just an ounce more than light models.

But before you get an idea that trout are singularly receptive to fly-fishing methods and you spin anglers threaten to set my book aside, I ask you to follow the path of this discourse for another bend and discover your writer is aware of the spin fisherman's joys and sorrows. For spinning is so well suited to fishing Minnesota rainbows that many anglers use spinning gear to the exclusion of all else. An angler, guided by instinct to the shores of some remote Minnesota pond in early summer, casts knowingly into the clear depths with a heavy spoon sure that his is the way to catch rainbows. Another spin crank who would catch big trout trolls the far side of the lake where the water drops into abysmal darkness. Both will catch rainbows.

Rainbow trout can be taken from many Minnesota lakes all summer by trolling with light tackle and early season anglers can take nice trout from shore between the May opener until around mid-June. Spoons are the chief prescription for curing rainbow fever, bright-polished spoons of silver, copper and brass. But trout will also hit Flatfish, Brooks Reefers and Lazy Ikes at times. An F6 flatfish is hard to beat for trolling. During the opening weeks troll your spoon or plug very slowly because rainbows are sluggish while the water is still very cold. A spoon idling along the bottom of the lake is tried and true rainbow medicine. This is an all-day technique, one employed by anglers waiting for the evening storm of mayflies and works effectively under sultry summer suns and endless rains. Most anglers take along spin and fly-fishing tackle when in rainbow country. Usually they troll or cast with spinning tackle until a hatch indicates a switch to flies. Rainbows have a weakness for flashing spoons when they're up near the surface, primed for a fly hatch. One particularly deadly spoon for rainbows is the quarter-ounce Wob-L-Rite made by Seneca Tackle Co., New York. Another is the Torpedo spoon produced by the National Expert Co., Minneapolis.

Fishing steelhead rainbows in the torrents of North Shore streams calls for a husky single action reel like the No. 1498 Pflueger Medalist. The 1498 weighs 8¾ ounces. It's also made in No. 1494, a smaller capacity reel, which weighs exactly 5¼ ounces.

The first time I took my wife out on trout water for prehatch spinning she hooked a good fish on her second cast. The fish hit the spoon and was out of the water in the same swift unbelievable second, flying into a topwater tantrum reminiscent of a mad man on a trampoline, going four ways at once and still holding a collision course. Pat watched the fish flower into the sun like a bright silver lily, cartwheeling five feet through space. As she stared in fascination at the big rainbow her line tightened, then grew slack.

"Did you see that?" she asked me, pointing in the direction of the flickering rings left by the fish. "One jumped right there!"

A man in a boat nearby laughed. "That fish was on the end of your line, Ma'am." he said.

She looked at me inquiringly. "He's not pulling your leg," I admitted. "Rainbows don't jump like that for exercise, only when they feel a hook in their mouth. But don't let it bother you, a lot of anglers who see one jump for the first time refuse to believe the fish is at the end of their line." She felt better.

Average Minnesota rainbow trout measure 14 to 18 inches long although a really big one comes to the creel of a spinning angler now and then. Spinning-minded fishermen interested in heavy rainbows spend their time working the mouths of streams that flow into Lake Superior. The Brule, Devil's Track, Split Rock, Knife and Reservation are some of the more accessible streams. These are coaling stations for big steelheads. Here an angler tossing heavy spoons can hope to feel a strong-jawed fish punch his lure and shatter the cool air in three-foot leaps.

These fish come and go, in and out of the stream mouths, feeding and retiring to deeper water at different times of the day. If you try them often enough or every time you go by, your reward is apt to be greater than you expected.

I once watched an Iowa fisherman at the mouth of the Knife take three bright fish, each over five pounds. He was wading cautiously on the shifty gravel and casting a red-eyed spoon slightly upstream, fishing just fast enough to keep his lure from hanging in the rocky bottom where he'd already lost three spoons. Before he was aware of who had who, a polished fish with a crimson stripe shot from the coffee-toned river and threw potfuls of brew in all directions. As the fish fell back the fisherman's rod curved to the water. A series of line plunges spiked with short aggressive runs were followed by gysering broad jumps before the trout began to yield slowly to the gifted anglers play.

When you spin for rainbows on these Lake Superior streams, use light four or six-pound monofiliment line for maximum casting distance. Normally it's the angler who can reach way out that will catch fish. A light line, coupled with a compact quarter-ounce Wob-L-Rite or Tor-P-Do spoon, will put you on the right track. Unfortunately you'll lose some spoons before you get the hang of this kind of fishing and you'll continue to lose them afterwards. Luckily the lures best suited to this kind of angling are rather inexpensive, well under the cost of bass and walleye plugs.

Many fishermen, especially natives, are drawn to the rainbow parties that begin in early April, even before the ice is off Minnesota lakes. This is a special season granted to hardy steelhead anglers, allowing them to fish the lower reaches of many Lake Superior watershed streams up to the first natural barrier, or three-fourths of a mile upstream, depending on which comes first. This is some of the most exciting steelheading in the country, where half-frozen anglers, line guides full of ice, stand in frigid water presenting red yarn flies and salmon eggs to willful, spawn-heavy fish.

Although a number of fishermen, full of young blood and fishing fever go out before the ice jams pound toward the big lake in mid-April, experienced steelheaders wait until the second or third weekend of the season when the water has warmed and the big run starts. Probably the best indication of a run is seen in the silver horde of smelt that ascend these same streams during the peak of Minnesota's steelhead exodus. Then smelters by the light of fires, throb up and down the stream, dipping here and there until a strike is made. During the day when the smelters, exhausted by cold baths, good fellowship and sleepless nights, retire as bats to the caverns of nearby motels, pink-cheeked city anglers and leather-necked woodsmen crunch the gravel, feeding terminal tackle to a hungry river already gorged on fat fish.

Fishermen prefer fly rods for this work because a long rod enables an angler to handle his bait or lure more effectively. It's also easier to feel strikes on a fly rod than with spinning gear or other tackle. To help counteract line drag in fast water some fishermen use monofilament line on their fly reels rather than conventional flyline. This is a good method in warm weather but has a major disadvantage that is sometimes overlooked. Fishing in sub-30 degree weather dulls the feeling in your hands and it is quite possible during the play of a fish, to get a digit or two hopelessly bound by your monofilament. The heartless twang of a snapping line as a great steelhead powers away with your rig is a painful lesson.

Two Duluth fishermen display beautiful steelhead rainbow taken while spinning the Knife River in mid-April.

A few anglers still cling to salmon eggs for steelheading. But recently most of them have converted to red florescent yarn flies, tied on single, double or treble hooks. Like other fishermen I buy red yarn and tie my own. There's nothing complicated in this since the fly is merely a tuft of yarn tied to a hook with a few turns of thread. There are a lot of custom variations of this red fly, all of them presumably tied to imitate salmon eggs, a natural food of steelhead in their native western waters. Color seems to be more important to the fish than shape. As a matter of fact, fishermen who have followed the early season for a few years carry several shades of flies in both red and chartreuse-green. I know a number of anglers who are so fussy about color they have steelhead yarn flown in from Washington's steelhead country to get the exact shades that they want.

The technique here, though it sometimes puts anglers in a somewhat unfavorable light, is considered necessary to feel striking fish. Usually an angler casts cross-stream and works the fly toward him slowly, but fast enough to keep a tight line. Weighted by a sinker attached to a dropper line the fly crawls along the bottom catching rocks and debris. Upon feeling any resistance the angler strikes back, hoping that what he felt was a light strike. More often it's a rock strike and the fisherman loses fly, leader and sinker. But occasionally it's a fish and the angler is faced with landing him in the raging current or treacherous wading conditions as he follows downstream. As the sound of "FISH ON" is heard above the roaring water other anglers pull their lines and watch as the fisherman and his rainbow rock-hop from pool to pool until one is beaten.

Frigid water and cold weather are no obstacles to early season steelheaders who fish the Sucker Hole of the Knife River on Minnesota's North Shore.

Be on the lookout for cable barriers erected from shore to shore a short distance below the natural falls. These are erected to prevent anglers from fishing among the trout concentrations below the falls where snagging possibilities are extremely high. Snagged or foul-hooked fish which are taken below the cable barrier now and then are usually released. The presence of other anglers makes this almost compulsory, but few anglers would want to keep snagged trout anyway.

Trout anglers who use salmon eggs and night crawlers account for a lot of rainbows in smaller trout streams where fly-fishing is not practical. Those who

This Duluth angler is landing a bright spring-run steelhead in the raging Knife River.

pick up the spinning habit or fish with flies during the brief but productive mid-summer season know that rainbow fishing in Minnesota is first-rate trout fishing. But with the emphasis on other species, few nonresidents and only a handful of residents realize that Minnesota has untapped rainbow fishing in a setting that makes chasing rainbows in the state's lakes a memory of mythical quality with concrete results.

CHAPTER V

Smallmouth Bass are Murder

Minnesota has so much bass water that no one has bothered to separate it into large and smallmouth territory. Some of the range of the smallmouth, in fact, overlaps that of his bigmouth cousin. The original range of this species includes the major rivers of the Mississippi River drainage and smallmouth bass are common in the main stream itself. It's especially common in the Brainerd - Pillager and Monticello - Elk River area and above Lake Pepin near Red Wing. It is also quite abundant in the St. Croix River, a river that is on the way to again becoming one of the country's best smallmouth rivers. Other good smallmouth water includes the Rum, Kettle and Snake Rivers. Lake Pokegama, Miltona, Spitzer, Little Rock, Bad Medicine, Elbow, and White Bear are good smallmouth lakes of long standing. And recently bass have been introduced into the border lakes between Minnesota and Ontario where smallmouth thrive in apparent harmony with walleyes and lake trout.

Smallmouth bass are easily distinguished from their more generous-mouthed relatives by dark verticle bars along their sides. They have slightly smaller mouths than the largemouth and the upper jaw of the smallmouth never extends past the rear margin of the eye. On the largemouth it always does. A smallmouth's eyes are red and the body is mottled like polished walnut. The belly and fins are often grainy gray leading to the name gray bass in some areas of its range. There is no prettier creature on earth than a shiny, wet smallmouth bass just lifted from the water.

Alan Maxson with mottled St. Croix River smallmouth he caught on a bucktail jig.

He's a beautiful fighter too. There may be a difference of opinion about the fighting qualities of the two bass species, but anglers who specialize in fishing smallmouth are inclined to rate them with rainbows in fighting ability. A smallmouth is to me a terrific fighter. He jumps so easily and well and with so little prompting that an angler who has once tangled with one will be hard put not to favor them a bit over the largemouth. A smallmouth will punch holes in the sky tirelessly and still fight strongly to the last. A big one will rattle your plugs until the paint chips. They often hit so fast you don't know you've had a hit until you've been bucked off.

Smallmouth bass grow pretty fast. A six-year-old fish will be twenty inches long and will weigh about four pounds, in the right kind of environment. In some lakes where conditions are not suitable and reproduction gets out of hand they never reach a large size. This condition is true to some extent in largemouth lakes, too, and people advocating year-around bass fishing for Minnesota, as practiced in more southern waters, often refer to these crowded lakes as proof that we aren't taking enough fish. While a few of these lakes could stand heavy fishing, people wouldn't fish where there were only small fish. They would fish bass where it is doubtful that reproduction and growth rates would sustain early fishing pressure at least in more accessible waters. But in spite of the year-around advocates in favor of quick reforms, fisheries' administrators are now maintaining a wait-and-see attitude, having already set the opener back a couple of weeks. If year-around bass fishing becomes a reality it should be only after fisheries' men have studied the problem in Minnesota and have determined to their own satisfaction that our bass can stand such a season. Certainly they should not set seasons based on the results of studies in any other state.

Actually the biggest reason that more bass aren't harvested lies in the plain fact that bass fishing gets too little publicity. Bass are fairly abundant but emphasis on walleyes and other fish cause anglers to forget about bass.

Fly-fishing provides the real thrills in smallmouth angling. Fly-fishing for bass is unequalled by any other method.

And significantly it is often the most effective way of catching them. Bass that I've taken on flies average smaller than those caught on lures, but I catch more of them. This is especially true in the north central part of the state where fabulous mayfly hatches occur, and true to a lesser degree on bass rivers.

In the cold deep water of Hungry Jack Lake in Cook County, average-sized bass probably enjoy eating mayflies more than any bass I know of. I've often wondered if Jack means bass in the language of the natives who are trying to keep the appetites of the fish in their local bass lake a secret.

I'll never forget the day I first fished Hungry Jack with Rod Bell. Rod stumbled across this fabulous lake during a trout-fishing jaunt. He had taken dozens of nice fish while standing at a little portage landing dock as clouds of mayflies rose from the water during the July hatch.

Now we were putting my light-weight canoe in at

the same landing, but it was too early in the day for a hatch and except for a few desultory flies bursting into the late afternoon sunlight, the lake was lifeless. Rod talked of the millions of fish that would be swirling all over the lake at sunset and his wife nodded and laughed with excitement at everything he said.

We set up our fly rods and paddled around the lake. I was getting nervous from the stories Rod was handing me and began looking around anxiously for rises. Rod pointed to a log-strewn bay opposite a hundred-foot rock promontory on our side of the lake.

"Let's wait around over there," he said and fairly lifted the bow of the canoe from the water as he thrust a great eddy of water behind him. "We caught some good ones over there last summer. Remember that big one you missed when you bumped your reel trigger?" he asked his wife.

"Yes, darn it. And you laughed too," she replied, and Rod laughed again thinking about it.

Off to the right in the reflection of the cooling sunshine, I spotted a rise and I let my paddle trail in the water, turning the bow in that direction.

"Did you see that?" Vi asked and she began stripping line from her reel.

"Take it easy," Rod advised. "One rise doesn't make a hatch."

When we got nearer the bay we saw a number of big sail-winged flies coming from the water against the dark cedars and spruce along the shoreline. Subtle rings indicated fish feeding just below the surface, probably taking pre-molting mayfly larvae before they could rise to the surface.

We began making short, exploratory casts. Rod and I pitched on one side of the boat while his wife cast on the other. Things went smoothly enough until Rod saw a rise close to the boat and without warning changed his casting direction. Our lines all met in mid-air and fell neatly on top of his wife in the middle of the canoe.

"Been fishing long, boys?" she asked very politely. "I hope one of you thought to bring a flashlight," she added as she began to unsnarl our lines.

We continued to fish and bass began taking flies all over the bay. One slammed my deer wing fly. I missed him! Then Rod's line swished through the guides and a spunky smallmouth squirted from the lake and rebounded high into the air. He charged the boat and circled the bow. Then, cutting inside his own circle, he bounced beside the boat.

"Who's winning?" I asked, without looking up, as I heard the fish dive beneath the canoe. I forgot to listen for an answer because a bass that sounded twice the size of Rod's sliced a thin piece of my fly, just enough to catch the barb. He sky-rocketed and back-flipped in two directions and took off on a crazy run for the scraggly weeds that grew near the shore. I snubbed him and he barrel-rolled, then backlooped again and came right at me.

"I got one," I heard Vi say, and could hear the fish jump on the other side of me. "Oh darn, he got off!"

Now the place was crawling with hungry bass. Circle widened to meet feeding circle and new rings appeared in between. Out in the middle of the lake things were a little slower but brisk enough. Fish were chopping up the big flies and you could hear them bang away on every hand.

We were all getting fish at once and as fast as we could cast. I paddled the canoe slowly in a circle with one hand and cast with the other and still I caught fish. It became too dark to see but they rose everywhere. I couldn't guess how many fish we caught and released that week in early July but I know it ran into hundreds. Most of them were under two pounds.

The techniques described in the chapters on large-mouth bass and rainbows will work as well for small-mouth bass too. A fairly heavy fly rod combined with a level or bug-taper flyline gives you a working tool that is very useful in lake and river fishing, particularly where you plan to wade or sit in a boat or canoe.

I'm partial to hair-wing flies for bass fishing simply because fish don't reject soft flies as quickly as they do standard-tied patterns. This gives the angler a bit more time to strike back. Hair-wings are very good floaters too, something well worth considering when you buy flies for bass fishing. There are many good flies of this general description, although some are very difficult to cast. Big, hairy, streamer-shaped flies like the Muddler Minnow, made famous by A. J. McClane, and the Slim Jim, have good casting design and are pleasant to handle. And of the dozens of poppers, hair frogs and mice are good at times. Where frogs are plentiful, hair frogs are hard to beat. Small poppers are always handy anywhere in bass country.

A long leader is unnecessary in the brown water of most Minnesota rivers. But when you fish the clear lakes in the Mississippi headwater area tapered leaders are helpful and quite often necessary. A seven footer tapered from twenty-pound to eight-pound stuff is about right. It should be made up of equal lengths of twenty, fifteen, twelve and eight-pound test material. While such a heavy leader is not needed to hold your fish it will straighten better when casting. It will also turn fish from weeds in emergencies. When fishing clear water it's then easy enough to add a couple of feet of six-pound monofilament to your present leader. If you encounter shy fish, this is often necessary.

Smallmouth bass seem to prefer a little more action with their dinner than their smarter brothers and usually a fly that is twitched gently at intervals will get best results. Imagination is often required to encourage fish to hit. So mix it up a little if stock retrieves or fly presentations don't work.

The new bass waters of Minnesota's wilderness like Rainy, Basswood, Moose, Knife and a number of others on the border chain are still practically untouched by fly-fishermen. Occasionally big bass are taken by walleye anglers and now and then you see a plug caster at work, but flyroders haven't really discovered this region. These lakes have miles of steep rocky shoreline with down timber lying in tangled masses along most of their margins. I've never fished there during a hatch but even when no flies are in evidence it looks like streamer water from way back. A maribou streamer fluttered beside the dead submerged trees that line these lakes is an unexplored opportunity wide open to experimental anglers. The bass are there for I've taken some good ones on surface lures at different times. But unfortunately I've never had a chance to spend time toying with them. When this water becomes known to bass-buggers they'll find miles of unfished smallmouth water in a setting matching the wild mood of the fish.

During part of the summer when the surface water is dead and bass are feeding deep and flies can't reach them effectively, spinning tackle answers the clear call to duty and fills the ranks decimated by seasonal change. River bass lying deep can be coaxed out of their cool shelters behind rocks, downed trees and wing dams by bright little spinning lures. Newer lures like the Mepps and Abu Reflex, an outgrowth of the fly and spinner combination, or a buck-tailed Heddon Spinfin fluttered along the bottom, are all ideal for taking bass in deep water. These lures are compact and go deep fast. The spinning blade helps keep them from hanging up even while moderately retrieved, although they're not strictly weedless. Fish these lures rather slowly and interrupt your retrieve by a gentle fluttering action.

I've also had good luck in rivers when using a light pearl and metal fish-shaped wobbler for smallmouth bass. When they're scattering minnows on bars and in slow places, the way they do along the shore in early summer, a pearl spoon is deadly. Try casting a pearl wobbler ahead of rising fish and begin working your lure as soon as it hits the water. If you cast well ahead, about six or eight feet in front of him, he'll see the lure as the school of minnows parts. If things go well, you'll be waltzing with bass until the dinner music stops and the dance is called off.

Another answer for anglers faced with minnow-chasing fish is embodied in the prop-driven surface

This pair of hefty smallmouth bass fell for a nightcrawler tumbled through a pool of the Mississippi River.

lures that well imitate the expiring antics of a wounded baitfish. Even when feeding bass are not in evidence this lure can be used effectively along stumpage and rock banks. Sometimes it will draw the fire of lethargic, disinterested bass. But remember to fish top-side lures very slowly and with great patience. When your plug first hits the water let it lie motionless for several seconds before you move it and then twitch it very slightly. As I mentioned before, smallmouth are more responsive to a traveling meal than old bigmouth and will paste a lure that is moving at a good clip. Try slow careful retrieves at first and change your pace until you get some action.

During September and October and again during the early part of the bass season when bass are feeding near the bottom and are somewhat sluggish, a bucktail jig bounced very slowly along the bottom will often recharge the weak batteries of droll fish. Jigs should be fished just fast enough to make them look alive, giving your fish all the time he needs to respond. I use a small white spinning bucktail jig for river fishing. However, I've taken some on yellow and light blue jigs as well. A bucktail jig should be fished by first

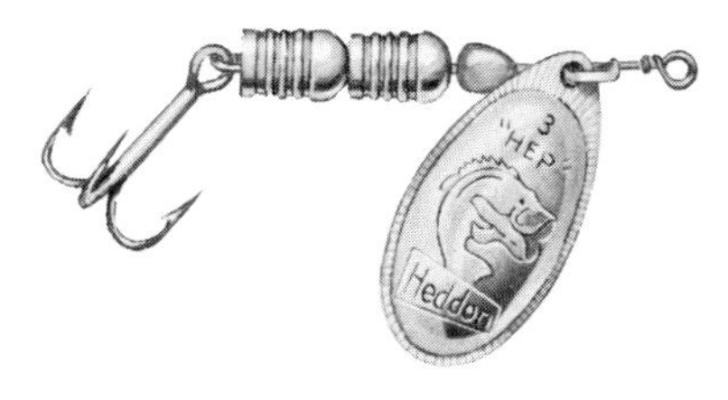

Heddon's "Hep" French-type weighed spinner comes in several sizes from 1/16 to 3/8 ounces. Excellent for trout, silver bass and walleyes.

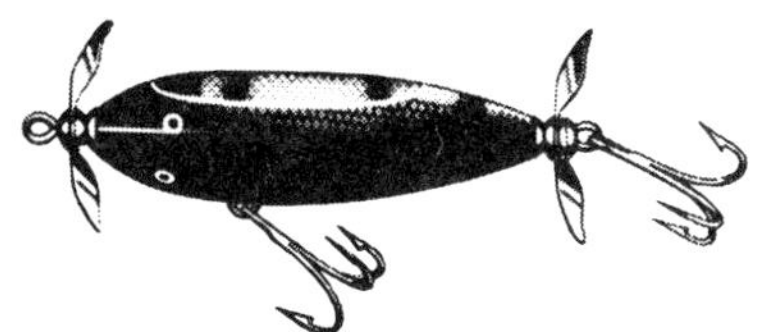

Lures like this spinning edition of Creek Chubs Injured Minnow account for a lot of smallmouth bass in midsummer.

letting it settle to the bottom. If no weeds are present, retrieve by raising your rod in a short abrupt manner followed by a turn of the reel handle. This causes the jig to jump, or hop, for a foot or so and settle back to the bottom. It is jumped again in the same way until the cast is fished out. Strikes will come as the lure begins to settle back to the bottom. This is a lure that is fast becoming a key fish-getter in Minnesota. After the rage started by myself and several other anglers and writers during the summer of '57, it looks destined to change the fishing picture especially where spinning is concerned. I've taken nineteen different species of fish in Minnesota on jigs and a spinning rod!

Deep-lying lake bass can be often reached by trolling or casting deep-running plugs along rock banks, gravel bars and weed beds outside drop-offs. Most of the useful plugs, except those having metal bills, are designed for medium depth and weight should be added for casting. But they can be trolled effectively if you let enough line out. You know you have enough line out when your lure bumps bottom now and then. When casting plastic-bodied, sinking plugs you should count slowly to give them time to sink. Keep changing your count until you begin catching fish or are fishing right on the bottom. Remember that lures made of wood usually need a couple of split shot to get them down. But a wooden plug has better action at slow speed, so when a very slow retrieve is called for you'll catch more bass on a wood-bodied lure.

There is a closer relationship between lure color and catching fish than many anglers suspect or are willing to admit. Generally speaking light lures are more effective on bright days and dark lures will catch more fish faster during dull days and during night or late evening. This theory has more to support it than is generally understood until you poke around into the secrets of biological records. Some of my best catches of smallmouth bass support the theory including a four-and-a-half pounder out of Knife Lake.

Most of the heavy bass I've caught have been feeding deep and were taken on 1/8- and 1/4-ounce spinning lures. These aren't the huge plugs used by bass anglers a decade ago yet they seem to supply a pleasant mouthful even for lunker fish.

I've also found spinning tackle is ideally suited to fishing smallmouth bass with live bait. You can cast nearly weightless minnows and night crawlers a long distance on spinning tackle with ease. Before spinning came along, anglers were using a chunk of lead to get any real casting distance with live bait. Even then the effort required to cast nearly always killed the bait or it would fly off the hook and onto the other bank of the river. Spinning has changed things and it has added a lot of pleasure to baitfishing for bass and panfish. Now you can cast minnows and other live bait long distances without losing or injuring it. Open-spool, foreign-type spinning reels do the best job of handling tender bait, but you have to use a light monofilament line. Four-pound line is about right. Unless you have a weed or snag problem four-pound line will hold the biggest bass even in fast water. Using heavier line on a spinning reel for bait fishing, while it may be much better than casting gear, defeats to some extent, the advantages that spinning offers. Spinning with live minnows, crayfish or nightcrawlers is a deadly way of taking smallmouth, from fast, wadeable Minnesota bass streams. A weightless nightcrawler drifted freely looks natural and it seldom becomes hung on rocks or snags. I like to fish live bait by casting slightly across and upstream, taking in line as the bait drifts toward my position. As it passes below me, I feed line out again so the bait will continue to drift naturally, and at the same time I follow its drift by keeping the rod pointed toward the bait. I can tell when I have a hit because the bait will begin moving unnaturally against the current as the fish scoops it from the bottom. There is always plenty of time to set the hook when fishing live bait in fast water except possibly when a fish hits as you begin to retrieve your bait for another cast. Then a fish will either hook himself or strip your hook. But normally all that is required to set your hook is to simply tighten up on your fish and you've got him. With just a little experience you'll learn to know the difference between the hesitation of a snag and a taking fish.

Fish swirling eddies and behind bars and wing dams by letting your bait drift into them on a slack or lightly-controlled line. This way your bait will be carried to the fish in a natural way. When a fish takes your bait the line will begin moving up or across the current and you will have plenty of warning and be able to set your hook.

Minnesota offers smallmouth anglers a lot of good bass territory to explore. Even lakes close to the Twin Cities, White Bear Lake, for example, produce five and six-pounders almost every summer. Rivers on every side of the Twin Cities have bass in abundance and catching them is mostly a matter of knowing where they can be found and what to use. You'll have to work to take one over three pounds because fish that have grown to that size while facing man and his lures have better than average IQs. But the bass are here and the methods outlined when accompanied by a little work will have you catching bass in short order.

One thing you should keep in mind. I've often seen anglers stubbornly plug away with deep-running lures when bass were taking flies on top of the water. The mistake here is so obvious that it shouldn't have to be pointed out, yet it's a common one. Conversely, don't beat your brains out bass-bugging for smallmouth if you have reason to believe they're deep. While a bass will rise about eight feet to smack a lure or fly, this reaction is not always dependable. And when nothing you're read here will catch fish, think up something new or apply a technique you've heard about. Tie a fly on a dropper behind your plug or hang a strip of balloon or half-a-night crawler on the middle hook of your plug. Fish your lure dead and retrieve it in fast jerks. When fishing seems off, try very tiny spoons or some of the outsized plugs of by-gone days.

If you're in bass water, there are very few times some of the methods discussed here will fail you. And once you've crossed wires with a sizzling, red-eyed smallmouth the memory of his jumps and his fighting ability will keep you going on the few lean days when bass are sulking.

CHAPTER VI

The Deceptive Walleye

An angler, much like a college student after a coed, has more fun if his quarry is artfully deceptive, the chase and acceptance predicated on the terms of the pursued. This is the thread, perhaps, which weaves the robe of success by holding the interest of the pursuer at a high level.

This deception explains, at least in part, the popularity of walleye fishing more than anything else. Walleyes could never be classed with bass or northerns as fighting game fish. Rather the key to their popularity is directly linked to their crazy, screwball behavior. Abnormality is normal with walleyes and anglers who fish for them exclusively have developed a broad philosophy in order to retain their sanity in the face of unexpected success and failures.

Although walleyes are poor fighters compared to almost any freshwater fish you could name, I think, they've been a little under-rated by anglers who use heavy tackle. When caught on either a fly rod or on spin-gear, walleyes make fishing more interesting and put on a pretty fair show. Even if you find them to be passive, slow fighting fish that seem confused by what's happening to them, they are great fun to catch when they're biting well.

You'd think a fish that ate a thousand smaller fish for every pound of body weight would be easy to catch anytime, but this isn't quite true in most walleye water. Success varies greatly from lake to lake and some anglers get skunked opening day while anglers in another lake boast the best luck in years. At times dead lakes come to life following the opener in May and water that was hot earlier has cooled completely. But when walleyes are on a rampage there are few fishermen who complain about not catching fish! When walleyes are hitting in Lake of the Woods, Upper Red, Leach, Winnie or Mille Lacs Lakes anglers take limits with ridiculous ease! When walleyes refuse to hit none but a few of the more gifted and preservering fishermen catch fish. Fortunately the walleye rampage every summer lasts long enough to give weekend and visiting anglers at least one good chance at schooling fish during the course of the season. Sometimes these splurges last nearly all summer. Other years the hot fishing lasts only a few weeks. But normally the best walleye catches are made during the last week in May and throughout the month of June. If I were driving to Minnesota with walleye fishing in mind, I'd put up with the mosquitoes of early and mid-June to get in on some of the best walleye fishing found anywhere in the country. For while walleyes are unpredictable they're much less so during early summer.

Walleyes are in no way related to pike although the name pike is often added. The true pike in Minnesota is affectionately called northern with the word pike lobbed off. In some areas of Minnesota the name pike alone is used when referring to walleyes. This sometimes gets pretty confusing! I heard a Canadian and Minnesota angler discussing fishing one time and watched them almost come to blows. The Canadian was referring to walleyes as pickerel, as they do in Ontario, and he was calling the northern a pike. The Minnesotan called the Canadian's pickerel a pike and his pike a northern! Finally they got so confused I offered to act as interpreter. But before I half finished explaining they were both ready to count coup on my scalp and fillet me for a walleyed pickerel! In spite of efforts of the Outdoor Writers Association to standardize common names of fishes, the people name the fish and if they want to call bass sardines nobody is going to stop them!

Walleyes are slightly bug-eyed, rather slender fish with mottled bronze and gold markings and have a white belly. A white rim on the lower edge of the tail, a black spot on the back part of the dorsal fin and sharp

Minnesota's No. 1 fish—the walleye.

dorsal spines coupled with a mouth full of deadly-looking teeth and razor-like gill covers well identifies this species. The sauger or sand pike, found schooling with walleyes, are very similar but are identified by a more slender body, by a black spot at the base of each pectoral, or side fin, and rows of black spots on a spiney dorsal fin.

Walleyes are as abundant in Minnesota now as they ever were. This is especially true of the larger waters centering around the Mississippi River headwaters and all the major rivers of the state have good walleye populations. Even with the growth of industry most of Minnesota's walleye's water is still relatively unpolluted. The only place where pollution seeems to be a real problem at present time is in the Mississippi River below the Twin Cities and the lower fifteen miles of the Minnesota River. Groups organized to combat the dumping of poisonous materials in the rivers and lakes of Minnesota are working hard to control pollution. When the value of the sport fishing and boating in even this small area is considered, it's surprising industrial pollution is tolerated. A clean river is an economic asset and restoration of the Mississippi below St. Paul means better fishing and dollars in the coffers of river towns.

Stizostedion vitreum is a wandering fish and lives best in large lakes where there is plenty of room to roam. This wandering characteristic is one reason why walleyes are considered unpredictable. This is especially true in early summer when walleyes are sometimes found in the most ridiculous places.

A few summers back Rod Bell, Tom McCutchan

and I drove to Mille Lacs for a few hours of walleye fishing and discovered the big lake was rough enough to blow a cruiser out of the water. But we decided we'd try plugging in a little channel at the entrance of Father Hennepin State Park, a sheltered spot near the town of Isle on the southeast end of the lake. Here the water running through a culvert creates a tidal rise and fall between a backwater and a protected bay of the lake. We'd often taken walleyes in this deep channel before. An hour of plugging that day brought us nothing for our efforts. Getting restless, Rod pulled on his boots and started along the shore toward a green-ash swamp.

"Where you going?" Tom asked him and he leaned into the wind blowing off Mille Lacs to sift the words that came back to him.

"Just looking around," Bell answered and he slogged across the marshy place that led to a small point projecting into the main lake.

We forgot about him and continued to cast the channel until we heard a whoop on the neck of land where Rod stood. It sounded like there was a scalp dance going on at the neighboring Chippewa's reservation.

"Well, how do you like that?" I asked Tom.

Rod stood in the weedy shallows of the point with big waves from the lake splashing above his knees. He was holding a walleye up for us to see. The wind carried his torn voice our way.

"COMon OveR!"

Tom dug his boots out of the trunk.

"You coming?" he asked, pulling off his shoes.

"No boots," I told him. "I'll watch and see how you do."

We heard another yip from Rod's direction and Tom hurried with his second boot and took off through the slough grass.

I fished along on the road and caught nothing while I saw those boys take fourteen nice walleyes from over a storm-lashed weed bed. They told me later that they were pitching Lazy Ikes and were getting hits only when they reeled as fast as they could. When they tried retrieving slower the fish refused to hit!

Normally anglers faced with a situation of this sort will go home disgusted, although there are undoubtedly times when they could capitalize on bad weather and take a few fish home with them. Walleyes feed in the queerest places and fishermen who can forget some of their pre-conceived ideas of fishing can often catch them when other anglers with less imagination tell you they're not hitting.

On opening weekend boats troll merrily all over walleye lakes, picking a few walleyes off the bars and points, but few of them explore inshore possibilities. Yet walleyes will often feed right next to shore during the late spring.

When they're feeding in shallow bays over weed beds or on shallow bars you can often spin for walleyes right from shore. Walleyes feeding in shallow water are suckers for almost anything you throw them. In fact I've caught them on dry flies in Northern Lights lake and I've seen anglers catch them on bass poppers when they're feeding in close to shore.

The universal method for locating walleye feeding grounds is obvious to veteran anglers, but beginning fishermen will often overlook the obvious in the face of confusion. However, few experienced walleye anglers overlook the boat concentrations as a first approach to their problem because they know boats almost always mean walleyes are hitting. Of course, there is often more than one feeding ground in a lake and at times boats will be piled up on all of them indicating the hot spots. This is where the casual anglers would do best to start. You can be sure these boatsmen know there are walleyes here or they wouldn't stick around. At times when action is fast, boats anchor on these bars or flats but when things are slow and the wind is right for drifting they commonly drift to locate scattered schools or at least to pick up some strays.

White sucker minnows are the most common bait used by drifting and still-fishing anglers. Some prefer shiners when they're available but when they become scarce following early spring seining fishermen have to settle for fatheads and suckers. Actually fatheads are as good bait minnows as anything you can get but shiner purists don't believe it. Other species that are useful as walleye bait include the common creek chub and the hardy, diminutive relative of the northern pike, the mud minnow. All these minnows except the mud minnow are lively on the hook. All except shiners, keep well in your bait bucket. Shiners are okay in early summer and will live pretty well under winter fishing conditions where they're extremely popular.

I use a medium-action spin-stick coupled with an open reel full of four-pound test monofilament line when I drift for walleyes. I like a No. 4 or No. 6 Big-Bend style hook, depending on the size of minnows available. The sinker prescription has to be filled at the fishing scene, according to your rate of drift or current. I fish from a canoe and the drift rate is much greater than that of a heavier boat. As a result, I use several heavy split-shot if there's any kind of breeze stirring. The faster your boat drifts the more lead you'll need to get your bait to stay near bottom. In an anchored boat you can get by with just weight enough to pull your minnow downstairs.

Minnesota walleye anglers often drift to locate fish—when netting walleyes lead fish to net—not net to fish.

When drift fishing keep your bait close to the bottom. The best way to do this is by opening the bail of your spinning reel or by taking your thumb off of your reel spool. Remember if you bump bottom now and then you're fishing just right, but if you're dragging bottom constantly take in a little line. A successful drift angler is seldom the picture of reclined relaxation. His work is cut out for him if he expects to use up his minnows. When you catch a walleye while drifting you can come around and drift over the same spot again or anchor upwind from the location. If you're fishing a big mud flat like those of Mille Lacs, you'll have a hard time pin-pointing the exact spot where you caught your fish, but if you're lucky you can come around and hit the spot again. Then still fishing will pay off. It's usually hard to relocate a school unless you have an anchor float to drop over when you take your first fish. A lot of anglers carry an air tight can or a big bobber with a heavy sinker attached to a long line and use it to "hold" a school of fish.

Trolling Strip-On type leader-spinner combinations often get results. Such a leader has a needle-eye end which can be slipped through the minnow. A double hook is then fitted through the needle eye keeping the minnow in place behind the spinner. This is a favorite river rig and it has a place in casting as well.

If you're a live bait angler, don't overlook nightcrawlers for walleyes. I've used them to decorate the treble hooks on plugs and as a trailer on a Mepps or Waterbaby spinner with deadly results. This is an old-time trout technique that has caught the fancy of walleye anglers, and known as a "Mille Lacs Cocktail".

Some anglers learn about night crawlers accidentally like a friend of mine who was fishing bass in the Rum River near Anoka. He hooked a fish he was convinced was a carp and played it indifferently. When the carp turned out to be a six-pound walleye he nearly flipped!

I've found crawlers a life saver at times too. Adding them to the treble on your plug can work miracles.

Two years ago I was talked into a wild-rice harvesting expedition to Big Winnie. When we reached the rice country we discovered the lake we intended to harvest wasn't ripe yet and hadn't been opened for ricing. While waiting around a day or so for the crop to ripen, Bruce McCutchan and I launched his canoe in Cutfoot Sioux Lake north of Winnibigoshish. We paddled out to join the admiral's fleet on a gravel bar across the lake. The boys weren't catching walleyes. We didn't have to ask to learn that. A few boats were anchored, but everyone looked like the low-man. Bruce and I tried drifting but our canoe behaved like an Arab mare in a Percheron race and we had to mend our course between every cast.

"Let's drop the hook and cast a few times before the wind drifts us off the bar," I suggested.

"We might as well try it," Bruce answered, and he splashed our home-made cement anchor into the drink. There were boats anchored within forty yards on both sides of us but they were still-fishing so we had a pretty fair piece of water to ourselves for casting. I cast a black deep-running Cisco Kid and it landed about forty feet behind the nearest boat. After a ten count I began to retrieve. Bruce worked the other side of the boat. I kept pacing my retrieve and after fishing a few minutes without a hit I thought about our emergency fish rations—the night crawlers.

"Think I'll tease 'em a little," I told my partner. But he shook his head and grinned.

"Maybe they won't work," I answered, reading his thoughts, "but you don't know until you've tried."

"Go ahead," he razzed, "you're the expert."

I continued to work the same water, trying to bring my lure across the edge of the bar, teasing it along the gravel bottom. On the second cast I got a strike the minute the lure came to life and it looked like I was going to tangle lines with my neighbor in the next boat. Just to be sure it didn't happen I stopped the fish's runs by increasing the tension on my reel spool. The fish wasn't having anything his way and after a couple of bewildering spurts I brought a two-pound walleye to the canoe. Nearby anglers looked mildly interested but they weren't getting excited about one little walleye. When the next cast collected another frisky two-pounder I heard a guy in the next boat say something about his fish.

"You better start fishing on the other side," Bruce suggested. "They don't appreciate your catching fish from right under their boat."

"Guess I wouldn't like it either."

We began casting away from the boats and caught two more walleyes before we decided we'd better head for camp and get things ready for the following day's ricing.

Since the advent of the Helin Flatfish over a decade ago, and subsequent patented variations, notably Kautzky's Lazy Ike, trolling and casting for walleyes with plugs have become an increasingly popular and productive technique. While there are a lot of good walleye plugs of this general design I think it's significant that the Lazy Ike is the only one still made of wood. If you've ever seen a plastic-type lure and a wooden lure of this design worked next to each other, you'd immediately see that the popularity of the Ike is no accident. A wooden lure "starts" sooner than a plastic one. As a result the wooden lure can be trolled or retrieved slower than a plastic one of the same design. Quite commonly, extremely slow trolling is the only way to catch walleyes. The Lazy Ike is constructed with a very slow retrieve in mind. And according to the Ike people they'll continue to make it of wood until they can come up with a plastic model that will start at the same slow speeds. The Lazy Ike is in a class by itself as the number one plug for Minnesota walleyes.

Other heavier lures, those especially designed to go deep and the floating diving metal-billed models have a place in the fishing scheme as well. Heddon's River Runts, both jointed and solid models, the Cisco Kid series, L and S Lures and Brooks Reefers are all producers. These are the best current lures and have been for a number of years, although not the only plugs an angler can expect to catch walleyes on in Minnesota.

How about lure color? Experienced anglers cannot always agree. In fact, they're often miles apart where color choice is concerned. There are obviously times when gorging fish will hit a lure of any color and choice based on these rare occasions alone leads only to complete confusion. In an effort to develop a general pattern of color choice I've spent a lot of time

For the walleye angler who trolls for his fish, a rugged reel like the Pflueger Akron shown here is recommended.

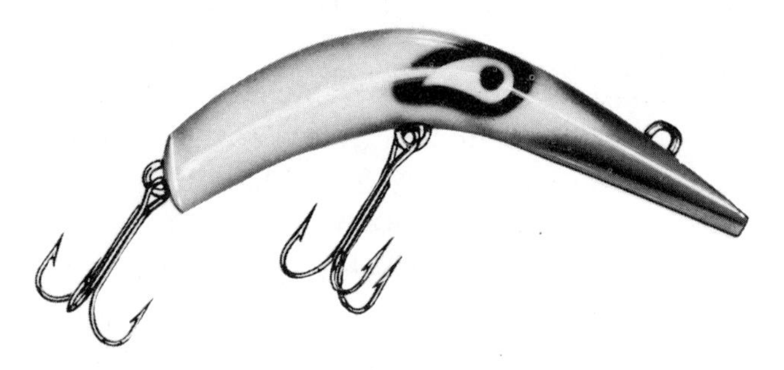

Kautzky's Lazy Ike, one of the few walleye lures still made of wood, is the favorite of anglers who troll and cast for these fish in Minnesota lakes and rivers.

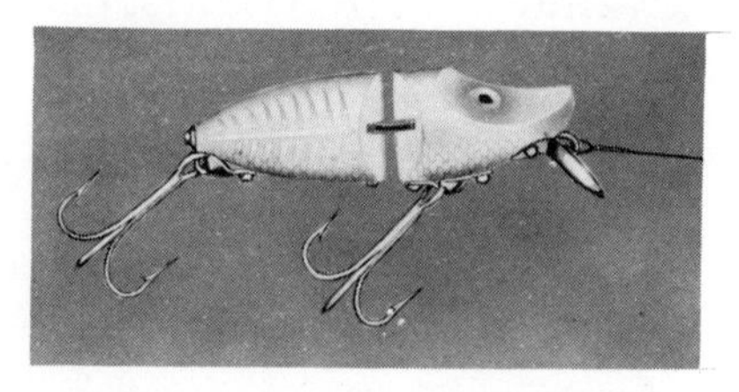

Heddon's Jointed River Runt "Spook" in both floating and diving models and many sizes have long been excellent walleye and pike lures in the hands of Minnesota fishermen.

7/16 ounce deep running Cisco Kid is dependable lure for dredging.

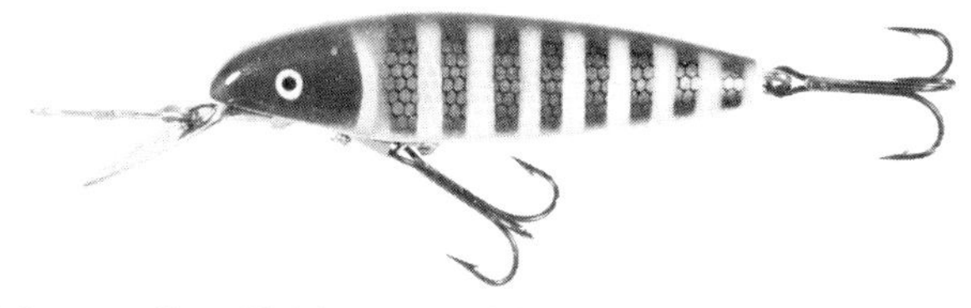

5/8 ounce Cisco Kid lure is good for bait casting and deep trolling.

This 3/8 ounce Cisco Kid is one spin fishermen and light baitcasters use for walleyes.

Spin Cisco Kid is strictly a spinning lure. Weight 1/4 ounce.

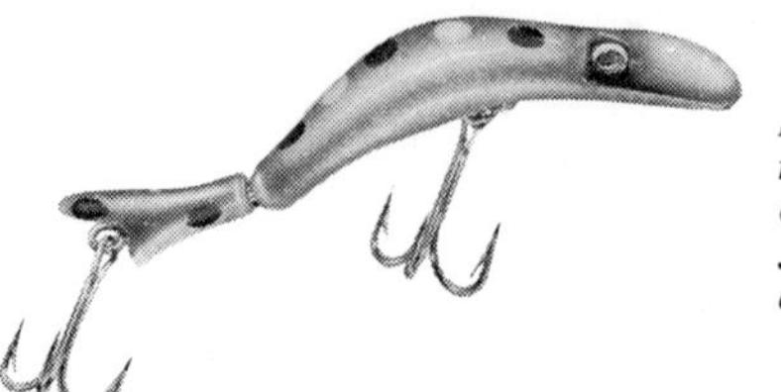

Brooks Baby Reefer is a spinning natural for Minnesota walleye fishermen. Brooks 3/8 ounce Reefer or Jointed Reefer are best for trolling or baitcasting.

experimenting with different lures. Sometimes I've had good results. At other times, all I've brought home were additional pages of notes. But a lot of fooling around has indicated that light-colored lures have more fish appeal during the day, particularly when the day is clear. Toward evening or during the night, walleyes prefer darker-colored lures. This rule, general as it appears, is sound, and perhaps as specific as one can get. There are anglers in camp who take the other view placing their confidence in light lures for dark days and nights and dark-colored lures for bright daylight fishing.

This light-dark theory has some basis in fact that is hard to refute. A case in point is the common white sucker. This fish is perhaps the most abundant forage species in Minnesota. They're found in all walleye lakes and are the staple in walleye diets. The white sucker along with the yellow perch makes up a greater part of the walleye's food supply.* Both are also active during daylight hours only. When night comes white suckers stop feeding in the deep water and retire to the shallows where they lie dormant until morning.** Yellow perch also hit the weed patch at night and snore

*A study being conducted by the Minn. Bureau of Research and Planning indicates walleyes feed much heavier on perch than had been suspected and further that they feed mostly on insect larvae until midsummer when the young-of-the-year perch are big enough to be eaten.

**Dr. Samuel Eddy, Minnesota Fisheries Research Investigation Report No. 37.

until dawn. The color of these fish certainly suggest some of the lighter-colored lures and lend some support to the theory. On the other hand bullheads and their close relatives, the madtoms, feed at night, supporting this theory even more. In fairness it must be pointed out that tullibee or ciscos, an important forage species, are active day and night punching a hole in the light-dark idea but also helping account for the many exceptions to the rule. Nevertheless, discerning anglers will find this a workable system and will boost their catch rate if they apply it with an open mind and with an eye for exceptions.

Modifications are in order when fishing clear lakes during bright days. I've noticed then that smaller lures will take more fish and that large bright lures will often scare them. On the other hand I've taken walleyes from discolored lakes and rivers under bright daylight conditions where large light lures worked to my advantage, probably because they were somewhat more visible than a smaller edition would have been. In the end the color question is resolved by experiment in spite of the rules of the game. If you want to catch walleyes consistently, you have to combine experience and technique continually. Real walleye anglers aren't made during the early summer slaughters when fish are constantly hungry. They develop slowly through observing and learning and then applying what they learn, always trying something new.

Almost any light spinning or casting gear is suitable for walleye trolling. However, I think your reel should have special attention. Your casting reel should hold a hundred yards of 12 or 15-pound line. Langley's

Top Cast is an inexpensive reel that will do the job well, especially for the man who wants to mix a little casting with his fishing. But for the troller who finds casting a pain he can't find a reel that will do a better job than the slightly more expensive Pflueger Akron. The Akron is a heavy duty reel, ruggedly built to stand the strain of constant drag against the gears.

Your rod should be a medium stiff pole. Trolling all day with a light rod makes fishing very poor sport. You'd be surprised how fatigued you will be after fighting a plug on the end of fifty yards of line for a few hours. A stiffish rod eliminates some of the work of trolling. When you set the hook on a striking walleye, a stiff rod will also compensate for line stretch, making it easier to hook your fish.

I like to use three feet of nylon monofilament material, 10 or 15-pound test, between my lure and line with a No. 5 snap-swivel on the business end. Some anglers use a longer section of monofilament to further disguise the connection between line and lure.

My favorite trolling weapon consists of a medium action spinning rod and a light reel filled with 6-pound monofilament line. Most of the time I attach a snap-swivel directly to the end of the line. I don't use a leader except when I'm trolling obstructed water or where I may make contact with a heavy pike. Where big northerns are apt to be encountered I use a 20-pound nylon leader. This in turn is fitted with a 4-inch piano-wire leader as precaution against their sharp teeth.

Be sure to keep your lure close to the bottom when

trolling. To get down where the fish live, let out line until you think you're hitting bottom. If you get hung up all the time you've got too much line out. Your lure should be working just off the bottom, knocking the tops off the high spots and coaxing fish out of the hollows. Naturally when you cross bars, you'll have to take in line or change your trolling speed to avoid snagging on them.

When you get a fish, swing around in a circle and try the spot again and again as long as they continue to bite. If you hit walleyes in one spot, you can sometimes anchor nearby and have more fun casting for them. Or to save trolling time getting over the spot, make a fast turn after you cross the school and as the boat turns you can retrieve your line easily and quickly. Complete the turn and swing around within a hundred yards of your fish and pay your line out again. Slow down just before you cross your hot spot and you can make another pass at your fish while they're still hungry. This way you avoid the time consuming and unproductive slow circle each time. But don't try this if there are other boats around because they won't understand or appreciate your approach!

Troll at a very slow speed when you begin. Too much speed seems to be the cardinal trolling sin. Try slow trolling until you're sure your speed is the reason you don't catch fish. If you're going faster or slower than boats nearby, and catching nothing while they fill the boat, you can be sure your speed is all wrong. Try pacing your speed to the boats around you and watch what they're using. Try plugs of different colors starting with light-colored ones. Run down the scale from light to dark until you get some action.

Walleyes are unpredictable to the point that if I told you they like slow-moving lures 90 percent of the time you might go for weeks when they wouldn't look at a lure doing anything less than five knots. Walleyes are diabolically endowed, alternately, with the cavernous hanger of a northern pike, the shyness of a brown trout, the moodiness of a largemouth and the impulsiveness of a bullhead. At times a lure can't possibly go slow enough and at other times you could troll from a torpedo boat and not go fast enough. This was true the time my brother Howie and I were canoeing out of Basswood Lake in a miserable endless rain. Fishing had been poor all week and we were more interested in getting to the dry clothes we had in the car at Winton than we were in fishing. After we portaged into Fall Lake my brother picked up a paddle and didn't put it down again until we reached the far end of the lake, six miles away.

Two men can urge a canoe along pretty fast and Howie grunted something I took for "Knot head," when I suggested trolling on the way in.

"Go ahead if you want to," he said without turning his head or breaking stroke. "But I'm not going to slow down for you."

I flipped a shiner scale, plug overboard and let out 30-feet of line. Then I braced the rod against a cross-brace, holding the rod handle against a rib of the canoe with my foot. We traveled so fast my medium-weight rod was bent double and vibrations from the heavy lure made it hard to hold it in place. I trolled a hundred yards over the deepest part of the lake and then got a jolting hit.

"Got one, Howie," I informed him. He continued to paddle as if he hadn't heard me, and paddled harder if anything. I finally worked a walleye to the boat and derricked him aboard.

I let out line once more and had another fish almost immediately.

"For crying out loud, quit slowing us down!" Howie growled. "Some guys just don't know when to come out of the rain!"

I felt a little sorry for him doing all the work and missing the fishing but I was having too much fun to remember we'd been wet all day long. Before we pulled up to the Winton landing I'd taken a half dozen fat walleyes—six walleyes while trolling at top speed in the middle of a deep lake at midday during the warmest part of the summer! What those fish were doing all over the lake a few feet below the surface is hard to say. Walleyes are just plain unpredictable!

A change of pace in trolling can sometimes work wonders. A slow turn will often get strikes. As the lure changes speed after coming out of a turn, fish will often take a crack at it. You can try pulling your rod forward quickly now and then too, or reel in some line and let it out again very fast. At times the only fish I've caught have been taken this way, by changing the speed of the lure.

Walleyes are most active at dawn and dusk although daylight fishing is seldom a waste of time. But if you don't like getting up early, fish right into the night. Night fishing has gained an impressive following in

Minnesota's larger lakes for several good reasons. First, walleyes are skilled night feeders and have no difficulty catching food after dark. Perhaps too, night fishing has the kind of appeal to anglers that blindman's bluff has for youngsters. While a psychologist might explain it better than we who practice the art, it's doubtful that he could resist night fishing himself after being exposed to a moonstruck patient. The world of darkness, where sounds alone transmit a new picture of what we have seen before in daylight, adds fascinating new dimensions to the black world that surrounds the imaginative angler.

Returning to reality, state law requires night fishermen to have a white light on their boats, as a precaution against collision. It must be a light that can be seen for two miles in all directions. This, of course, is a sensible idea on walleye lakes because often boats are as thick as ants at a picnic during the early weeks of the season.

I think you'll have better luck at night fishing if you get the lay of the water during the day. And you'll find your way back to camp easier in the darkness after you become acquainted with the shoreline.

Minnesota anglers are learning that spin-casting at night from shore or from a boat is a sporting and very effective way of catching night-feeding walleyes. You can catch fish from docks and jetties or right from the bank if you're willing to move around a little. The first time I plugged from shore at night it was a hit-or-miss affair, but I had fair luck. Since my first try I've taken walleyes from shore a number of times from Mille Lacs and other lakes. Walleyes often follow baitfish onto rock bars and into shallow bays. They corner minnows over weed beds and sometimes between the weed beds and the shoreline. Try fishing the mouths of streams, along rocky shorelines and shallow points of land. Casting is the best way to harvest these shallow feeders. Trolling anglers never troll where these fish are feeding. Rocks, weed beds and other inshore obstacles keep trollers out from shore.

Nothing has done more to promote light tackle fishing in Minnesota than the homely little saltwater bucktail jig. This little newcomer is fast becoming standard walleye fare and is destined to play an increasingly important part in the spinning picture. No combination is more compatible with catching walleyes than a small Upperman bucktail jig tied to the end of your spinning line. An angler seriously interested in catching Minnesota walleyes should have some white jigs in the 1/10 and 1/4-ounce sizes in his tackle box when he steps into his boat. Two winters ago I caught river walleyes on bucktails from November until the first of March. Winter spinning is new and hasn't caught on yet. It will probably never become really popular. When Minnesota's lakes freeze solid, the Mississippi, St. Croix and a number of smaller rivers are still free of ice. Some accessible spots remain ice free most of the year, freezing over for short periods but opening again with the first sunny spell. During November and December and even into January, river walleyes have hollow fins! They hit fast and furious and average much larger than walleyes caught by summer anglers.

One evening Alan Maxson and I took our limit of twelve walleyes at the mouth of the St. Croix River in a half hour's time. Everyone of them weighed over three pounds!

The technique is simple and anyone willing to endure the discomforts of late-season spinning should be able to catch some good fish during the dead of

Tom McCutchan grimaces as he unhooks jig from the mouth of a hardfighting St. Croix River walleye. Scene was near Hastings in December.

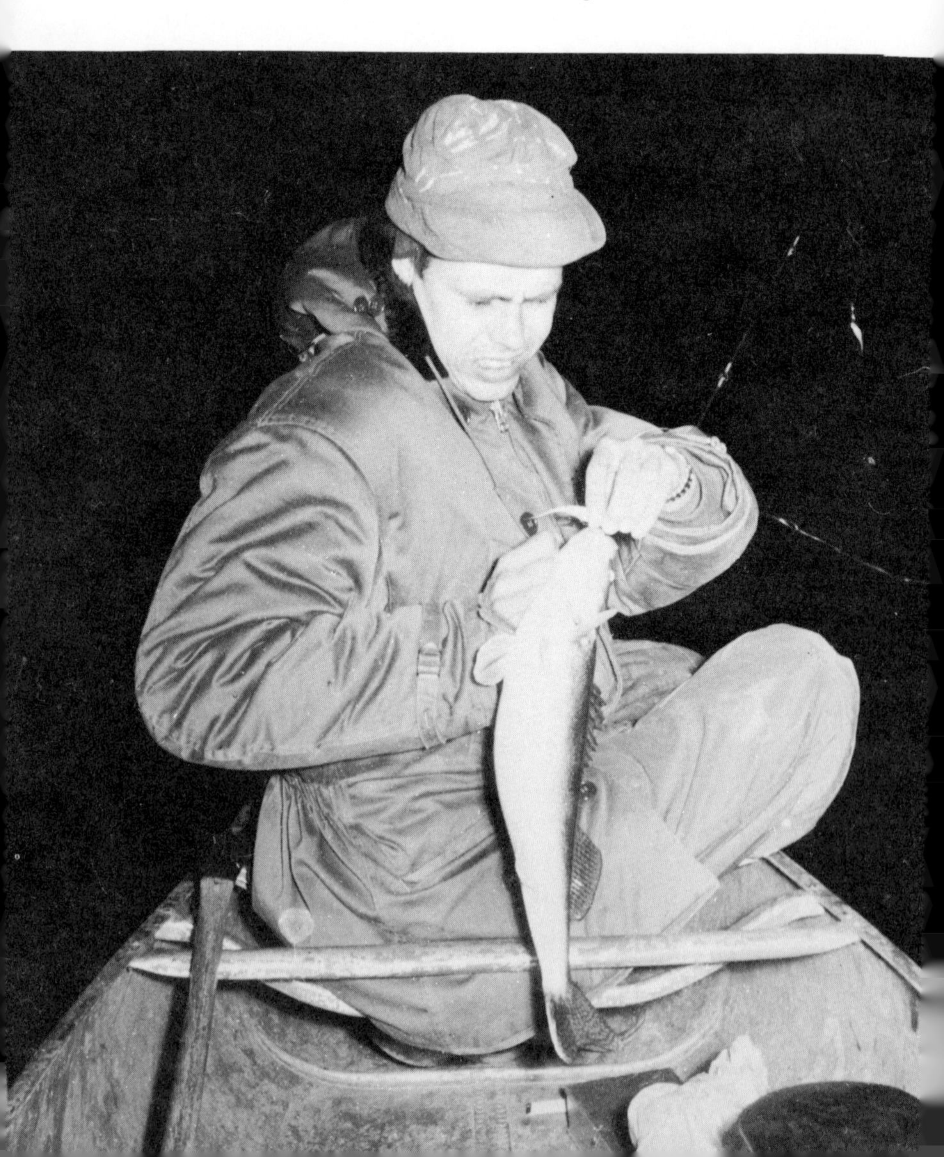

winter. The secret weapon is the deceptive little bucktail jig. And the best fishing I know of is at the confluence of the St. Croix and Mississippi Rivers. To catch walleyes there, anchor your boat near the Minnesota side of the St. Croix fifty feet upstream from where it mixes with the Mississippi. Start fishing about sundown and you'll be there when walleyes begin roving the rocky point downstream. Cast and let your lure hit bottom before jigging it back to your boat. Jump it off the bottom by twitching your rod tip with every turn of the rod handle. A painfully slow retrieve gets best results most of the time.

A light spin-stick and a bucktail jig produced this big river walleye for Al Maxson while night fishing the Mississippi.

These walleyes are willing enough if you just give them the retrieve they want. It's hard to fish slowly when the thermometer reads 28 or 30 degrees because your hands get numb up to your shoulders. But once the fish begin to hit you'll warm up fast.

When you're dodging cakes of ice you know the fish are going to be cold too so take a gaff along. It's impossible to extricate your hook from the net mesh when your hands are numb. With a gaff you can avoid the added discomfort of wet hands.

There are always times when the steady hop-hop retrieve won't get a look and you'll have to think of something else. Another retrieve I've used successfully is a variation of the first. Let the lure sink as before. But instead of starting it back right away let it lie quietly on the bottom for about ten seconds. Then begin retrieving your jig very fast. This will send your lure darting for the surface. Now stop reeling and the lure will settle back to the bottom. This really excites them!

Once when Danny Sams and I were casting against a strong south wind, and the walleyes had been ignoring our jigs in favor of the gizzard shad they were scooping off the point, I began experimenting with different retrieves. Before long I started to pick off walleyes on this stop-and-go kick.

"Pretty lucky," Danny complained.

"Possibly," I admitted, and began another retrieve nailing another walleye. I pointed out the retrieve I was using.

We took eight fish on this retrieve and then they quit cold. We continued to cast. Nothing doing! Nothing happened until Danny absently lapsed into the straight-hop retrieve and caught a fish.

"Hey, I got one!" Dan announced. "The crazy fish have changed their minds again!" By going back to the standard retrieve we filled our legal limit in a few minutes!

One pleasant aspect of winter spinning is the absence of speed boats and cruisers. In the summer fishing is a difficult proposition in some river areas but in winter you can launch your boat across the river from Point Douglas and row across and fish without interference. You can even watch ice fishermen standing on the ice of Lake St. Croix just above where the lake constricts and funnels into the Mississippi!

Most anglers have been inactive through the fall months, but when winter comes they drag out heated minnow buckets, flight pants, custom fish sticks and ice chisels. They chip away just outside summer weed

Winter fisherman Harry Anderson with 12-pound walleye he caught in Lake Minnetonka.

beds, over the same flats and bars where they trolled in May, or at the edge of a dropoff. Generally walleyes bite best during early winter. As the snow deepens on the ice and spawning time approaches fishing tapers off. By February walleye fishing is usually pretty dead.

Native fishermen who know the winter movements of walleyes in their local lakes set up permanent fish-houses. Often these are good spots for you to fish first. Ask questions at filling stations or resorts to locate good spots. These people can save you time if you take time out to talk with them and they are usually willing to help.

To avoid wetting hands in icy water Tom McCutchan uses gaff to hoist winter walleye into boat.

Walleyes like this one lying on the floor of Harry Anderson's fishhouse are one of the rewards of winter fishing in Minnesota.

The best ice-anglers I know avoid concentrations of fishermen. Instead they prowl around the lake punching holes in the ice until they begin catching fish. The biggest objection to joining the social gatherings in the "villages" stems from the noise of cars coming and going, slamming doors and chopping holes. When fish are biting well noise doesn't bother them, but when walleyes get fussy or they're in shallow water, then commotion really goofs your fishing.

But noise is only one consideration of the successful ice angler. By the time the ice is heavy enough to walk on, the water is settled and clear and as a result it's extremely important to use extra-light terminal tackle. This is especially true when you fish during daylight hours. Lakes that are discolored and roily all summer filter out when wave action stops and they become beautifully clear. Anglers who use six-pound monofilament and a No. 4 or No. 6 hook lose some of their big ones on their light rigs but catch more average-sized fish and have much more sport and action. Unless you're just interested in trophy walleyes keep your tackle light for the most fun and action in ice fishing.

Fathead minnows are the most popular bait for winter fishing although some anglers insist on shiners when they can get them. As I pointed out shiners are more sensitive to temperature changes than fatheads and suckers and harder to keep alive. Unless you have a heated bait bucket or carry them in a bottle on your hip they'll freeze. They get too warm in a house and die from the heat! The size of your minnows is more important than the species you use. Two-inch fatheads or suckers are just right although it's a good idea to have a few other sizes in your portable aquarium. Lively minnows usually work best. An old Chippewa trick of flicking them on the head with your finger slows the most ambitious minnow to a quiver. And when walleyes are touchy this can often make it easier to catch them. Sometimes just adding a piece of red yarn to your offering will work. Try hooking your minnow in different ways. Hook them in the side, by the tail or even through the lips. Weight the minnow just enough to achieve a delicate balance between the minnow and bobber so the slightest strike will take it down. But don't set the hook until your fish stops fooling around and starts away with your bait. Strike when the bobber has gone down a foot AND IS STILL GOING AWAY! If it starts back up you're too late so DON'T TAKE IT AWAY FROM YOUR FISH. Give him another try. If you don't get another hit in a minute or two, pull up and check your line. Chances are that he took your minnow and went his merry way.

Carry a clamp-on sounding weight in order to know exactly how deep you're fishing. This is a handy item for the summer angler too. Let your weight down to the bottom, then raise it six inches. Attach your bobber so when you begin fishing your minnow will swim six inches or no more than a foot from the bottom. At times fish will feed only a few feet below the ice and if you don't catch something near the bottom begin working upward, a foot at a time, before you move to a new spot. If you know the lake, you can afford to hang around a good spot and wait for the fish to come in. But if you've never fished there before, it's better to move around because walleyes move from week to week

Alan Maxson lifts seven-pound walleye he caught on a bucktail jig through the ice of Dead Lake narrows, near Detroit Lakes.

or even from day to day. Don't depend on holes cut ten days before.

You might want to try a new kind of winter fishing that worked pretty well for me last winter. After having such terrific success with bucktail jigs the past two seasons, I tried them for walleyes on Dead Lake last winter. Originally Alan Maxson and I had been trying for crappies but the streak tapered off. But we caught three walleyes, the largest seven pounds, and five small northerns—without getting our hands wet! So if you get chapped hands from dipping out minnows try jigging!

During that same early December weekend two brothers named Kelly were jigging another kind of lure on Mille Lacs. With a Swedish Pimple on the end of a jig stick they caught ten walleyes in a few hours! The trend to artificials for ice fishing is clear, and there will surely be others on the market before this volume is dry on the presses.

Winter fishing is great sport for anglers dressed to face cold winds, blowing snow and cold ice underfoot all day long. It doesn't require a great investment for the beginner to get started. Begin with one of the inexpensive ice sticks sold in tackle stores. Before your first winter you'll think of ways to improve your present rig or build a fancy one of your own. An ice chisel is your most expensive item and I'd advise getting one of your own. If you borrow one, be sure you have a piece of line tied to it so you won't have to crawl back to apologize and buy a new one because it slipped out of your cold hands and went to the bottom. Inexpensive heated minnow buckets will keep your bait from freezing in below-zero weather and a half dollar will buy an ice skimmer for keeping film ice from immobilizing your bobber.

You can drive to their favorite reefs and flats during the winter if the ice is safe and resorts on most lakes plow roads to fishing spots right through the season! But whenever you drive on ice you're apt to get into trouble if you don't take a few precautions. Drive slowly on lakes and keep your doors open so you can jump if you have to. There aren't many cars that find their way to the bottom, but play safe by staying away from heaves and following only trails that have been most recently traveled. The ice in Minnesota lakes is never safe before the middle of December. Some years it may freeze up a few days earlier but this is the average date for safe ice. Even when walking it's a good idea to test the ice ahead of you with your chisel as you walk. If your chisel chunks through ahead of you, find another way to where you want to go.

Walleyes are undisputedly the most popular fish in Minnesota waters, summer and winter. Their reproductive ability coupled with management know-how of Minnesota's fisheries' men, makes the walleye everybody's game fish. Minnesota is THE outstanding walleye state in the country!

One more thing. Fishing in the rain might be uncomfortable but it can often mean some of the most exciting walleye angling you've had in your life. When a gentle rain is falling walleyes often go on a feeding binge. So bring your rain gear to Minnesota. And to get the most out of your fishing, use light tackle.

Walleyes give a much better account of themselves on spinning tackle than on heavy gear. Spinning is the real key to walleye success and fishing pleasure because it adds up to more fish per trip and more fun per pound!

CHAPTER VII

Speckled and Brown Trout

The day I first creeled a mess of plump native trout from a Minnesota stream I had fished a dozen different creeks before I caught a fish.

It was nearly dark and I was headed back to our house trailer in Gooseberry State Park south of Beaver Bay on the North Shore. As I crossed a little alder-covered stream near Lax Lake I slowed down to look at the water, although at the time I didn't know a good speckled-trout stream when I saw it. I'd crossed this trickle a half dozen times without bothering to fish it. This time I decided I'd have a look anyway and see where it went. Standing on a little wooden bridge I could see the stream widened into a deep pool that was partly concealed by alders, raspberries and wire grass, and it was hidden too by the way the stream made a bend. The water running under the bridge was just an overflow from the pool. I hunched along the bank and standing well back from the stream I flipped a worm into the marly creek. The eruption that followed was so unexpected that I recoiled and instinctively raised my rod. A big fish stripped the worm from my hook, splashing half the water out of the pool in the process. I tried another worm and prepared myself for a mad strike that never came. I worked up stream then until

I became hopelessly tangled in alders. While mosquitoes chewed the rind off my ears and black-flies played jack-straws with my eyebrows I fought my way out. Again I tried the first pool and caught two three-inch specks which I released. I scrambled for the car and returned to explore the stream on the following day.

In full daylight I noticed that there was no indication the stream had been fished that season. The grass was straight and unbroken except where I'd been walking the night before, no trampled paths or parking sign. I squeezed into the jungle until I reached a position where I could look over a flat pool. Several ten-inch brook trout were lying in the middle in two feet of water. When I extended my rod it cast a shadow and the fish dissolved.

At the foot of this pool I noticed water running into a chute beneath some logs. On closer investigation I discovered a decaying log bridge with brush growing on top. Ice jams and decay had torn the bridge and water boiled under it, eddying on the lower side. I walked cautiously on to the rotting logs, staying in the shadows of the alders. Lowering an angleworm into a small rift in the bridge I saw a strong fish snap it just as it touched the water. Even though I was prepared for a strike my leader was too light. When I tried to keep him out of the logs and limbs that lay in rows beneath the bridge, it snapped. Nervously, I tied on a new hook and a heavier leader and fed a new worm into the opening. The response was the same but this time I was able to hold the fish without breaking him off. The heavy speck bounced off every log and snag in the creek before I finally hefted my first keeper from under the ancient sod-covered bridge. A beautiful 14-inch speckled trout!

There's no substitute for fishing specks in these small personal streams to give the beginner confidence. Contrary to popular belief there is a lot of know-how involved in catching brook trout consistently. An angler starting in small streams can see his fish hit and learn quickly which are productive-looking pools and runs and those which are a waste of time to fish. It's a fact that a good live bait angler can usually give the fly-fisherman a run for his money. By beginning with worms in a small stream you will soon learn a great deal about Minnesota trout.

Author holds speckled trout taken from one of the small lakes in Cook County in extreme Northeastern Minnesota.

I remember one old duffer from Duluth we met along the Baptism River who had a creel full of 13 to 15-inch speckled trout he'd taken on worms and a snoot full of Old Muskellunge. Tom McCutchan and I were eating lunch by the stream below the ranger's cabin at Finland, when he walked over from his tent to talk a spell and show us his fish.

"You didn't get those in the Baptism," Tom stated flatly when he looked into the man's creel. "Not around here," he added, pointing vaguely to the wide stream below us stocked with browns.

"Well, son," the angler admitted, "I got these specks the hard way but they came from the Baptism."

"That's pretty hard to swallow," Tom said, "but if you caught 'em, you ought to know."

The man took a bite of the sandwich I offered him and pondered Tom's last comment.

"Tell you what," he said, "I'll show you where I got them if you'll keep it quiet."

This didn't sound fair and we told him we didn't have to know, that we believed him.

"It's all right," he said getting to his feet. "Let's have a drink and get started." And he produced a bottle from his pocket.

"Better keep it to yourself," I suggested, referring to the secret trout spot and not the whiskey. "They're not easy to find anymore."

He persisted so we followed him for several miles until he pulled his car up beside an old pair of khaki pants that hung on a tree limb beside the road. He hauled out his flyrod and motioned for us to stay back. Then he slipped up to a culvert that ran under the road.

As we watched he snaffled a twelve-inch brook trout from a deep roadside pool.

"Ya see! You boys probably been over this little crick a hundred times and never knew it was there!" he explained looking very much like a university professor lecturing on the philosophy of Nietzsche.

"Did you get them all here?" I asked.

"Come on," he said. Ignoring my question he plunged into the heavy cedar and alder swamp on the far side of the road. We came out on the edge of a deep "slack" water stretch less than fifty feet from the road. We watched him cast a worm expertly to the edge of the sin-tangle that grew along the far side of the dark, lifeless water. His rod bent violently and we saw him play a beautiful big speck into his waiting net!

A Minnesota brook trout for some reason forsakes all caution if he sees a meal going by. Specks can be plenty smart when they know there is danger but their memory is poor when the turkey is passed. However, what he lacks in common sense a brook trout makes up for in fighting ability. Brook trout have a peculiar fighting style that gives an angler the sensation at first that he's hooked a powerful coil spring. All muscle and bone, they're one of the gamest trout found anywhere. Playing a fourteen-inch native speck in a small brushy stream requires the same miraculous luck needed to hitch a wild stallion to the leg of a kitchen table. They can tangle in roots and snags so fast you're not sure exactly what happened until it's all over. That's part of what makes specks so interesting!

Minnesota's native brook trout, referred to as speck, brookie and speckled trout is a beautiful fish. His back is dark amber green, sometimes almost black with lighter olive vermiculations. He has a light, sometimes pinkish belly, and his sides are speckled with red, orange-rimmed spots. The margins of his fins are black on the lower edge with a touch of orange on the inside. The tail is so slightly forked as to be almost unnoticeable. As a result, older specimens are sometimes referred to as square tails.

Eastern Brook Trout—Minnesota's only native stream trout.

At one time brook trout were extremely abundant in North Shore streams of Lake Superior, tributaries of the St. Croix and streams running into the Mississippi River in the Red Wing area. Minnesota's lakes had their share of specks too. Old timers say they can remember catching five-pound natives from Kimball Lake forty years ago. Some big ones are still around, although not as plentifully as in the old days. The angler who is willing to work hard can still catch two and three-pound specks in the more remote and hard to reach beaver ponds and streams. Every summer three and four-pounders come from Lost, Monker and Pike lakes. Kabekona Creek northwest of Walker, the Isabella River southeast of Ely and Mud Creek north of Grand Marais give up outsized specks. Many of the little trickles your car crosses in Lake, St. Louis and Cook counties present opportunities for good catches in spite of their diminutive size. An occasional heavy-speckled trout is caught by fishermen who hunt browns in the pools of the North Shore streams in late September. Lake Superior specks, called coasters, move onto reefs and into rivers to spawn about the same time as lake browns start upstream to perform the same duty.

Although baitfishing is extremely well suited to smaller trout waters, large Minnesota streams are ideal fly-fishing water. Even some smaller streams have meadow stretches where flies can be presented to fish without serious trouble. When fly-fishing meadow stretches, stand back from the bank and cast. Or stay above a pool and let your fly drift to trout that are watching for food to be carried over the lip of the pool. For speck fishing I use dry flies that imitate mosquitoes. Among my favorite flies are Grizzly King, Adams and any small palmer-tied bivisible. Most of mine are tied a little larger than natural mosquitoes on No. 10 and No. 12 hooks. Smaller flies are sometimes useful too. I've actually caught specks on a tiny No. 20 a few times. Such small hooks don't hold fish well and anglers don't very often use them where trout run over ten inches. I fish them when trout are gorging on tiny midges as they sometimes do in midsummer. If you carry a stock of gray, brown, black and white flies tied palmer style (hackled the length of the hook shank) in sizes from No. 10 to No. 16, and you present them right, trout will come to your flies.

Don't overlook wet flies and streamers. Natives along the North Shore use a soft hackled, yellow or orange-bodied wet fly tied on a heavy No. 8 hook. One of my best producers is a streamer fly tied to imitate a slim-bodied stickleback minnow, a small fish which is at times very abundant in slow stretches of trout streams and beaver ponds. The Stickleback fly has a body of olive floss with close lying wings made from guinea hen feathers. Hackle consists of a whisp of soft hen tied below the head. When trout are feeding on these minnows this fly is often a real life saver.

It's difficult to describe just how to present a wet fly because many of Minnesota's wet fly streams are so covered with alders the best an angler can hope to do is simply part the branches cautiously and drop his fly to the water. Where there's casting room, cast the fly upstream from the place you've selected as your target and work the fly slowly toward you. The Stickleback should be worked in darting motions by stripping in about eight inches of line at a time. Conventional wet flies that imitate insects should be allowed to settle deep. Retrieve a wet fly by working it jerkingly toward the surface or crawl it VERY SLOWLY along the bottom. Water insects move slowly in the larval stage and a wet fly moving too fast usually gets the fishy eye from trout. On occasion I've taken trout on wet flies that were traveling anything but slow. So the rules suggest exceptions now and then.

Fly-fishermen haven't begun to weigh the advantages offered by spinning tackle in stream angling. Others are aware of its possibilities but prefer sportier but often less spectacular catches with flyrods. But minnows fill a lot of little pink bellies and we less esthetic fishermen find the charm of trout water enhanced by an occasional fish for the skillet. An ultra light action rod like the Ted Williams 503XL adjustable ring style, or Heddon's Mod. 126 light action six-footer, allow you to cast lures from 1/10 to 3/8-ounces without effort. For the same money you can build a standard ASP 54R-2 Sila-Flex 5½-footer that will handle lures as light as 1/12-ounce. The spin anglers will get a lot of fun using one of these light wands and he will be able to present the lightest lures to trout that may be interested in eating something besides caddis cases. This kind of spinning demands nothing heavier than four-pound line for best results.

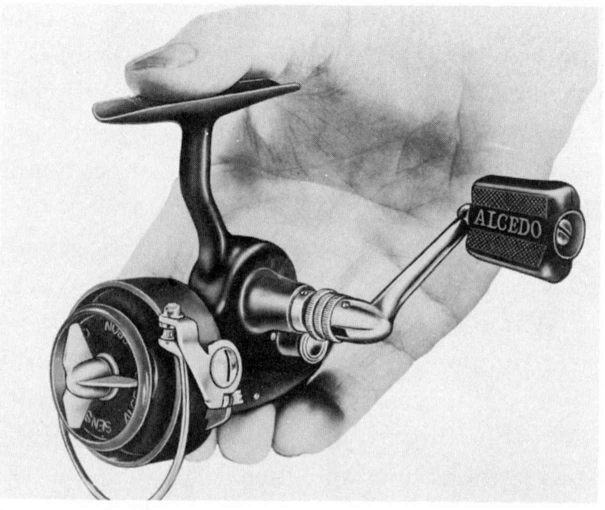

Alcedo's tiny microne, high-priced precision made reel for light tackle pleasure.

This little Ted Williams 300 reel weighs just 7½ ounces and holds 200 yards of four-pound monofilament line. A perfect companion for the Mitey Mite TW spinning rod which weighs just 2 3/8 ounces, and ideal for Minnesota trout water.

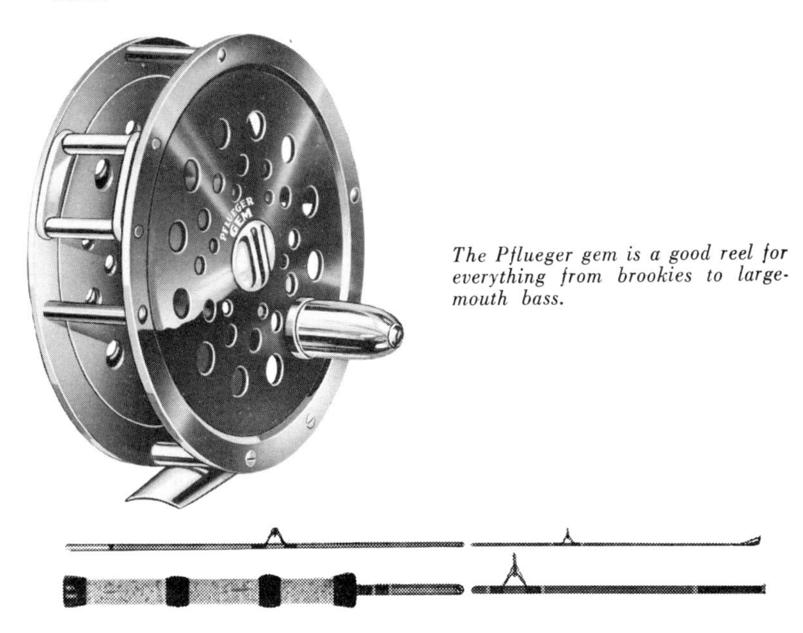

The Pflueger gem is a good reel for everything from brookies to large-mouth bass.

Ted Williams medium action spinning rod will do a creditable job for a Minnesota angler.

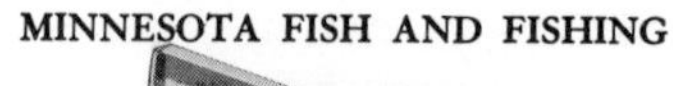

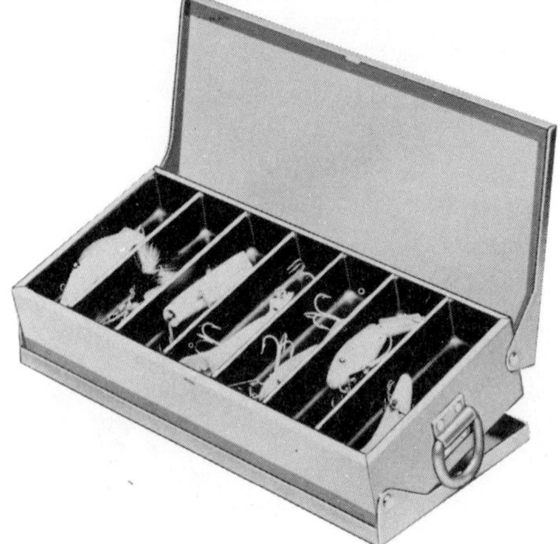

A handy belt-type (or shoulder) aluminum tackle kit—ideal for spin fishermen. Two sets of lure compartments each independently covered. Will carry several dozen small spoons and lures. Umco Model 10 Port-A-Tray.

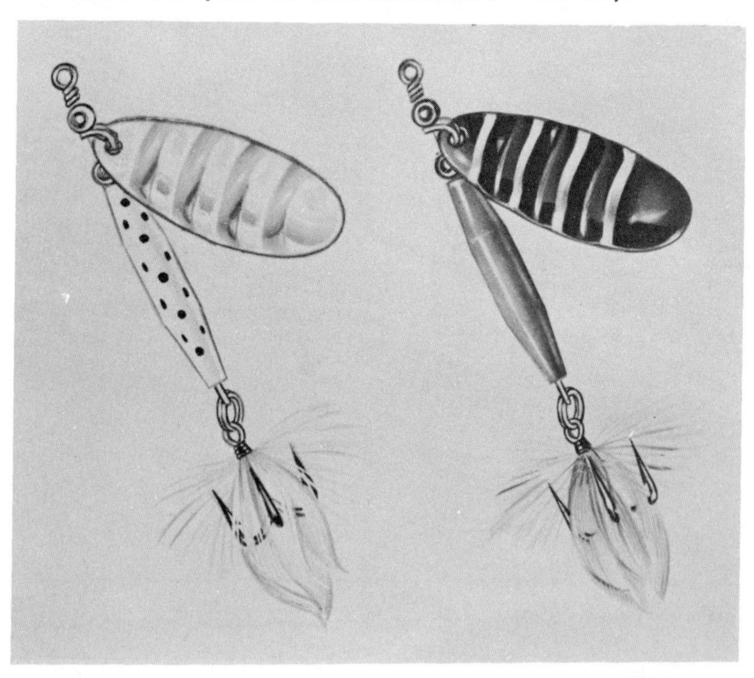

Abu French-type spinner by Garcia. Abu are excellent lures for beaver pond specks and browns.

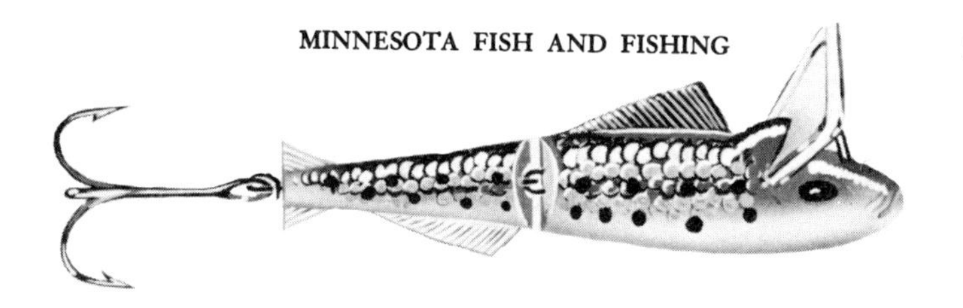

Pecos Dace by Garcia is deadly for beaver pond speckled trout. (Several times actual size)

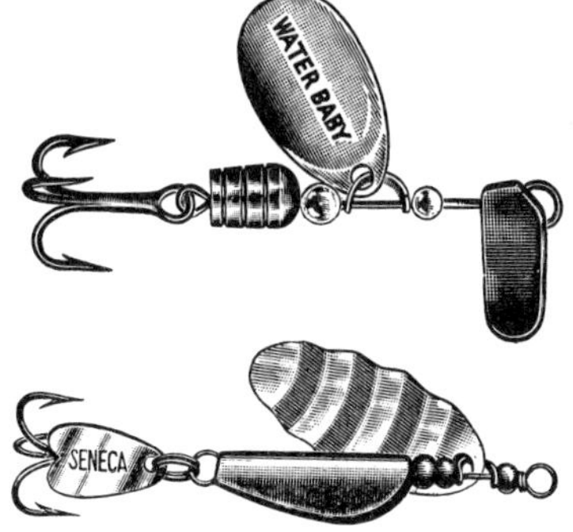

The little non-twisting Water Baby is the Seneca Company's answer for spinning for specks in beaver ponds.

The Spin-A-Lure is one lure stream trout, especially browns, find tempting.

If you're fishing beaver ponds, be sure to begin retrieving the moment your lure hits the water. Otherwise, you'll lose spoons right and left to deadfall placed strategically in the path of your every cast by some ingenious beaver. Ponds and slack water are best fished from a canoe because their margins are impossible to wade. Without a canoe or rubber boat you can still reach some of the deepest spots by fishing along the top of a dam. Beaver ponds produce best in early summer, up to about the end of June. By July, trout have started moving upstream to cooler water and by September they're in the headwaters and feeders checking into the maternity ward.

Spinning tackle is absolutely tops for fishing the little speckled-trout lakes that dot central and northern

This 12-ft. Mod. E Aluma Craft is an ideal cartop boat for small roadside trout waters.

Minnesota eastward from Park Rapids. Duck, Bogus, Rat, Thompson, Esther and many others I haven't had time yet to fish, provide elbow room for the growing spin army. Fish these lakes with a small silver spoon, letting it settle to the bottom. By counting until your lure stops, you can tell how long it takes to get down. Begin your next retrieve before the lure gets fouled on a rock or log. Brook trout normally like a slow retrieve so you want to fish slowly. Fish just fast enough to keep your lure up about a foot. I always carry lures of several weights and finishes when fishing these lakes because trout are not always on the bottom—only MOST of the time. Silver, copper and black-finished spoons will take care of almost all water conditions. My favorites are small compact Wob-L-Rite or Nebco spoons that sink fast and stay deep while retrieved at a moderate rate. Wob-L-Rite has a high-gloss polish that is really important to a trout fisherman. A 3/16-ounce Wob-L-Rite casts well on four and six-pound line, and I think it's the best all-around trout spoon on the market. I've noticed that silver spoons produce best in clear water or during bright weather, gold or copper spoons are better suited to muddy and discolored lakes. Black spoons have a place in dark day fishing and I feel unprepared to meet all fishing conditions if I don't have one or two along.

Keep your hooks sharp. Trout have tough mouths but they're soft enough for easy penetration if you dress your hooks occasionally. I've replaced the hooks on some of my spoons with single Siwash, or salmon lure, hooks with long slender barbs. American treble hooks seem too blunt for good penetration especially the nickled kind that are supplied on most lures. The best treble hooks are those that come on some foreign lures. They have a wide, hook gap and slender, pointed barbs. A few lure-makers, like Seneca and Pflueger, have made single Siwash-style hooks optional equipment on some of their spoons.

There are a lot of good beaver ponds in the trout country northeast of State highway No. 1, but most of them are hard to find unless you spend a little time asking questions or fish with someone who knows their way around. Filling stations along the Shore, especially those in Grand Marais and Finland, are willing to direct you to the most accessible ponds and probably offer to show you there where they're afraid you may get lost. Don't expect them to divulge secrets of a life-

Small brooks like this afford first rate speckled trout fishing. This fisherman using spinning tackle and worms is catching trout in sight of a road.

time, but you'll get some good tips that will save you days of searching on your own.

Trout from Minnesota's beaver ponds are as fat as butterballs and pretty as the brightest tropical fish you've ever seen. Your light-spinning rig applied in these dark ponds with a Mepps or a waterbaby French-type spinner attached to the end of your line, is right in its element. It's hard to find trout fishing that offers more pleasure than drifting among the deadfalls of a beaver pond casting a spinner into the black-looking water for hard-fighting specks.

Fishing browns is usually another story. Most of the brown trout in Minnesota inhabit the southeastern part of the state. They're also found in a few streams and trout lakes of the arrowhead counties. Many big browns are caught during the spring steelhead run and during a special fall season. During the month of October browns and other trout are legal below the first natural barrier or within three-quarters of a mile from the mouth of most North Shore streams.

Late fall spawning runs are pretty hard to predict and they're spotty at best. Only the natives really know how these runs are progressing since a good run depends on the water level in the stream. If streams are high, there will be a good run. But some years when there is very little rain—1956 for example—a run never materializes.

The square-tailed, sleepy-eyed brown trout is among the wariest and paradoxically the most aggressive trout in Minnesota streams. It is identified easily by large almost course body spots. The body is light brown fading to cream or light yellow beneath. Brown trout, like rainbows, are not native to Minnesota but according to Eddy and Surber in *Northern Fishes* were introduced from Europe in 1883. There seems to be no evidence to support the common belief that the German brown, and Loch Leven introduced from Scotland later, are distinctly different species. Undoubtedly Minnesota browns are a mixture of both. The name brown trout is now applied to both since only biologists can identify them and even they become confused at times.

When speckled-trout fishing declined in many southeastern Minnesota streams, browns were stocked experimentally in the hope they might tolerate the warm silt-laden water and thrive there. They are now common in the Whitewater-Root-River watersheds where they provide the major sport fishing in several

Brown trout were introduced to many Minnesota lakes and streams before the turn of the century. Record brown for Minnesota: 14 pounds.

southeastern counties. Browns seem extremely tolerant of warm water and mild pollution and they have found their way up the Mississippi, St. Croix and Minnesota Rivers to creek mouths and tributary streams. In fact, some beautiful heavy fish come from the mouth of Eagle Creek near Savage, on the Minnesota River. They migrate from no-one-knows-where and spend a few weeks each summer feeding at the creek mouth. There is reason to believe there are other streams flowing into Minnesota's rivers where browns may follow this same pattern. Where they go during the rest of the year is anyone's guess and a source of discussion and debate among local anglers.

Bait fishing with nightcrawlers and worms is a dependable means of catching brown trout in Minnesota trout streams. Minnows and grasshoppers make good bait too. Native fishermen along the Blackhoof catch some real lunker trout on minnows by still fishing deep pools both early in the morning and late in the evening. However, smaller trout will sock a worm drifted by them under a noon-day sun. Occasionally even a fat cannibal can be coaxed out from the bank during midday. I recall a heavy brown that shot out from under a stump and gobbled some worms I was waving before a school of suckers. He came out in broad daylight right to the middle of a clear pool even though I was standing on the bank in plain view.

If you're fishing from shore in large streams like the Baptism and the Manitou, try likely-looking spots closest to the bank first. Work gradually toward the far side of the stream. Try to fish so your casts quarter upstream. By fishing your bait slightly upstream from you it's unnecessary to add weight except in very fast water or where a run is both deep and fast. Follow the bait with your rod tip keeping pace with it as it flows swiftly past your position. A strike will come in the form of a slight hesitation followed by an upstream surge of the line as the fish runs with the bait. Because the current keeps your bowed line tight a slight strike will hook your fish. A lot of fish will actually hook themselves.

Waders make stream fishing in Minnesota so much easier that I wouldn't think of fishing trout without them. Most streams have wadeable riffles where you can cross and often get into better position to cover cutbanks and pools that are impossible to reach from one side of the stream. Often, too, walking becomes impossible in the alder jungles and you have to cross the stream to go on. In places you will be confronted by insurmountable canyon walls and without waders you will have to retrace your steps to the nearest bridge. A pair of inexpensive light plastic waders and a pair of ordinary tennis shoes, a size too big, will certainly improve your day on Minnesota streams.

The best fly-fishing streams in Minnesota include the Straight, Baptism, Blackhoof, Whitewater and

Manitou. There are others, too, like the Grindstone and Root rivers, Hay and Duchee Creeks. Some of the best holes are easy to find—others you'll have to pry from the natives. Minnesota's brown waters have some unbelievably huge fish but to get them you've got to work for them. State game warden Bill Jubarian, who fishes the Straight River with Park Rapids sports shop owner, Bob Fake, tells me that when the mayfly hatch begins in the middle of June, fish under 20-inches aren't considered keepers! Many Straight River anglers never keep a brown unless it's mortally wounded. Such things seldom happen while fishing with flies and most of their trout go back to be caught again.

When a hatch occurs on a stormy summer day trout sometimes go on the wildest feeding sprees a fisherman is likely to witness in his lifetime. Once I fished browns during a spree like that while I was on a bass-fishing trip.

We'd driven up to a little lake on the Gunflint Trail in early July to catch smallmouth bass. Before leaving Grand Marais, at the foot of the Trail, we stopped for gas and groceries. The weather was unsettled and it looked like a storm brewing. As the attendant stoked the gas tank we questioned him on bass fishing.

He looked at the noisy sky, "should have been here last night," he said. "Good catches on Bearskin and Hungry Jack. Looks like it might storm now."

Sure we should, I thought. This guy's a genius!

We fished hard all morning catching nothing but a few squirty bass and a pair of unquestionable keepers for lunch. This was the big Fourth of July weekend and we'd driven 300 miles to be rained out. We tried for bass again that evening through wind shifts and calm with full moon and empty creel.

We slept late next morning as thunder rattled and rain pounded on our mountain tent. As the thunder clapped loudly it came to me! This is trout weather!

We had stopped Friday evening at the Manitou to take a shot at the fat browns that hang around the upper bridge. It was too late to do any serious fishing then, but in the afterglow we had heard and seen big fish rising all up and down the river.

It took an hour to eat and break camp and another hour's drive to reach the upper bridge on the Manitou. Big trout were rising in the pool upstream as we arrived. A half dozen more were feeding on minnows in the riffles. They wallowed and fussed like hogs in an oak grove.

Nervously I tied on a couple of large palmers. But the trout didn't seem to notice them as they drifted by. Danny Sams, who was new at the trout game, pounded the stream with an assortment of flies with negative results. I lengthened my leader by adding a two-pound tippet section and tied on a No. 16 bivisible dry fly. Gently I dropped a cast above a good rise. As it passed the fish's hold, a rowdy trout tightened the knots in my light leader—a pretty spotted 14-inch brown.

Trout fed all over the river that day hitting both wet and dry flies when they were presented right. When they failed to hit our dries for awhile we switched to a wet Light Cahill, and began catching bigger fish!

This was a very pleasant ending for a souring bass trip because we had fortunately remembered what

Minneapolis Tribune outdoor writer Jim Peterson with five-pound brown trout he caught in Southeastern Minnesota stream.

experienced trout anglers have long known about weather and fishing—what's bad, weather-wise, for pike and bass is often best for fishing brown trout!

Browns can be depended on to respond to spinning lures as well as to flies, perhaps better and more consistently than speckled trout. The best time to feed them hardware is when streams are still fairly high in late spring just after they've warmed up a bit. Any good brook trout spoons catch browns. I use a heavy gold or brass spoon that will show up well in the dark slack-waters of the Baptism. Here browns are often feeding in the company of brook trout among the pad growths below a chute of fast water. I've never taken a truly big brown from these waters. Big brown trout fall only to the most artful, calculating angler. Sometimes a bright spoon going by is just the right appetizer to bring a big one to your net. Often a big fish will expose himself

The author and Rod Bell tie flies in preparation for an evening of fly fishing on Trout Lake, near Grand Marais.

Minnesota streams hold some lunker speckled trout. This one was taken by Vi Bell from stream in Beaver Bay area of the North Shore.

if a white fly is drifted over his hole during the day. Then you can toss him a spoon toward evening when his guard is down.

Remember when casting to trout that your fly should drop lightly and ride naturally over the fish. If that old demon, line drag, takes your fly along faster than the current carrying your feathers most trout will smell a spitball and shy away. To avoid drag, cast across and upstream. As the line straightens over the water give your rod tip a side-to-side action. This will result in the line falling in a series of S's and will be unaffected by line drag until your fish has accepted or rejected your fly.

When you begin fishing for specks or browns don't hesitate to use bait in order to get the feel of trout fishing. As you become more confident you'll gradually begin placing your faith in artificials, depending less on live bait.

Minnesota has so much trout water that the best streams are never crowded after the opening weekend. When the general fishing season opens, usually about May 15, trout waters are practically deserted although trout fishing is then normally just getting good. Approach trout streams with a light foot. If you see the fish, remember he's most likely seen you too! Boggy-banked brook trout waters are very sensitive to heavy boots so slink along like a chicken thief on a bright night. Keep the silhouette of a tree or some brush behind you. As you sneak in close to a pool don't consider dropping to your knees a bit undignified. The biggest trout fall to the sneaking, crawling angler who knows how to get the most from a small stream.

CHAPTER VIII

They're Called Lakers

As a kid I used to listen to my dad and old bachelor Bob Gusse talk in platitudes about the ways of lake trout. I often became engrossed in their talk of metal lines and stiff, hollow steel rods. I was bug-eyed to learn that huge, heavy spoons were required to catch these trout. There seemed to be only one way to catch lake trout. You had to go to the end of the road in Ontario, and make several heart-stopping portages. You had to carry gallons of gas, tents and the biggest boat you could drag, across the height-of-land. Then you would fish in 200 feet of water. It was exciting to listen to them speak with great authority and I planned for the time I could join the men and explore the wilds of Canada.

The part about the portages and deep fishing, I found had an element of truth in it and no one would deny that Ontario has been lake-trout country from the time these deep lakes were spawned by the last glacier of the ice age. Still I never quite got around to going that far north for lakers. The fact is I've been so busy rediscovering the lake trout waters of Minnesota that I've lost sight of the original objective.

Minnesota has comparatively unlimited lake-trout

water. Lake Superior and numerous inland lakes make up the best laker range anywhere in the country where big lakers, while not abundant, are still common. Partly because the streams of the Minnesota section of the North Shore of Superior are rocky and unsuitable to lamprey spawning, fishing in this area has been the least affected by these jumbo, salt water blood-letters.

Some of Minnesota's best and most accessible lake-trout water is found at mouths of streams flowing into Lake Superior. The most productive and easily reached streams are the Cascade, Devils Track, Brule (incorrectly called Arrowhead by the chamber of commerce —Brule to the natives and most anglers*), Baptism and Split Rock.

Pretty, strong lake trout in the 2-to-5-pound class, known as "reefers" along the North Shore, work near these rocky stream mouths during odd hours of the day throughout the months of July and August. If you happen to be there when they come in, you'll have a good chance to lead a hard-fighting, light-spotted reefer to your net. If you hit them right, you'll experience a new thrill in trout fishing. A laker in 50-degree water is very strong and fast. When you get them near shore they shy wildly and are equal to any rainbow in fighting ability. What they lack in acrobatic style they make up for in brute strength and, when after a good battle, you hold an ice-cold reefer in your hand you'll do so with a sense of accomplishment!

Your first fish may come hard because reefer fishing is quite often a hit or miss proposition. Skin divers

*Originally called the Bois Brule (burnt wood) by the French in the early 1840's, also mentioned as the Brule by the Owens Expedition in 1848.

diving for lost lures at the mouth of the Cascade River said they watched reefers come and go as they worked at prying lures from the rocky stream bed. Reefers swam into the river mouth, cruised around feeding a little and left. You have to keep trying. Confirmed reefer fishermen are a very strange breed. They stream-hop along the shore until they find a stream where trout are feeding. Sometimes they may fish the same river all day long fishing and resting or working in shifts. A man and wife or a pair of fishermen working in half-hour shifts are sure to catch some trout if they work one of the good reefer streams during normal summer flow. When reefers are hitting well, tackle shop owners in the Tofte-Grand Marais area will know about it and be able to tell you.

I've found spinning tackle ideal for handling reefers. For one thing, spinning makes it possible to cast light spoons a long distance. Long casts are important in order to reach these fish most of the time. I've had best luck on reefers using heavy gauge ½ or ¼-ounce Seneca Wob-L-Rite in bright chrome or silver finish. Copper and gold spoons are at times also useful. Carry an assortment that includes several finishes of Wob-L-Rites or Nebco Tor-P-Do spoons including some in red and white. The same lures you use for northern pike will double for reefer spoons if you happen to have the wind at your back. With the wind behind you, you can use light hardware but you'll have to retrieve them a bit slower to get to the trout than when fishing a heavier Wob-L-Rite. Have enough lures with you because you won't catch reefers without losing a spoon now and then. But a few lures is a small price to pay

Despite inroads made on the lake trout population of Lake Superior by the sea lamprey invasion, anglers who spin the mouths of North Shore streams continue to catch reefer trout like this one the author is leading to net.

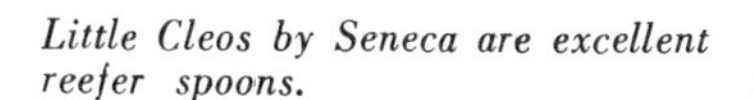

Little Cleos by Seneca are excellent reefer spoons.

Nebco Tor-P-Do spoon, a compact lure ideal for lake rainbows and reefers.

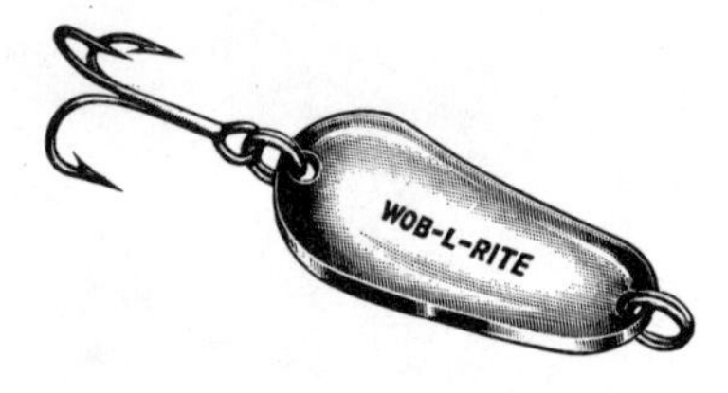

I've had best luck on rainbows and reefers spinning with a ¼ or ½ ounce Wob-L-Rite in bright chrome finish.

"Reefer" country. Here the author casts for reefers and steelhead rainbows at the mouth of the Split Rock River northeast of Duluth.

for the rewards you'll realize if you hit them right just once!

If you don't consider casting in your line, you can launch a boat at the Devils Track or some other river. At Grand Portage you can often rent a safe boat and an outboard from one of the commercial fishermen who live there or you can put in your own boat. There are a number of Indians at Grand Portage who know the trout reefs around Grand Portage and Susie Islands. Don't expect them to work for nothing because guides that know where lakers hang out and how to catch them are aware of their value. After you learn the reefs you can go out by yourself. When you go be sure to have a big, safe boat. If an onshore wind is blowing while you're out, keep an eye out for fog from the southeast. Superior is too big and cold to fool around with, so get off the lake if bad weather is brewing. Five minutes in the 40-45 degree waters of Superior is more than you could stand!

You'll never get a big reefer, but Lake Superior has some mighty big trout if you want to go for them. Most of the big lakers, those famous 30 and 40-pounders, are taken by deep trolling out in the main lake. The little town of Hovland, at the foot of the McFarland Trail, is the focal point for "deep sea" lake-trout fishing. The boats that take anglers out on Superior are well-built inboards designed to take the buffeting the old gal deals out. Don't try to follow them in your 12-foot skiff. If you go out on one of these boats, be sure to dress for winter weather. Even when it's 80 degrees on shore it is often very cold on Superior. Superior's water never gets more than ten or twelve degrees above freezing

Boats like this 19-foot outboard cruiser are designed for big waters like Lake Superior and Lake of the Woods.

and some years it never reaches maximum temperature required to mix top and bottom water. It's a liquid refrigerator that is never warm enough to swim in as many fishermen find out when a roller piles over their boot tops!

Although the gear used for deep trolling is heavy and cumbersome, as far as I know it's the only effective means of reaching trout 200 to 300 feet below. Most charter boats furnish tackle. However, you can bring your own if you have a suitable rig. A large spool star-drag reel, that holds at least 900 feet of 40 or 50-pound monel or woven stainless steel line, is required. Your rod should be a fifteen thread, or medium action 5½-foot rod that can take the beating of trolling instead of the angler. A long, whippy rod simply won't handle the heavy load of line and lead needed in deep sea fishing.

When you troll deep, lead is added according to how deep you have to fish. Sometimes more than a half a pound of lead is added to get your lure deep enough to catch lake trout. The most popular laker spoons for deep fishing include the Doctor, KB, Red-Eyed Wiggler and Daredevil. There are others too, but these are among the best lake trout spoons ever invented. The Doctor particularly has excellent action at slow trolling speed. And to catch lakers you have to troll very slowly! The slower you can go the better. As long as your lure is moving you're moving fast enough.

Most of the big trout come from the offshore fishing grounds—here a Lake Superior skipper lands a "deep sea" laker.

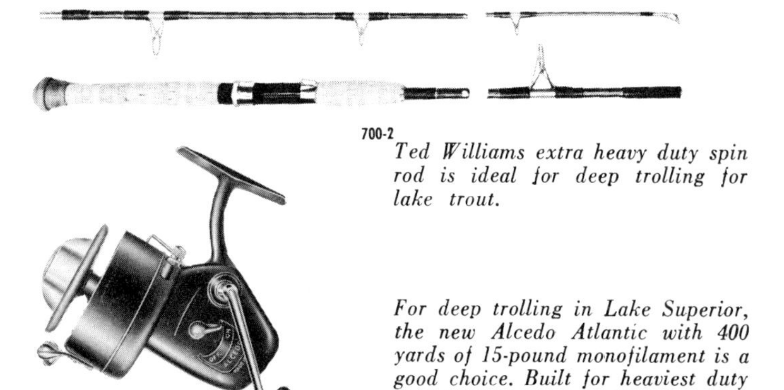

Ted Williams extra heavy duty spin rod is ideal for deep trolling for lake trout.

For deep trolling in Lake Superior, the new Alcedo Atlantic with 400 yards of 15-pound monofilament is a good choice. Built for heaviest duty use. Matched heavy duty rods are available.

You might think big lake trout would be hard fighters, but they're not when caught by deep trolling. Still this is the only way to catch them. Although changes in water pressure take the starch out of these fish as they're brought to the top the game is still exciting. The thrills come from the hardships; fighting heavy tackle and long hours on the cold lake required to catch a trophy.

My favorite lake-trout fishing is found in the many cold, deepwater inland lakes of Cook, Lake, Itasca and Koochiching counties. Here lie most of the wilderness area trout lakes that make up the vast rock-bound canoe country on the Minnesota-Ontario border. The best accessible ones are Snowbank, near Ely, Big Saganana at the end of the Gunflint Trail, and Greenwood and Trout Lake near Grand Marais. There are also smaller lakes like Echo and Caribou lakes which are easily reached by road. Here trout are on the small side but fun to catch. Still others, Flower and Clearwater for example, have some heavy trout in their depths, but the introduction of Lake Superior herring or ciscos, makes them extremely hard to catch.

To get to the best laker waters in Minnesota you should plan to take time for a trip into some of the wilderness lakes. A day's travel and a couple of easy canoe portages will take you into some of the remote lakes where you'll catch big trout. Try jumping off at Ely where an outfitter can furnish you with canoes, camping gear and even guides. Make a jaunt into Frazer, Ameober, Cherry or other wilderness trout waters where you can have a whole lake pretty much to yourself and where trout run heavier than in roadside lakes. Guides are sometimes a good investment if you've never done any laker fishing. If you're an experienced lake-trout angler, you might have more fun and just as good luck without one.

In some lakes and at certain times of the year trout feed best very early in the morning, even before sunup, and just about dark. In early spring lake trout move in close to shore and stay near the surface from ice-out until the water begins to warm up. They stay in comparatively shallow water until the end of June. Most of the small spring-fed trout lakes are less than a hundred feet deep and many under sixty feet in depth. If you're a light tackle angler, here is where you can catch trout all summer long. Starting with ice-out you can catch trout on streamers, spoons and dry flies following them to the depths with light tackle all the way. You can use ordinary spinning tackle for this kind of fishing. Your reel should be fitted with 6 or 8-pound test monofilament line and your spinning rod should be a medium action stick. You don't need heavy tackle. When I fish trout this way I use a standard freshwater reel equipped with 6-pound monofilament. By attaching an ounce and a quarter sinker two feet above my lure I can get down a hundred feet, deep enough for most inland trout lakes.

When you troll with this light rig, go slow! Troll no faster than required to get action from your lure. Use a Doctor spoon or one of the other wobbling spoons that will work at drifting speeds or the slowest crawling speed of your outboard. Another lure that is particularly deadly on lakers in deep inland lakes is the paper-thin Sutton spoon made by Sutton Lure Co.,

Naples, New York. Before I learned where this lure was made I cut some workable spoons from coffee can lids. Rough looking as they were the results justified a great deal of respect. The original Sutton spoon is even more effective. The design of this lure coupled with its lightness results in a lure that has vigorous action at the very slowest speeds. It can be trolled much slower than conventional spoons of the same size. This spoon is the key to successful light tackle trolling!

A few weeks after I discovered this lure in Ontario and fashioned my own from a tin can I tried it in a small Minnesota lake. I was fishing out of Bud Kratoska's Trout Lake resort with Johnny Peitso. Johnny, who has spent more time probing the depths of the lake than many of its inhabitants, knows the lake like a book. A hammered spoon man in his own right, John knows how to sell a mouthful of bare hooks to lakers almost anytime he wants a few trout to go with his beans.

I'd been telling John about the spoon copy I had and as he fished for a minnow in his bucket I dropped my "canlid" over the side and watched it waggle beside the slow-moving boat. I caught my first trout before we'd trolled 200 yards and had a second and third fish before Johnny connected. To be sure it wasn't a fluke. We tried the same experiment the following day, John using his relatively deadly spinner-minnow combination and I using the wafer-thin spoon. The results were nearly the same.

Winter fishing for lakers, which is becoming more popular each season on inland lakes, has been practiced for a hundred years or more by natives of the North Shore. Trout bite best in winter but bad weather and deep snow often makes reaching remote lakes a feat of endurance, at times an impossibility. As a result fishermen fish roadside lakes and Lake Superior. Natives do a lot of fishing on Superior and Ben Hervig of Grand Portage tells how people there catch trout by "bobbing" for them through the ice. The trick, Ben says, is a hard one since lakers are then in several hundred feet of water. Anglers use seaman twine with all the stretch taken out of it and they fish a chunk of herring or cisco meat right on the bottom. Bobbing would be impossible with a stretchy line because you couldn't feel the fish take the bait. A half a pound of lead or more goes down with the bait and the line is bobbed up and down by hand. When the fisherman gets a bite he sets the hook and starts running across the ice as fast as he can in the deep snow. Anglers generally don't go alone on Superior in winter any more than they do in summer so you don't have to try this alone. As one angler takes up line his partner guides the last part of the line with his hands and hoists the fish over the lip of the ice when it appears in the hole. Line must be fed back into the hole carefully because it freezes solid on contact with the air. If kinked, it would snap like a matchstick.

This winter-fishing technique is similar in inland waters except that most anglers use live minnows in place of herring. They fish with minnows just as they would if they were fishing walleyes or crappies. Just enough lead should be added to get your bait down quickly. Trout in these lakes are near the bottom during the winter in 50 to 150 feet of water or depending on the depth of the lake you're fishing.

There is another method that will catch trout during the winter months. Lawrence Downy of Two Harbors has found the weighted Swedish Pimple will catch as many lake trout for him as live bait. This silver minnow-shaped lure is specifically designed for ice fishing. Anglers who fish for lake trout through the ice on Big Saganaga Lake have very good luck on this lure. It's a good one to keep in mind where minnows are hard to get in the winter. Best winter trout waters are Snowbank, Gunflint, Loon, Clearwater and Saganaga.

Fishing lake trout can add greatly to your fishing fun in Minnesota. There is a special thrill that comes with mastering deep-trolling with light tackle. There is

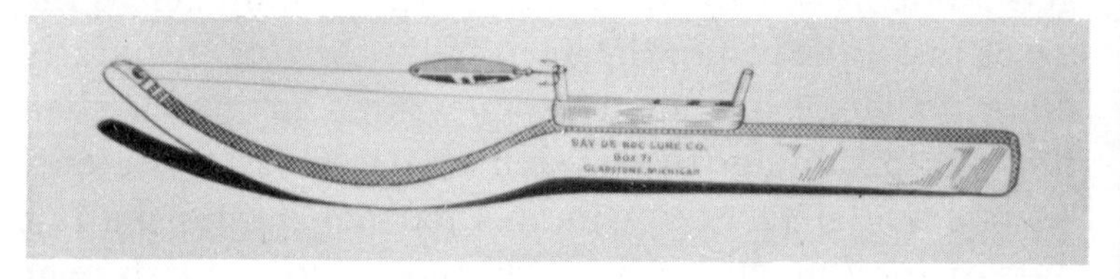

The Pimple Pole is a convenient rod for jigging with Swedish Pimples and bucktail jigs.

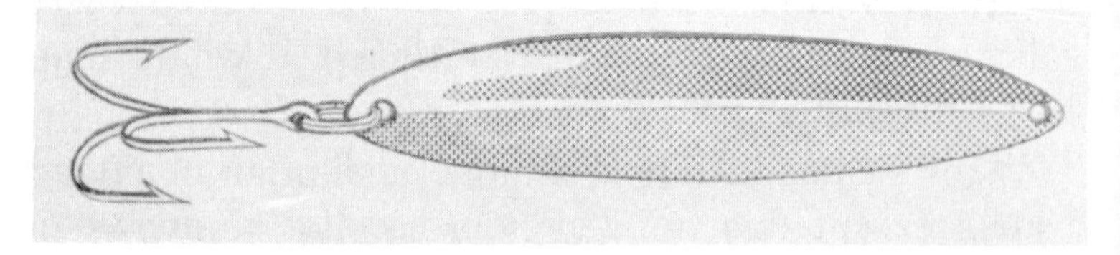

The Swedish Pimple, an old Swedish lure used by North Shore lake trout fishermen for years, is now becoming popular for walleyes and panfish.

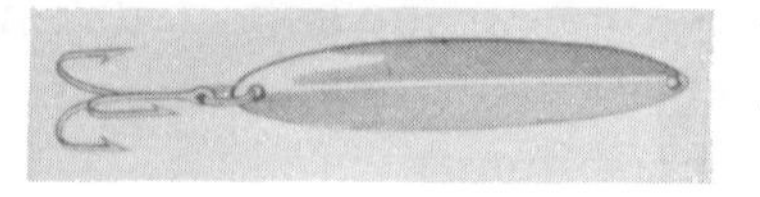

Same as two—Panfish size.

Lake trout from Frazer Lake, north of Snowbank Lake near Ely. Inaccessible lakes provide best fishing for lakers.

real fun in fishing trout when they're still near the top in early spring and in taking reefers along the North Shore. Unfettered by heavy sinkers and big spoons lakers provide the light tackle man a stubborn and long remembered battle. Go back into some of the inaccesible lakes where you'll catch big trout. Little Saganaga, Tuscarora, Star, Ogishemuncie, Ameober or Agamak lakes are good ones. Or spend a day fishing the easily reached waters of roadside lakes. How do you know lake trout water? Well, it's almost a sure thing that lakes with unpronounceable names are good lake-trout waters. Maybe a fish with an Indian-sounding handle such as *Christivomar namaycush namaycush* wouldn't have it any other way!

CHAPTER IX

Catfish Are Heavyweights

The St. Croix River was at least five feet above normal when Tom McCutchan and I began fishing crappies inside the ice-break of the railroad bridge below Point Douglas, Minnesota, a small river town. Fishing was slow, walleyes and silver bass apparently scattered and obviously difficult to locate. That was why we'd decided to try for crappies.

We slipped our boat between the beams of the tarry superstructure where we knew minnow fishermen had caught some beautiful crappies a few days before. I dropped a white bucktail jig into the square opening between the beams and let out about twelve feet of line before the lure hit bottom. I closed the bail on my spinning reel and took in a foot of line. Tom did the same in the next frame. I had a hit right away and I started the fish to the top.

"Crappie already?" Tom asked. "Looks like this is going to be easy."

I thought so too until I cranked a sheepshead up through the forest of timbers. I tried again. And again I had a hit right away. But this time when I tried to bring the fish to the top my rod took on a rainbow shape and the fish pulled hard for the river bottom. Each time I gained a foot the fish doubled my light rod and took a few feet of line against my drag. Finally I began gaining ground and we were both pretty sure what kind of fish it was although we'd never seen one taken on a jig before. It was like fishing in a stovepipe. A walleye, we knew, wouldn't stand for such foolishness; he'd run out into the river and saw my light line on the rough timbers. But not this fish, he just wanted to play elevator. At last I pumped him to the surface and the water parted as a broad-headed mudcat or shovelhead catfish, splashed in the dark water.

Tom took the big cat by the gills and hoisted him aboard. "Get out the smokehouse, Kit!" he grinned. "Always heard smoked cat was really good." And it was! In spite of his ugly mug and his grubby habits, the mudcat and his more handsome cousin the channel cat, are exciting to catch and good to eat either fresh or smoked.

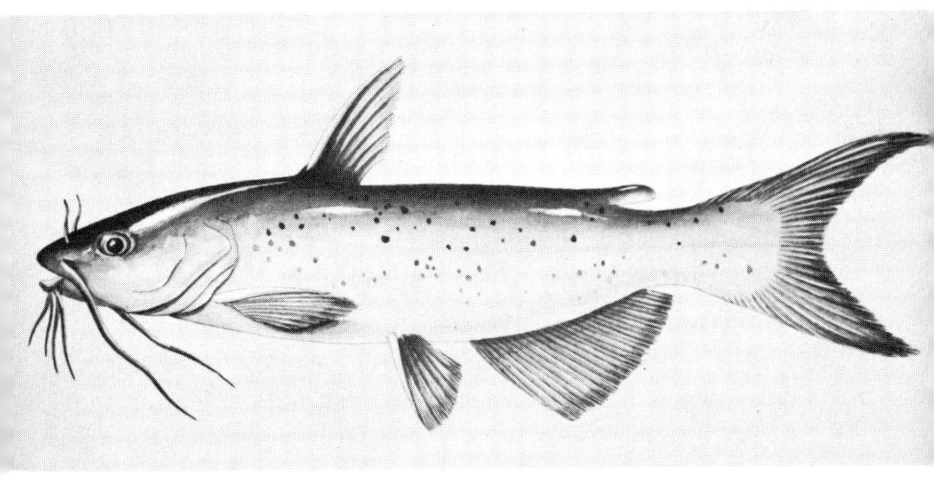

The channel catfish is the most popular and abundant catfish in Minnesota waters.

Catfish are quickly identified by their trout-like adipose fins, feelers on both sides of their mouths, scaleless bodies and sometimes by their great size. They have fierce-looking dorsal and pectoral fins that can inflict very painful wounds if handled carelessly. The channel cats are distinguished from bullheads by their forked tail and flatheads from bullheads by the backward extension of the lateral part of the tooth plates on the upper jaw, which forms a crescent shape. Cats are found in all three drainages of Minnesota, the Hudson Bay drainage, the Superior watershed and the Mississippi drainage. They're particularly abundant in the Mississippi watershed. They're uncommon in the others except the St. Louis River of the Superior shed. Blue cats that scaled better than 150 pounds were at one time taken in the upper Minnesota and Mississippi Rivers, but in late years they have been absent from commercial seines. The channel cat is the most popular and abundant catfish in Minnesota waters and makes up the bulk of the sporting catch. But the mud cat is the heavyweight of the catfish family and in the absence of the once plentiful great blue catfish, is the only big game catfish still found in the headwaters of the three great drainages that rise in Minnesota. He's also known as the Mississippi River bullhead . . . and a stubborn, boneheaded, bottom-pounding scrapper!

Fishermen as a rule find they have a big shovelhead on their line by accident and seldom do they strategically prepare themselves to win over odds favoring such heavy opponents. In view of this, if it were not for those who skillfully handle the fish they hook, and a few others who calculate to take big fish, the record would be noticeably barren of such catches. For very few people concentrate on catfishing in Minnesota. Biologists' creel census indicate that, while 29 percent of the total catch in Minnesota consists of walleyes and seventeen percent crappies, catfish are but an unrecordable fraction of the miscellaneous seven per cent that includes about twenty-five species!

Yet in spite of these statistics, the various catfish have disciples who pursue them in preference to any other kind of fish found in Minnesota. And among the devotees are practiced fly-fishermen and cane polers, spin anglers and star draggers who are experts in other tributaries of the main stream of sport fishing but who have found a new, different experience angling for cats.

Perhaps the days of the big cats are gone forever. But catfish like the 63-pounder taken from the St. Croix below Stillwater, or the 44-pounder caught by Eddy Kunz, from the Minnesota River at Bloomington, or the 36-pound shovelhead caught by a spin fisherman from the Mississippi, gives the catfish angler something to shoot at. Three years ago a group of night-fishing catfish artists, fishing with big sucker minnows set the fishing fraternity on its collective ear when they took about a dozen big mud cats between 25 and 60 pounds before the week-long spree came to an end!

Catfish eat many things. Blood baits, rotted minnows and various cheese-minnow-mash and dough combinations (in secret proportions) have spelled success for those who fished them in good faith. Experience and observation indicates, however, that most big cats, at least in Minnesota waters, are caught on large minnows, although those using other smelly concoctions have recorded success as well. They've also been taken on shrimp and crayfish, night crawlers and grasshoppers.

Selecting tackle for catfishing is often simpler than choosing bait. For the fisherman who works from shore a medium-action baitcasting rod and standard casting reel will handle them. But many anglers prefer heavier star-drag service type reels that hold more line. Catchummers as a rule prefer lines as heavy as 35 to 50-pound test in order to be able to turn heavy fish from snags.

A popular terminal hookup for your catfish rig consists of an 18-inch nylon leader made of material a few pounds lighter than the line with a No. 6/0 Eagle Claw or No. 2/0 Big Bend style hook attached to the end. By tying a heavy sinker to a still lighter, short dropper, and knotting it to the swivel to which the main leader is tied, the angler can keep his minnow just above the river floor where it is easily located by the fish. When the dropper is kept lighter than your leader you can often save part of your terminal tackle and sometimes even your bait when your sinker becomes snagged and you have to break off.

While this is standard tackle for catfishing it's by no means the only thing that qualifies as catfish gear. I've learned that when fishing for "fiddlers," a native name for young channel catfish, in relatively snagfree water, spinning tackle can be usefully employed with the increased pleasure peculiar to light tackle. A ten-pound catfish on a light spinning rod is a great fighter. I'm partial to a stiffish, slow rod for this kind of fishing. Using one with backbone I can cast a crayfish and a half-ounce sinker to midstream on the Minnesota River, even while spinning with heavy eight-pound line.

I use light line if the current is swift. Light line has much less water resistance to fast water. With four-pound line I often get by fishing with less than an ounce of lead, and still avoid the scourge of having my bait drift away. Cats as a rule feed very leisurely and if your bait stays put you can relax and play a waiting game.

When fish are hitting lightly, and this seems to be the rule, it's always best to use egg or football sinkers. Many fishermen use them all the time. To use them simply run your line through the hole in the sinker, then tie on a swivel to keep the sinker from sliding down the line to the hook. Attach your leader to the other end of the swivel. With this combination you can fish close to the river bottom and be in direct contact with those bait-snapping fiddlers. And because your line runs freely through the hole in your sinker, fish don't become suspicious until you've got a hook into them!

Some catfish specialists interested in heavyweights only, fish with a stout canepole fitted with an extremely strong nylon line and a 3-ounce egg sinker. This is a tried boatman's method, one that is effective and exciting. A big cat on a heavy short line is a contest of brute strength between the angler and a powerful, bullheaded fish determined to go uncaptured!

Fish for catfish early in the morning, late afternoon and evening. Look for them on a night when a gentle rain is falling and cats are on the prowl for food washed into the stream with the rain. Starting when rivers reach their normal flow, usually in late June, catfishing remains good throughout the summer, particularly during hot sultry days of late July and August. When fishing for more popular species takes a slump, catfishing is just getting started! Cats are warm-weather fish and when the river bank is baked and warm during late afternoon, a fisherman can count on some channel cats coming to his shrimp or minnows.

When you go in search of catfish water try stream mouths and near spring banks where the water drops off abruptly. Fish below dams and both above and below log jams. Investigate the water above deep holes and in sloughs and backwaters adjacent to the main stream of the river where a slow current exists. These are the haunts of *Ictalarus* and *Pilodictus,* the scientific names for channel and shovelhead catfish.

Minnesota's best channel cat hunting water includes the St. Louis River in the northeast, the St. Croix, below Taylors Falls, the Minnesota River and Mississippi River below St. Anthony Falls. Included, too, are a few southern tributaries of the Ottertail River of western Minnesota. Shovelheads are found in the St. Croix, Minnesota, and Mississippi, co-existing with channel cats. They are absent from the St. Louis River.

Although about half the food taken by catfish consists of aquatic insects, they eat minnows too and there are times when artificials account for some good fish.

The first time I saw a catfish hit an artifical plug, Tom McCutchan and I were floating the St. Croix River for the first time, between Taylors Falls and Stillwater. We'd had poor luck with smallmouth bass

Most Minnesota fish will hit artificial lures. This 10-pound mudcat that hit the author's jig was no exception.

in the main stream so we began working stream mouths and crystal springs falling from the sandstone cliffs along the river, windows through which, here and there, we could see the geometric, rocky bottom. Fishing one of these jewels of spring water, Tom got a jolting hit and he let out a holler that could have barked a river-bottom coon at half a mile.

"Man, he's a good one," I said as his rod rapped the metal gun'le and the fish depressed the rod into the water. "A bass like that ought to go about three-e-e----"

"A bass like that will what?" Tom asked starting to laugh.

"At catfish like that doesn't very often hit a plug," I managed, and grew pink around the ears as a silver-blue catfish bored and flashed beside the canoe.

Tom broke off his mild razzberry laugh. "Had me fooled too," he said. "Hard to believe a fish that size can fight so much like a big bass!"

Cats often do that. A walleye fisherman spinning in the Mississippi will suddenly find his lure has snagged a log and finally discover after prying and straining, that the log is actually alive! Some time later if he plays his fish patiently and keeps his head he may land the monster cat he mistakenly identified as a log.

There seems to be little danger of overfishing catfish and there is some strong indication that the annual catfish harvest is small in the Mississippi River compared to the available crop. And because cats are wanderers no one navigation pool (the area between locks and dams) is entirely dependent upon the fish in that particular pool to maintain its population. Areas of heavy fishing are restocked naturally by fish traveling through locks from one navigation pool to another. In fact individual fish have been known to travel down stream through eight locks and upstream through two locks of the lock and dam installations on the Mississippi.* Apparently these locks don't represent a barrier.

If you're a light tackle enthusiast, try fishing catfish with your flyrod. There are a number of places where a flyrodder can have a time with baby channel cats from one to eight pounds particularly if you fish from a boat. There's a good spot on the St. Croix River, across from Beanies at Lakeland, called catfish bar. There are several places on the Minnesota River; the rapids at Carver, the Ferry Bridge near Savage, the mouth of Pergatory and Eagle Creeks and Credit River where you can fish cats with light gear.

You'll be a little surprised when you start traveling the catfish circuits to find you have no competition to speak of. While the lakes are crowded with water skiiers and fishermen in some areas on a Sunday afternoon, the land of the catfish is often a lonely place. You can actually have miles of river all to yourself!

Once you find yourself on the bank of a Minnesota catfish stream watching your line throb in the steady flow of a good current, your rod resting in the fork of a willow stick, you'll discover for yourself that catfishing presents a challenge few died-in-the-mud anglers could refuse to accept!

*Information from the Upper Mississippi River Conservation committee report. This committee in a tagging study has also learned that catfish will travel great distances. Of greatest interest and significance are 158 tagged fish caught outside of Lake Pepin. Forty-five were caught above the lake, having traveled an average of 21 miles. Eighty-three were taken below the lake having covered an average distance downstream of 44 miles, with a range of from 9 to 180 miles!

CHAPTER X

Black or White Crappies

I saw the fish inhale Jim Elder's minnow and watched him set the hook into a "jumbo" Lake Miltona black crappie. Several other fish came from among the reeds to follow the platter-sized crappie as it fought resolutely, and Jim's rod bent sharply under the weight of the broad fish. I eased a net under it and lifted it into the sleepy sunlight of midmorning.

"I'll take crappies any time!" Jim smiled, "I didn't know these guys could fight so well!"

We continued to catch heavy panfish and Jim, who has a partnership in an oil business and has a lot of time to fish, repeated his allegiance to them each time one reluctantly swam into our net.

Jim is far from alone in his opinion because crappies are everyone's favorite. And for a very good reason. Crappies are distributed statewide and bite well all through the year. They aren't discriminating fish and the average fisherman is equally undiscriminating, accepting either black or white crappies without prejudice. Black and white crappies are taken with equal eagerness by a large army of anglers in the state. But geographical segregation is the rule. White crappies are found mostly in lakes and the larger rivers of the southern half of Minnesota while black crappies are found mostly in the north and central areas, excluding some of the deeper lakes of the northeast. Both kinds are occasionally found in the same water. It's easy enough to know which you've taken, often by color alone. When in doubt just measure the distance between the eye and the forward edge of the top, or dorsal, fin. This measurement is much larger in white crappies than black, being greater than the length of the fin. Then, too, white crappies can be identified from their northern cousins by a more depressed brow.

White crappie found primarily in Southern Minnesota, black crappie more commonly in the northern half of Minnesota.

Excellent crappie fishing water is plentiful in Minnesota, particularly in the great central Minnesota panfish area that makes up thousands of square miles of fishing water. You never have to go far to catch crappies!

Lake Osakis and Miltona, near Alexandria; Crane and Pelican near Orr; Green, Chisago, Dead, are statewide samplings of some good crappie lakes. There are

Black Crappie

many others far too numerous to mention. If you fished ten different good crappie lakes every year for fifty years, you'd have fished 500 lakes and have only scratched the surface of the state's panfish water! All the major rivers have crappies too, although locating them is another matter . . . crappies are really everywhere!

Crappies move and feed in schools just as walleyes do and where you catch one there are more nearby. That's one reason why crappies are popular among all kinds of anglers. Kids catch crappies in the residential lakes of St. Paul and Minneapolis. Families vacationing or spending a weekend at a lake cottage catch them from the dock or from a small boat or from shore. Flyfishermen stand in shallow bays or in boats and pluck fish from the aquatic cabbage patch like girls gathering daisies in a meadow. Spin anglers cast white bucktail jigs or small bright spoons and everyone catches fish most of the time!

Often the best crappie fishing occurs when they move in close to shore in early spring to feed on the insect life that begins stirring in the ooze of the shallow bays. As the ice recedes fly-fishermen stand waist-deep in bays and inlets where the water warms first. It is here where many a fly-fisherman has learned his trade. For at no other time are flies and crappies more compatible than from ice-out to early June. As fish move into deeper water they are sought by boating anglers over weed beds and along bars and dropoffs. Crappies sometimes go quite deep in midsummer often retiring to thirty feet of water. They feed heavily on minnows all summer and early winter. As baitfish become scarce each winter and daphnia, or water fleas,

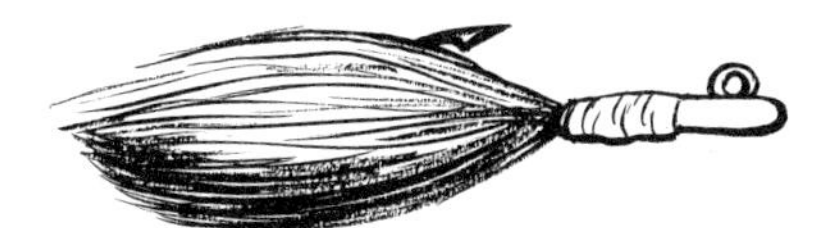

One-tenth ounce Upperman Bucktail jig is pure murder on schooling crappies.

Big black "slab" crappies like this one Rod Bell caught while fishing Lake Miltona are abundant in bass-panfish lakes of West Central Minnesota.

become plentiful they begin gorging on these pin-head sized animals. Then anglers wearied of their perversity, give up until ice-out. As the water warms, water fleas, which thrive in cold water, become scarce again and crappies begin to move into the bays where they grub for dragon fly nymphs and damsel fly larvae on dead weed stems and in the bottom muck.

Of the popular crappie-catching methods fly-fishing presents the most interesting and by far the most productive means of taking them. Perhaps I'm too impatient to tease them with minnows and for me casting has more appeal.

Starting right after the ice goes out you can follow crappies with a flyrod like a schoolmaster chases his kids to the library with a ruler, defending your rash action by the end result. Crappies are the darndest fools about a mouthful of feathers and a seductively-dressed white fly will have crappies falling all over each other to get at your fake. There are a number of standard panfish patterns. Crappies are normally inclined to favor the light patterns most of the time but occasionally dark patterns will pay off too, so carry some of each. Most crappie flies are tied on No. 8 hooks but since sunfish often feed at the same counter, I use smaller flies. I've found No. 10's just right. For streamers I like to use No. 6 or No. 8 long shank hooks. I've taken many hundreds of crappies on a white No. 6 streamer right from shore on lakes within sight of the Twin Cities. Fish a streamer like a swimming minnow, in long darting motions, and pause slightly between darts. The streamer will flutter in a life-like way and fish will come to it on the double.

Crappies are schooling fish. That's why they're so popular with natives and non-residents alike.

Tom McCutchan reaches for exhausted jumbo Lake Miltona crappie. Crappies are found in all parts of Minnesota.

Don't forget to use poppers. You'll catch baskets of crappies on small cork-bodied bugs from early spring right on through the summer. When Cal Standish first introduced me to ice-out fishing for crappies with flies we used poppers almost exclusively. Cal had a way of knowing what crappies would be hitting just by looking at the water. He knew from several years of practice that when it was warm and calm it was time to tie on a small, dark popper. On cool days he fished wets. Casting to a rise he'd drop a green or black popper within the circle made by the fish and let it rest motionless until a wild crappie would smash it as if it were a sinister enemy. Or he would cast to a weed pocket near shore where a fish was nearly always compelled to hit in self-defense seldom having time to weigh the right or wrong of it all in view of the emergency.

What, you now wonder, makes a good panfish rod? Simple enough. Any rod you now use for bass bugging or for trout fishing will do a good job on crappies. While wetfly actions are better suited to most panfishing than a dry-fly rod it would be a waste of money to

The author holds black crappie. A small bucktail jig holds the secret of successful crappie fishing in Minnesota.

consider buying one unless you are going to do nothing but wet-fly and nymph fishing. So much of the better fly-fishing is found topside in Minnesota lakes and rivers that a wet-fly rod is just not practical for all-around anglers who will fish bass, trout, and panfish with the same rod. Most of the low-priced bargains you see advertised are wet-fly rods dealers have been unable to move at regular prices. The rod mentioned as an all-around rod in the chapter on tackle will do a fine job on panfish with a lot to spare.

Your line and reel requirements are the same, too, but you could use a bug-taper if you have one. Don't get any special equipment for panfishing because crappies simply won't appreciate it. Leaders can be similar to those recommended for trout since tapered leaders are easier to control. They don't have to be as long as trout leaders but the taper should be about the same. If you want to use a level leader, use one stout enough to complement your line. A heavy leader will straighten out better than a light one and won't fall back on your line as one that is too light will do.

When casting a wet-fly or streamer there are two basic retrieves that will catch crappies. A wading angler can begin by dropping his fly a short distance out from shore, as far as he can comfortably cast, let the fly sink and begin retrieving very slowly. Normally the easiest way to take in line is by the hand-twist method, where the line is grasped between thumb and forefinger and the hand is rotated toward the body. Then the other three fingers are placed over the line and rotated back and the line is brought against the palm of your hand. The process is repeated until the cast is fished out.

Fish prefer this retrieve most of the time but if you're not getting any action better try another one before changing flies. Because sometimes reluctant fish can be urged to hit when your fly zips along as you strip line in swiftly with your free hand. To do this you place the line between your index finger of your rod hand and the rod itself, then placing your free hand on the line a foot above the rod grip, strip in a foot of line at a stroke. Be ready for a hit during the hesitation point when you reach for more line. Remember to hold your line just tight enough to hook fish as they hit but not so tightly that these paper-mouthed fish will tear away or break off your fly.

I think it's a toss up between minnows and flies as the most popular means of catching strings of crappies in Minnesota. If you fish with minnows, begin fishing just outside of the weed patches or a stand of reeds, or begin fishing just out from a point of land, or at the edge of a bar. Crappies usually patrol these areas during early morning and evening hours.

If action is slow, it's important to present a minnow in the raw state with no spinner and just enough weight to take a small shiner minnow to the crappies below. To get the best direct contact with your fish eliminate the usual bobber. If you don't begin catching fish in a few minutes, try another likely spot or pull your anchor and drift over a good bar or point. I like to use a fly rod while drifting for crappies. A light fly rod, a small hook and delicate leader makes a perfect combination for the drift fisherman. If you add lead, put on several shot and if you add a bobber, use a very small one. When crappies are hitting lightly they can be discouraged by a little thing like the resistance of a bobber. When you feel a fish, set the hook very gently.

Don't overlook the fact that crappies congregate around brush piles and docks in early summer and are often found near diving rafts and bridge pilings. Before you go swimming row gingerly to the diving platform and catch the crappies from under it.

A few years ago my wife Pat and I rented a place for the summer on a small lake where we discovered that dinner was no farther than the diving dock. We used to catch crappies first and go swimming later. Crappies are sociable animals we learned and by taking advantage of their fondness for civilized surroundings we enjoyed some fast fishing.

Spinning has undoubtedly added a new facet to baitfishing for crappies as well as for other fresh-water fish. This is especially true for thousands of shore fishermen who jam bridges and other access, to catch their favorite panfish. By using spin gear they can cast live bait without fear of it flying off their hooks and light tackle makes a good fighter of a fish that had formerly been considered to have a dishrag personality. Spinning certainly has no greater advantage than that it makes catching crappies easier for expert and novice alike. Kids have taken to spinning like a hog to beachnut ridge. There could be no better place for spinning tackle than in the hands of a young crappie angler.

It's easy to find a lure that will satisfy crappies. They go for a wide variety of lures. Small plugs and spoons are good, and particularly a spinning-size bucktail jig.

A 1/10th-ounce white Upperman bucktail is so deadly for crappies that an angler armed with a handful of these hairy minnow imitations could often catch ten limits a day. Fish your jig deep, right on the lake bottom and retrieve it very slowly at first. Jump the lure along by whipping the rod upward for each turn of the reel handle. If you get no response increase the tempo of your retrieve. Mix it up—slow for a few feet, then fast. And if this doesn't score, change to a yellow jig or a black one and continue to change pace. This little bucktail jig has a beautifully life-like action that stimulates hunger in crappies as it does with no other fish with the exception of walleyes which have a pronounced weakness for this phenomenal lure. Bucktails are inexpensive and easy to fish. Their single hook lends itself to snaggy waters because the hook rides upright as the lure darts through the water.

If you can get a handful of lead and a few deer tails, you can make your own jigs. You will catch as many fish on your homemade lures as you can on those you can buy. In fact I made several hundred of them before I began using commercial jigs and I took seventeen varieties of Minnesota fish on them in a single year, proof indeed that homebrewed jigs are potent!

You can catch crappies on spoons too. I like to fish a light-weight pearl, or a red and white spoon of thin metal. I use a spoon that can be retrieved very slowly without hanging in the bottom on every cast. There are a number of manufacturers that make them and they're all good if they're light enough. Heavy spoons have to be retrieved much too fast to work properly in this kind of angling even when crappies are very deep. Crappies like time to make up their minds. At times they're extremely timid and when a lure is fished too fast it will get the cold fin from finniky fish. Once in awhile a faster retrieve works, but start out idling your spoon along, because Minnesota crappies won't be rushed! Fish these lures in some of the same spots you'd try for crappies with flies and minnows and you'll get the same—sometimes better—results with much less time between bites.

Don't overlook crappie fishing in the winter when a foot or two of snow blankets your favorite lake. When temperatures fall below zero and a northwest wind licks Minnesota's lakes with its frozen tongue crappie fishing takes an upsurge. There are days in early winter when crappies bite so fast ice-fishermen are hopping all over the ice trying to keep track of two bobbers at once. Crappies are the most cooperative fish an angler will encounter throughout the winter. They hit well from the time lake ice is thick enough to bear the weight of a man in early December, until mid-February when fishing takes a slump. This late winter slow down, incidentally, is due primarily to an increase in water fleas which thrive during cold winter weather. As minnow surpluses decrease and water fleas increase, crappies become more interested in these little animals as food. During this slack period the best way to take crappies is to fish ice flies and grubs. Bait dealers carry mousee, golden-rod grubs and other larvae popular for ice fishing. When you fish these baits use a very tiny gold-coated, fine wire hook in size No. 10 or No. 12.

Put several small grubs or one large one on your hook and fish with a light jig stick. By jigging the bait up and down you can often attract crappies that have lost interest in minnows. If you use ice flies, add a grub to the hook as an attractor.

You can depend on crappies being in the same location winter after winter. If you find them in sixteen feet of water one winter, they'll be in that same area again at the same time the following year. But they don't stay in the same spot all winter long. As the season progresses they often move to deeper water. When I fished Lake Waconia with Bob Johnstone early one winter crappies were biting furiously just off the northeast end of the island. As the season advanced fishermen began chopping holes further to the northeast. Gradually the ice fishing village moved in that direction in an effort to keep up with the fish as they moved toward deeper water. As long as they stayed with them they caught crappies. So if your spot cools off move around. Chop some new holes!

Popular ice-fishing equipment for crappies is inexpensive. It consists primarily of a light, limber jig stick fitted with 4 or 6-pound test nylon monofilament spinning line, or an ice stick with a spike on the bottom end that can be driven into the ice while fishing. Your stick can be customized with a submersible reel that won't freeze up or you can make one that lights up when you get a hit. There are as many variations in ice-fishing sticks as anglers can dream up, additions that fit the particular angler's fancy or fishing style. Start out with an inexpensive stick and see what you want or need in extras after you begin fishing. Add to the jig stick and fishing stick, an ice chisel, some warm clothing, insulated boots, a heated minnow bucket and an ice skimmer and you can fish all winter in comfort. You can fish inside of a warm portable fishhouse or you can build a "winter home" with all the comforts and conveniences of a motel. Or you can rent a licensed fishhouse at many resorts for about two dollars a day per man. Most ice fishermen prefer to move around but they often take advantage of access roads plowed and maintained by resorters on many lakes. A nominal fee from fifty cents to a dollar is charged which includes a tow and addi-

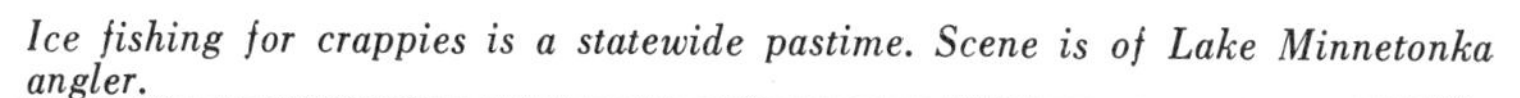

Ice fishing for crappies is a statewide pastime. Scene is of Lake Minnetonka angler.

tional plowing if the road fills in while you're fishing.

Most winter fishermen fish for crappies with small shiner minnows about an inch long. The minnow is impaled on the hook by running a No. 6 or No. 8 hook through the flesh behind the dorsal fin of the minnow, being careful not to injure his backbone. A shiner hooked in this fleshy area will swim about in a fish-attracting manner. I use the smallest bobber I can get for ice fishing so the crappie will discover no resistance as he takes the minnow. I add just enough split shot to get the minnow down. A single, or sometimes two split shot, are just right. Usually a crappie dances your bobber across the hole before taking off with your minnow so let him have time to take it! Wait a minute for the fish to start down with the bobber and strike ONLY when your float is still going down. Don't strike if it starts up again because you will only take it away from your fish. Wait a minute if the bobber comes back up and if the fish doesn't hit again within a minute or two check your bait because he's cleaned you out! Once you get the timing right and can set the hook when the fish starts down with the minnow you'll be able to catch fish when they're just mouthing your bait. But be sure to keep your tackle light. A light-balanced rig makes suckers out of suspicious light strikers.

Don't forget the little bucktail jig when it comes to winter crappies. A 1/13-ounce Upperman bucktail is a crappie getter in the hands of a confident fisherman. You have to keep working a jig to catch fish on it, moving it up and down in short jerks, or fluttering it with a jiggle of your rod tip. Fish don't always react to the same jigging movements so you have to experiment until you're working it the way they like it.

One more thing about crappies. In their fondness for civilization they've developed a pattern of feeding under lighted bridges at night. Last summer I took crappies on flies at the narrows of Lake Minnetonka when all the speedboat skippers were sleeping. My young son and his cousins were busy with cane poles and spinning rods as the crappies surged about under the navigation lights. I've also caught crappies at night under the lights of the Stillwater bridge where crappies follow baitfish in against the seawall and compete with ugly, long-nosed gar fish for their dinner.

So take along your fly rod and spinning tackle when you fish in Minnesota. Spin for crappies from shore or from a boat. Cast for them with flies and streamers during the spring of the year. Crappies are everyone's

Winter fishermen congregate on Lake Waconia during "hot" fishing days in early January.

fish and you never need to go home fishless if you're willing to shop around a little in almost any lake where you fish for bass or walleyes. All the lakes where other species get priority from anglers there's an underharvested crop of crappies waiting for your lures. If you fish in Minnesota and don't catch crappies by accident or design, it's only because you've been working the wrong kind of bars!

CHAPTER XI

Bluegills Act Big

If bluegills grew to the size of largemouth bass and walleyes, tackle makers would have been years developing spinning tackle that would handle them! Muskie fishing would be an also-ran and northerns would play third fiddle in the eyes of sunfish anglers. Because a husky bluegill on the end of a fly line is the sizzlingest fighter that could be conjured up if you were to thumb through your imagination for days. Bluegills, or sunnies to most fishermen, can be caught on the fanciest dry-fly patterns or common earthworms with equal success. The cane-poler and fly rodder can relax with the knowledge that here is a hard-fighting fish that takes very little time weighing the factors of barometric pressure, moon phase or wind direction. But that's not all! Besides being a good fighter and a willing customer to your bait or fly, he's the best eating of the saucer-shaped fish that make up the sunfish family. In the skillet I think he's tops.

Of the five native species of sunfish in Minnesota, bluegills have the widest distribution and are the most plentiful. There is hardly a lake or major river in the state that doesn't have bluegill fishing. From the Mississippi backwaters near Red Wing in the extreme

Small hardy "sunnies" like the one shown by the author abound in many metropolitan lakes.

southeastern part of Minnesota to little Lake Bronson, a WPA lake in the far northwest, bluegills thrive and provide fishing enjoyment for thousands. They're common in shallow weedy lakes, existing in harmony with bass and northern pike and all the major walleye lakes have bluegills although they are not abundant in the larger ones. Many ponds that aren't officially listed as lakes have good sunfish angling. If the weather is rough many fishermen concentrate on these smaller ponds where they can catch sunnies. Or if there's a slump in bass fishing they can still count on catching some bluegills to fill their strings. Bass may jump better, walleyes may be the state fish and most popular eating, but bluegills are the catchingest species found in Minnesota lakes next to the lowly bullhead.

Pugnacious looking, hard fighting bluegills are perhaps the most popular fish among anglers of all ages. Wide distribution makes them available to everyone.

Bluegills are the largest of the sunfish found in Minnesota. A few over the two-pound mark are taken occasionally although the average fish is less than half a pound. Most of these are termed "eatin' size," or about as big as your hand. They're very easily distinguished from other sunfishes, common punkinseeds, and green sunfish, by dark vertical bars. They have a black spot on each of their short ears or opercle flaps and bluish gill covers. During spawning season male bluegills take on a beautiful deep orange color on the breast. Bluegills feed on nymphs and small crustaceans including fresh water shrimp, and young crayfish. They occasionally eat small minnows.

A few fly-fishermen have long known that bluegills were easy to catch on wet and dry flies. With a year-around panfish season more and more anglers are beginning to see the light and are using flies to catch panfish. The sale of fly-fishing equipment for panfishing is far ahead of sales of the same tackle for trout. If you've ever tried catching sunfish with flies, you already know the fun this sport offers. A half-pounder on a weightless fly and a light fly rod is like taking a five-pound walleye on heavier tackle! These little fire-eaters can cut capers and a bluegill angler is in no danger of falling asleep with boredom. The best time to catch sunnies with an empty paunch and a big appetite coincides with the magic time between the trout opener and the weeks that follow when fishermen are busy preparing for the general fishing season of mid-May. When the ice goes out sunfish come in and join the crappie clan, flashing copper and silver in the backwaters like a handful of mixed coins. This is pan fishing to remember. When, in later summer, things have slowed to a walk you can think back on ice-out fishing and know you were in on the fish fry!

I'll long remember an early season jaunt to Lake Marion, with Al Morgan for bluegills. It was a raw and windy April afternoon when we eased the canoe into the icy water from the highway bridge on US 65 just west of Lakeville. Al was wearing a navy peacoat but complained of the cold nevertheless. When we reached the bay that held the jumbo sunnies it was a little more comfortable but still very cold and windy. We anchored to a muskrat house by keeping a foot on it to hold the canoe. It was Al's first time out for early bluegill fishing and so far he didn't appear to like it. We began casting to a weed-free opening on the down-wind side of the canoe but the wind made our lines nearly unmanageable and Al was condemning me for ever suggesting such a trip. While he was struggling with the urge to strangle me and tow me back to the landing with his fly rod, a fish straightened his leader and ripped slack through his guides like a streak. It snubbed itself against the rod tip causing Al's whole rod to tremble with shock.

"A bass, I'll bet!" Al half complained. But at least it made us both forget our painfully cold hands and the screeching wind that rocked the canoe and tore at our clothing. The fish maneuvered in typical bluegill style corkscrewing in tight circles and bursting into frantic runs, then renewing his circling again. I was positive it was no bass.

"If a largemouth could fight like that," I joked,

"people wouldn't spend so much time trolling for walleyes."

Al ignored my allusion to his favorite fishing technique until he landed his fish. He admired the glistening, barred sunnie for a moment and then placed it carefully in his creel.

"Pretty nice fish," he said. "Wouldn't mind catching a few more before we get pneumonia!"

"You won't notice the cold if they keep hitting like this," I reasoned. Just then a fish took my fly and began barnstorming the bow of the canoe. The heavy sunnie exhausted himself with a burst of power that brought him to the edge of the canoe and I slipped my hand on his back, stroking down his dorsal fin to avoid his sharp spines. Al hooked another heavy sunnie and lost it but had another one on the next cast. By allowing our flies to settle to the bottom we caught fish on nearly every retrieve or had hits. Al had forgotten the cold and was having the time of his life. When we got back to the car and had the canoe loaded Al asked: "Do they only hit on miserable days like this or is fishing good when the weather gets warm, too?"

I explained to him that fly-fishing in early spring isn't always a cold and painful business. The majority of the days are fairly warm this time of year and the best fishing occurs after a few days of warm, sunny weather when protected bays and backwaters have had a chance to warm up. A few warm days and the bays are teeming with fish which will hit almost any fly. They stop hitting, however, when a strong wind whips colder lake water into these bays. But since the wind can blow only in one direction at a time the bays on the

Bluegill? You bet, and fly fishermen couldn't get along without them!

lee side of the lake will be calm and fishable as it was the day we fished Lake Marion.

The same inexpensive chenille bodied single-colored flies that catch crappies will take bluegills although I've found that sunfish prefer darker colors. One of the top wet-flies for sunnies is the black and yellow bee or McGinty pattern, tied on a No. 10 hook. If you tie your own flies, use soft brown hackles that breathe and move as your fly inches along the bottom. The body of the bee pattern consists of black and yellow chenille wrapped alternately on the hook and the tail is made of red mallard quill or a mixture of red quill and a whisp of woodduck breast. The McGinty is a dependable fly, a day-in day-out killer on sunfish. Bluegills will hit it when other flies fail completely to stimulate action.

When sunfish are feeding deep as they are when searching for larvae it's a good plan to use weighted flies. One extremely productive weighted panfish fly, the Timber Wolf, was originated in the Park Rapids panfish area, according to outdoor writer, Jim Peterso. It's one a serious fly-fisherman should carry with him in Minnesota sunfish country. The first time I tried the Timber Wolf, Alan Maxson and I were fly-fishing on a small suburban lake. The sky was threatening rain and as we shoved the boat into the water fat blobs of water began pounding the surface here and there. Thunder rumbled in the distance.

"We're going to get wet for nothing," I told Alan. "Panfish won't hit during a storm like this and when it begins to rain there'll be as much rain in the boat as there is in the lake!"

My words had no effect on my companion although even now a gusty wind abetted his measured strokes with the paddle. This, I thought, was just one more of a series of tests a fishing writer is constantly put to. I said nothing more.

We anchored in the quiet end of a bay and started fishing. The rain came down in buckets and the thunder rolled loudly but our weighted Timber Wolves caught fish the way Jim had said they would. And thus my confidence in a new fly was established and the effectiveness of the Timber Wolf confirmed. Any fly that will catch fish under storm conditions is no ordinary offering. The Timber Wolf is tied with a yellow wool or chenille body and has a red egg-sac and no tail. The hackle is soft brown hen neck and is tied very sparsely. Lead wire is wrapped on the hook before the body is tied on giving the fly just enough weight to sink rapidly and stay deep when retrieved slowly.

These flies are two good starters but there are dozens of patterns that will catch sunfish at different times.

All-white, black, red, yellow and brown and combinations of these colors do a fair job most of the time. Many anglers have their pets but the two I've described are among the most dependable. Effective panfish flies can be purchased anywhere in the state. Inexpensive wet fly patterns are stocked in almost every Minnesota tackle store and many resorts and general stores have them.

Small sunfish poppers work very well even when there is no evidence of a hatch other than the mosquitoes that are chewing you to shreds. Just throw a dark popper out on that glassy water and watch what happens. I use a black fly for topside fishing almost all the time because I'm sure fish see dark lures better against the lighter sky, especially in late evening.

You have to fish these flies and poppers right if you are to get results with panfish consistently. The hand-twist method is the universal retrieve used in wet-fly fishing for sunnies. Most insects and larvae which make up the bulk of a sunny's diet are slow-moving animals that inch along the lake bottom or propel themselves to the surface in jerky movements much like the action imparted to the fly by the angler who uses the hand-twist retrieve. Sunfish seldom go for a fast retrieve so when fishing wet-flies for deep feeding fish KEEP YOUR FLIES DEEP AND FISH THEM PAINFULLY SLOW! Watch your line closely and when you see your leader begin to tense or straighten, then set the hook softly and you'll hit him going away with your fly. Bluegills will actually hook themselves most of the time if you just give them a little help. Sometimes a two-fly combination is a good way to interest difficult sunnies. Tie on a dropper fly of a contrasting color to your point or end fly, by means of a second short section of leader. Tie it far enough forward on the leader so the dropper fly will travel at least a foot ahead of the point fly. Using a dropper, or even two, can sometimes make the difference between good and only fair action and often you have the fun of actually catching several sunfish at once.

Tom McCutchan and I were fishing a little bay on Bush Lake in my home town one day when two fish per cast was the rule. Tom made thirteen casts and actually caught 26 pint-sized sunnies on as many casts!

Another time I could do nothing but watch while a more skilled fisherman took two heavy sunnies on almost every cast he made. Try as I would I couldn't work the combination even though I used the same flies and fished the same spot after he left. Some subtle difference I couldn't uncover caught fish for him on almost every cast while I caught only an occasional one.

Punkinseeds are the second most abundant and popular sunfish in Minnesota. They're found in most of the lakes inhabited by bluegills. However, they don't grow as large. Nor are they as abundant or as free from grubs as bluegills. The other sunfish, the great lakes longeared, and orange spotted, are not abundant enough to be important. Another kind, the green sunfish, seldom reaches a length of five inches. Kids with cane poles and a supply of worms can have a great time with a school of green sunfish but most anglers consider them a nuisance.

Although fly-fishing drops off during the warm months of July and August they will still take flies at certain times. During the very early morning hours and again in the evening big sunnies move inshore to feed. They come in from deep water to pick food from the stems of lily plants and other water weeds and catch free-swimming insects as they move about. This is the perfect time to catch sunnies with small palmer-tied dry flies or tiny poppers. Larger bluegills don't feed on top during the day at this time of year and if you want to collect some of them you have to get up in the morning ahead of the sun. Some summer fishermen actually get out for an hour of fly-fishing before they go to work in the morning!

The Bluegill is Minnesota's most abundant and largest growing sunfish.

Punkinseeds are not as common as the bluegill nor do they grow to the same size.

Find a bay or bar that has from four to eight feet of water and is overgrown with a sparse weed bed. Here you'll see fish rise or hear them kissing flies off the underside of lily leaves. The peculiar smacking sound they make gives them away when they're feeding. When you find a good spot watch for rises or simply drop the fly in open pockets in the weeds. This is hazard fishing of a sort and you might want to use a regular bass leader if the fish are large. Don't overlook the possibility that fish may move right up to the shoreline. If they're close inshore you will often see swirls along the beach as they feed. This kind of fly-fishing often produces some beautiful fish, fish that are little known to summer anglers. Lakes where only small sunnies are caught have some real surprises in store for the angler who works the weeds at dawn or on a calm summer evening. Use any of the No. 10 or No. 12 fuzzy-looking palmer tied bivisibles or tiny poppers. I use black, brown and barred hackle flies, all with success. Remember though, these aren't the same starved sunfish that you could fool with sloppy castings in April and May. They spook if you make too much commotion.

It would be hard to say how many people enjoy baitfishing for bluegills but it's safe to say that among the thousands of fishermen who come to Minnesota from other states this year, about 35 percent of them will fish for bluegills during their vacations or weekend fishing trips.* Fishing sunfish is undoubtedly the most relaxing kind of fishing offered in Minnesota's

*According to figures compiled from a survey of non-resident anglers, the bureau of research and planning, Minnesota department of conservation, concluded that while only 16 percent admit a preference for panfish almost twice that many fish for them and express satisfaction with their catches.

endless fishing acreage and it is at times the most exciting. While a handful of plug casters pound the weeds for bass there are armies of fishermen enjoying themselves fishing bluegills from a gently rocking boat with their hats protecting their eyes from the disagreeable reflection of the hot summer sun. For clock-punchers who have had to hurry all winter long, summer brings fishing for bluegills with a gob of worms and a bobber and a chance to enjoy his family or the company of his neighbor as he waits for some action from below. There are those who take their baitfishing more seriously but the average man goes for bluegills and has a good time whether they're biting well or not. This is fishing close to hearts of families and to those rare fishermen who actually take their wives along. No doubt about it, bluegills provide as much fun, pound for pound, as any Minnesota fish.

If sunfish grew as large as muskies fishermen couldn't buy tackle strong enough to hold them.

Cane poles are still popular in Minnesota for sunfishing mainly because they are simple and effective to use. You can be in business for a dollar with pole, hook, line and bobber. Another couple of dollars for a license and you begin fishing. There are places to fish where anglers can catch sunfish from bank or bridge. For this kind of fishing worms are the most popular bait. Just common angle worms that are dug by the young and ambitious and sold for a song. Use a small hook for sunfish since bluegills and punkinseeds have small mouths and if your hook is too large you'll feed them a dozen worms for every fish you hook. A No. 10 sproat or perfect bend hook is just right. Some fishermen prefer to use long shanked hooks because bluegills, like bullheads, have the disagreeable habit of taking bait with gusto often becoming hooked very deeply. I like to use short shanked hooks but always carry a pair of long-nosed pliers or surgical clamps to extract deeply imbedded hooks. Clamps, which are available at medical supply houses, have tight-locking jaws and are chromed or stainless so they won't rust.

Use a bobber that will go down very easily and hook on a worm or two by looping them on the hook, leaving the ends dangling to wiggle freely. By letting the bait squirm naturally you can sometimes persuade those suspicious old-timers to join the parade to the top. Find a spot near the outer edge of a weed bed or on the margin of a dropoff. Channels or narrows between lakes are good too. Fish about a foot above the bottom and give your quarry about fifteen minutes to show. If you get nothing more than perch, or still have your bait intact by the end of that time, move out thirty yards or so and try again where the water is deeper. Many anglers make the mistake of sticking to a spot all day because they caught some fish there a week before. Keep in mind that sunfish go deep like other fish when mid-summer water temperatures begin to climb and the water becomes too warm for comfort near the shore. When you locate a school of sunfish they'll most always be cooperative.

Fly rods have replaced the cane pole to some degree for baitfishing. Fishermen have discovered the added enjoyment a fly rod provides while still-fishing or drifting with live bait. Any fly rod and reel will do for baitfishing and the rod I've suggested in other chapters will do the job. If you don't plan to become drawn into the vortex of fly-fishing, then you can use your baitcasting reel on your fly rod. Spending a lot of money won't help you catch fish nor add much to your fun. The light rod is what makes the difference.

If you're a spin nut you have a very useful baitfishing rig for bluegills, particularly if you fish from shore. When fish are way out, spinning is the perfect way to deliver their dinner to them. Light tackle makes good sense in bluegill fishing. You can cast easier and farther if you keep your spinning line below six-pound test and use an ultra-light rod. Besides worms for bait, don't overlook crickets, grasshoppers and crayfish. Bluegills love them, especially crayfish. I've watched while crayfish were tossed into a bluegill tank and have seen the way these fish go after them. If you fish with crayfish, break off their claws so the critters can't grab a weed or a stick in their meathooks. Many fishermen know about crayfish as walleye bait but few know how well they attract big sunnies. Crayfish can be collected from almost any farm pond with a simple minnow seine and few farmers will object if you ask them for permission to remove a few for your personal use.

Don't put bluegill fishing out of your mind when winter comes. Fishing sunfish through the ice has been in the experimental stage for ten years in Minnesota. Still there are mysteries involving this relatively new sport that give it added appeal to the experimental angler. Fishermen know enough about it to be able to catch some sunfish at times but they're certainly more temperamental than crappies or walleyes.

Big Marine Lake in winter. When panfish begin to hit the whole family turns out.

Basic winter fishing gear is similar to that employed by crappie anglers. In fact, the jig stick was invented with the advent of ice-flies for bluegill fishing. The idea caught like wildfire when anglers learned that bluegills aren't dormant during the winter after all! Now winter fishermen carry a supply of mousee or goldenrod grubs in their coats in case they happen to run into a school of sunnies while fishing crappies or walleyes.

Ice flies were originated to imitate natural insect larvae. As a result the better ones have a close life-likeness. Rubber legs and maribou tails that move at the slightest jigging motion have made ice flies a very effective lure. Some of these flies are designed without a tail. These are made to be used with goldenrod or other larvae or grub on the point of the hook. Grubs are effective alone too and should be used on a very small hook. A favorite method is to impale several tiny goldenrod grubs on a tiny hook and fish near the bottom. A bobber can be used, but if fish are hitting lightly you'll have difficulty hooking your fish. Then it's best to hold the jig rod in your hand.

One last thing about bluegills. Some of those fat and sassy fish that continually escape the creel can be lured into hitting a worm and spinner trolled slowly behind your boat. Troll just fast enough to keep your spinner turning over slowly and fish deep, off drop-offs and over deep bars and reefs. Sunfish go into twenty or thirty feet of water during midsummer so you have to go down to reach them with bait.

It would take a book in itself to give all the details of every method, bait and trick for taking bluegills.

Bobby Standish lands a "sunnie" from Orchard Lake. In recent years winter jigging for bluegills has become almost as popular in Minnesota as summer angling.

There are local peculiarities I'll never hear about. New ways of catching them are being revived each season while old ways fall by the wayside from time to time. Spend a little time listening, talking and observing and when you get around to the fishing you'll be catching sunnies with the best of them. Minnesota has so many sunfish that consideration is being now given to removing all limits! The present limit is 30 per day and 30 in possession. Liberal limits have already improved fishing for other species in some overcrowded lakes and with the accent on spring fly-fishing and liberalization of limits no doubt fishing will continue to improve.

Use a fly rod, cane pole, casting tackle or dropline. Fish with bait or flies—just don't pass up Minnesota's eager bluegills if you want to have the fishing fun of your life!

CHAPTER XII

Rough Customers and Odd Fellows

There were already two anglers fishing at the mouth of Eagle Creek when I walked up. I asked them if the big browns that had been feeding there were still around.

"Got two beauties last week," one of them said, "but it's deader'n Columbus here today."

I decided to try fishing anyway. The river was up and conditions were right. Maybe I could try a different bait and do some business. The two other anglers were using minnows so I caught a frog and swam it around in the creek mouth hoping a change would be welcomed.

It wasn't long before something fastened to my bait and swam away strong. Big brown! I thought, and the guys sitting across the creek must have thought so too, because one came loping down to the shore with a net.

"Looks like a good one," he observed, "fights like a brown!"

The fish fought like a demon, dogging on the bottom stubbornly and not giving anything. I pumped him up trying to get a look at him. In response he splashed gray muddy water at me and shot for the bottom to resume his plodding battle. When I finally had the fish worn out and brought him in close I nearly fell off the creek bank.

"Kind of odd for a carp to take a frog," I suggested apologetically to the stranger who had abandoned his fishing to stand by with the net.

"The way he took it I wouldn't have guessed it was an old carp," the stranger soothed. "Fought like a brown all the way. Well, you had the thrill of a trout anyway; the only part you missed was the bragging."

I didn't like to admit it then but the stranger was right. Rough fish, notably the carp, have all the qualities of game fish except one. They don't ordinarily hit artificial lures; the standard by which game fish are measured. This holds true of many other Minnesota rough fish which seldom if ever hit fishermen's lures. Still they have a fighting heart on light tackle in spite of anything written to the contrary. Carp, sheepshead, silver bass, eelpout, garfish, whitefish, tullibee, goldeyes, mooneyes, buffalo fish, suckers, perch, redhorse, bullheads and dogfish make up a limitless roughfish population. Carp probably are more abundant in Minnesota than any of the others except possibly whitefish and tullibees and they bite more consistently than all the others except silver bass. Most rough fish excluding perch and bullheads are caught by specialized techniques or taken accidentally and occasionally by bait fishermen.

Carp are almost strictly bottom feeders although they can at times be seen feeding near the surface. They eat both animal and vegetable matter as they come to it, sucking it into their vacuum cleaner type mouths. They've long been guilty of destroying or causing damage to wild rice and other water plants, muddying up waters and destroying food for ducks and cover for forage and game species of fish. But it's obvious that we're stuck with them and have to make the best of the situation.

Carp are fairly easy to catch and in some areas where they're most abundant people have discovered they're not as bad eating as we've been led to believe. But eat them or not as you wish, Minnesota law requires anglers to keep the carp they catch, or at least not to return them to the water after you catch them. I've solved the disposal problem by planting them in neat rows between the carrots and onions and I've got the hottest organic garden in the neighborhood!

Although carp average from two to three pounds, now and then a real bruiser will latch onto your crawler and boil away downstream like a scalded dog. Then look out! For carp have an unusual strength for such ill-thought-of fish and it behooves the fisherman to make up his mind without prejudging because he may have to change it some day. A heavy carp in fast water below a spillway is a big smallmouth bass or a strong walleye until his identity becomes known to the angler.

An incident I always laugh about comes to mind that will well illustrate what I mean.

Alan Maxson and I were returning from a one-day trip to Mille Lacs last summer by way of state highway No. 56. It was late afternoon and as we crossed a tributary of the Rum River near Dalbo, we pulled over to make a cast or two near the bridge. I walked onto the old wood and iron crossing and couldn't resist planting a long cast midstream on the way across. Al went below the bridge and began casting for bass where the water eddied around the bridge abutment. On my first cast something took my bucktail jig, picking it lightly from the bottom even before I had started retrieving the line. I raised my rod against the strike and had the sensation of being hooked to a souped-up nuclear submarine. The fish peeled my four-pound mono like my grandmother used to peel Greenings—all in one piece! The picture of a giant smallmouth raced through my mind and I waited and wondered when he'd jump.

"What's that you've got now?" Al echoed from beneath the bridge, wondering what new and weird fish I was adding to the mounting collection of species our jigs had accounted for in the past few months.

"I don't have the slightest idea," I answered honestly as the fish continued to heat up the drag on my spinning reel. He was getting close to a bend in the river nearly 200 yards away and the line on my spool was almost gone—I had to turn him! I gritted my teeth and reared back on the rod slowly. The fish turned and began angling upstream in the direction of a jam of deadwood and overhanging drift along the left bank. I strained him away and as I did so he rolled and in the turbulence I could see nearly three feet of fish thrash for the bottom again. Finally, as I brought him up, I was getting all kinds of free advice from the crowd that had gathered to watch the show. But faces dropped when I led a very tired three-foot carp to the surface. A fish that weighed seventeen pounds and took

His un-majesty, the German carp, is found in the southern half of Minnesota.

nearly twenty minutes to land. A lowly carp had given me one of the best battles I've ever had!

Carp are found in the shallow lakes of southern Minnesota, the Mississippi River and its tributaries. Fortunately they're absent from the up-state lake region and the Lake Superior drainage.

You don't have to have elaborate gear although light tackle makes carp fishing exciting. In fact, a spinning outfit is well suited to carp fishing because of the way in which it handles bait. And spinning tackle makes even a small carp feel like a much bigger one.

Don't underestimate the carp because they spook very easily. Make as little noise and movement as possible, especially when they're feeding in shallow water. But don't be fussy about what you feed them. Most of the carp I've taken have been caught by accident on frogs, night crawlers, crayfish, shrimp, minnows, and an assortment of artificial lures. Angle worms and night crawlers are the best and most available natural bait, although prepared baits of dough and corn mash are used by some anglers with better results. Fish for carp in the eddies below spillways, in river backwaters and below creek mouths in the Mississippi, St. Croix and

Minnesota Rivers and their tributaries. Fish inlets to lakes and anywhere you see carp rolling or where they've muddied the water while routing for food. If you're spinning for carp you won't need to use a leader. Carp don't have teeth and can't cut your light spinning line. Use a light monofilament leader if you go after carp with a baitcasting rig because it lends naturalness to your bait. Carp have sensitive mouths from constantly sorting food from debris so it's a good idea to use small hooks. A No. 6 or 4 is just right.

Fish for carp right on the bottom, using just enough weight to keep your bait where you want it. They take bait gently and you seldom know they're around until your rod bows deeply and the fish is going away. Carp have tough mouths of cartilage and once hooked rarely throw your hook.

If you don't care for carp fishing or you think they're too easy, you can fish for sheepshead and other rough fish and still catch carp on the side. Sheepshead like carp inhabit the major rivers as well as a number of lakes in Minnesota. They're actually a fresh water

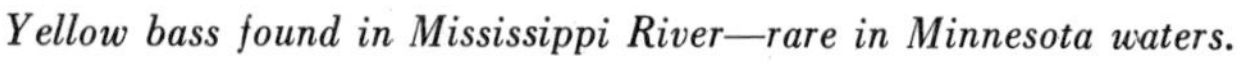

Yellow bass found in Mississippi River—rare in Minnesota waters.

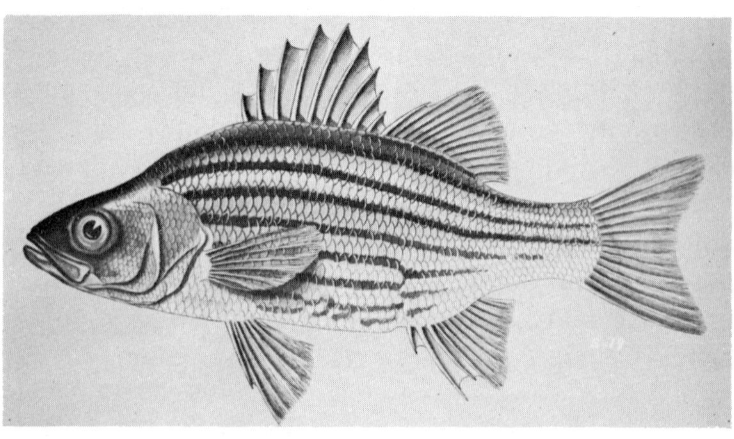

drum or croaker. Lake Waconia has a sheepshead population and some other southern Minnesota lakes have them. The best places to catch them are the slower parts of rivers and river lakes. Lake St. Croix and Lake Pepin on the Mississippi are particularly good. Sheepshead are ridiculous-looking fish with underslung jaw and strong mouths designed to feel for clams and snails in the river mud. They have a highly-humped back crowned with a studded dorsal spine, and a round, broad tail. Sheepshead are purplish green on top and silvery underneath. They come readily to worms and are at times caught on minnows. They congregate along seawalls and near bridge pilings and stream mouths. Sheepshead are strong fighters for a few hard runs, then they tire and collapse all at once.

But speaking of rough fish there's one within the reach of thousands of anglers in southern Minnesota, where game fish are less abundant than in the north. A fish that is one of the scrappiest freshwater species to be found in the sky-blue state. He's a chunky slice of finny giantism, a sharp-spined, razor-gilled, powerful fish known in Minnesota as a silver bass or just plain silver. The silver bass or more properly white bass, is an inland cousin of the striped sea bass, the prized salt-water heavyweight so respected by ocean anglers. Except for the yellow bass, silvers are the only true members of the bass family occurring in Minnesota. Large and smallmouth bass are actually members of the sunfish family. Silver bass are river fish for the most part where they attain a size near five pounds, and they inhabit a few lakes where they don't grow as large. Silver bass feed on insects and minnows and are the most willing and dependable species you'll find anywhere. There are very few times when an angler cannot locate and catch enough silver bass to keep him content throughout lean gamefish days. While most walleye anglers consider silvers worthless bait stealers and not fit for food, fishermen who are primarily interested in fun on light tackle love them! Silver bass will take dry flies and streamers and they eat small spoons and bucktail jigs like candy. Here is a fish that likes to chase anything that resembles food. Indeed the silver is a real game fish, one who has gained the respect of sport anglers in the past few years and one taking on more importance every day as hurried metropolitan fishermen find less time to make trips into the remote parts of the state for northern pike and walleyes. They take minnows and other bait but the man who goes for silver bass with a light spinning rod and a bucktail jig will catch many more fish and have a field day doing it.

Silvers feed on flats and bars in rivers and often where the water from creeks meets the main river. When they're feeding you'll see minnows flying into the air in all directions as wild fish blast through their ranks. That's the time to toss a bucktail ahead of a rise and fish it back fast—but hold on with both hands! They're very hard strikers and will strip line from your reel in quick downward dashes never giving an inch until they're completely subdued.

The first time a fisherman tangles with a silver bass he'll think he's got a big fish and will always express great surprise at the gaminess of this barbaric fighter.

The day I introduced Cecil Wilson, flight engineer for Northwest Airlines, to silver bass fishing the fish were slashing at minnows, making their peculiar hollow popping sound as they fed across a bar. The fish were so busy feeding they paid no attention to our boat anchored fifteen feet away.

As we cast into the busy school of silvers I watched Cecil to see what his reaction would be when he hooked his first silver. His lure hit the water twenty-five feet out and he had a strike immediately. He didn't say a word but his face grew grim. It was obvious he was enjoying the battle with his first hard-fighting silver bass that was as grimly determined as my companion. Finally he brought his fish up to the boat where it boiled and charged away on a desperate attempt to get free. Even for undemonstrative Cecil Wilson this was too much. He turned on a fish-charming grin and reached for the husky silver that lay quietly beside the boat. On the next cast he had another and the grin widened into a smile. "Best darned fishing I ever saw!" he blurted.

Finally, with 20 silvers, 30 short of the limit, on the deck of the boat, I asked Cecil if he had enough.

"You mean you want to quit?" he asked incredulously.

"I mean quit keeping them," I answered, "I'm going to throw them back unless they're badly hurt."

He looked relieved and we continued to catch fish and toss them back for another hour, releasing many more than we had kept.

A word of caution when handling silvers. Be careful when releasing them not to throw them since you can receive very severe slashes on your hands from their gill covers. They have no teeth but their spines and gill

Four hands are better than two as the author's son and daughter land a silver bass from the Mississippi River near Hastings.

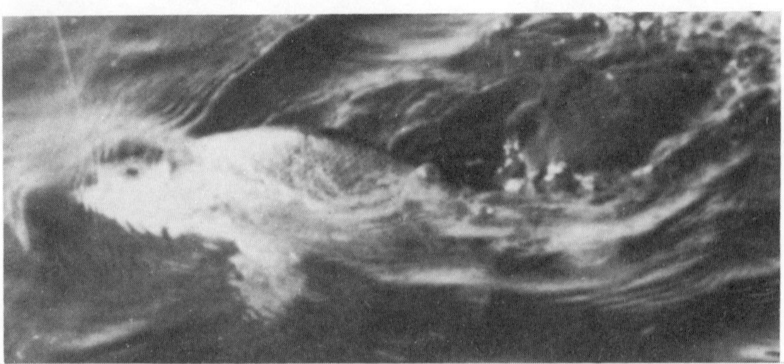

This scrappy silver bass hit a bucktail jig. Silver bass provide some fast and furious sport fishing for river anglers.

covers are dangerous. No leader is required when spinning for silver bass since they have no sharp teeth. I like to fish for them with an extra light rod and four-pound line. The light rod gives you casting ease and added distance when using light lures. A quarter-ounce Upperman bucktail, added to this combination and fished through a school of silver bass will make a silver bass artist of any angler in short order and provide him with a fast rough-and-tumble fishing bout he won't soon forget. So keep silvers on your emergency list when fishing is dull. They're ready, willing and extremely able!

If you're out of the carp-silver bass country, then you're fishing in northern Minnesota, the land of another little exploited but nevertheless exciting rough fish. Tullibees and whitefish are becoming to anglers in northern Minnesota what their counter-parts have become to southern Minnesota's casual fishermen. These two fish belong to the whitefish family, a group that includes the newly introduced Montana grayling. However, there's a distinct difference between them. The true whitefish has an overhanging snout and an inferior lower jaw while the mouth of the tullibee is equal when closed. Tullibees and whitefish are two of the most important commercial species in Minnesota, and tons are shipped to eastern markets each year. Yet in spite of their abundance and the fact they have no closed season they've been discovered by very few anglers. You can take home all the tullibees and white fish you can catch. They're beautiful fighting fish, but they're not popular because most anglers don't know how to catch them. Probably, too, fishermen have no idea of their range and abundance.

Starting at Mille Lacs, about a hundred miles north of the Twin Cities, both of these fish are found in most of the deep lakes all the way to the Canadian border. Cutfoot Sioux, Leech, Winnibigoshish, Red Lake, Lake of the Woods and many others including Lake Superior, have whitefish populations that exceed the numbers of walleyes and trout. Here is a sport fishing resource that hasn't been tapped! A new sport fish that has never been exploited!

You won't have trouble locating whitefish water in Minnesota. Just ask around and you'll quickly learn which waters have whitefish or tullibees. In some places tullibees are referred to as lake herring, in others as ciscos. Actually they're all tullibees. Sub-species definitely exist but even among icthiologists there arises a question often about the differences. Certainly you'll never know if you have a northern cisco, a Twin Lakes cisco or a blueback and you probably wouldn't care.

There are a few whitefish taken on lures and minnows by winter walleye anglers and a few dozen fishermen catch tullibees at Lake Kabatogama and other lakes on dry flies during the mayfly and pine mosquito hatches of late June. This is unbeatable fly-fishing. Fish boil and roll all over the lake surface, hundreds of fish rising at one time. During this hatch anyone can catch tullibees on dry mayfly imitations or anglers can collect a jar full of naturals and drift them on the surface with the same end result. Tullibee fishing with flies smacks of fly-fishing for specks except that tullibees take flies with a delicacy not duplicated by any fish but their recently introduced relative, the Montana grayling. Some day anglers will become aware of the fabulous fishing that awaits them at Kabatogama or remote Gunflint lake, and uncounted other waters. Some day these gamey fork-tailed fish will find a spot high on the game fish list in spite of their present rough fish designation.

The author with Kabetogama tullibee. Tullibees are hard fighters and can be taken easily from border lakes during the mayfly hatches in July.

I strongly suggest a light action fly rod for tullibees because they don't run very large. Most of them weigh between a pound to two pounds. A ten-pounder would be a record. With light tackle you'll have real sport with the average fish that come to your mayfly imitations. Mayflies in these waters are dark, brown sailwing flies that drift like derelict sailboats on a calm sea. They're very poor fliers and get airborn with difficulty, flapping their papery wings clumsily until they climb from the water and fly shoreward. When mayflies begin to emerge from the water tullibees move inshore and pop them as they appear on the surface, taking them in a delicate dimpling manner, leaving only slight rings as they rise, expose their backs for an instant much like a porpoise playing, and disappear. They take flies leisurely, so leisurely that you can often cast no more than a foot ahead of a rise and draw a strike from the fish. They move methodically like feeding rainbows but a great deal slower. As a result you have time to determine their line of advance and time to present your fly. Use the same mayfly imitations you'd use for trout, Slim Jim, Muddler and the grotesque but effective Shaving Brush. When a hatch of smaller pine mosquitoes requires a smaller fly, tie on a number 12 or 14 Adams or other mosquito imitation. Sometimes when both mayflies and pine mosquitoes are hatching at once I use an Adams as a dropper fly and a Shaving Brush for the point, or end fly. Often when there's a light hatch, as there was the first time I fished tullibees, they feed on both mosquitoes and mayflies. Using two different flies gives the angler a much better chance to score. Tullibees don't seem to be leader shy

The sheepshead or freshwater drum is often taken by river and lake anglers while fishing for more desirable species.

The sheepshead, an odd-looking humped backed fish found in Minnesota rivers and a few lakes. Abundant in Red Lake.

nor are they boat shy to any degree when they're feeding. But unless they're feeding heavily it's very hard to interest them at all. When the hatch is light, strikes come few and far between and a surprised fisherman can easily set the fly too hard, for tullibees have soft mouths and the hard strikes resulting from surprise too often result in lost fish. Set your fly gently, just raising your fly rod against the fish and you'll have him.

Yes, tullibees are game fish regardless of their commercial classification and a fisherman who has tried fly-fishing for them will know just how game they are. Once hooked, a tullibee goes insanely wild, wallowing on the surface in a series of erratic charges until he finds the water again. Then he begins to bore and pound in hard-jabbing runs.

But you don't have to be a fly-fisherman to catch tullibees. That's perhaps the most enjoyable way, it's true, but fly-fishermen have no exclusive corner on tullibee fishing. Tullibees can be taken on a cane pole supplied with a length of monofilament and a small hook. You simply hook on a natural mayfly and dab it on the water among the feeding fish and catch tullibees! Sometimes tourists catch them on casting tackle in almost the same way. They tie a small hook on their lines, collect some mayflies from the side of their cottage and use a matchstick for a float. The light float makes it possible for the fish to take your soft-bodied mayfly without creating enough resistance to tear it from the hook.

But you don't have to confine your tullibee fishing to topside and in some lakes during the summer uncertain results can be expected by fishing in the deeper parts of whitefish lakes with small live minnows. This can be a fascinating kind of fishing and bound to become more popular as resort people on whitefish and tullibee waters awake to a totally unexplored potential sport-fishing frontier.

These species bite in winter too, of course. In late winter, during the dull days of February and March, when the season on walleyes is over and fishing doldrums that last until mid-April begin, fishermen are learning they can have some of the hottest angling of the year in northern Minnesota lakes. Whitefish and tullibees are in comparatively shallow water then and when they're hitting you never had such fast fishing in your life! And when you hook a heavy tullibee or a bruising whitefish you're going to wonder whether the term rough fish applies to their fighting ability or their sport fishing status!

A crazy but effective fishing method, revealed two years ago by Al Brown, Elk River bait dealer, and related by outdoor writer Jim Peterson, is worth mentioning. Al started a tullibee-whitefishing rage at Cutfoot Sioux, Bowstring and Lida Lakes in Itasca county that is spreading to other northern lakes. To attract tullibees, he uses a red and white fluorescent bobber which is attached to a separate weighted line. Just why these fish gather around a bright red bobber might never be determined. Perhaps the fish are curious for I've had them follow a white bucktail jig right up to the canoe even though they had no intention of taking it. With the decoy in the water he fishes near it with an icefly or a tiny ice-spoon baited with mousee, goldenrod or golden grubs. The bobber which is attached to his foot is in constant motion at fishing depth to keep the fish interested. This might seem like an odd way of fishing but it provides some furious tullibee-whitefish action if you're able to locate the fish. In late winter when walleyes quit cold you might find it worthwhile to spend some time prospecting for tullibees. The trick is to locate the fish. If they're biting, you'll get fast action and some very good eating fish. If you've ever eaten smoked tullibee or whitefish you know what I mean. If you haven't, you don't know what you're missing!

There's no need to go into the heart of the northwoods to catch good eating fish, however. Bullheads and perch which in some Minnesota lakes grow to unbelievable size are readily available to the dock, bridge and boat fisherman in untold numbers. But in Minnesota where a host of more important species get all the attention, bullheads and perch are frowned upon as being too unsophisticated; scavengers that don't merit mention in our fishing picture. How wrong can you get! The common yellow perch, a carnivorous relative of the walleye, is a yellow and green vertically-barred fish of insatiable hunger. Perch grow to weights in excess of two pounds. The average, however, is much smaller. They're considered a nuisance in most Minnesota lakes where they compete with more desirable game fish and eat the young of other species. In many lakes perch are so numerous their entire population is stunted. But in Mille Lacs, for example, and other large waters of the state they reach maximum size. Perch spawn in April, laying from 10,000 to 50,000

Minnesota perch grow to weights over two pounds in Mille Lacs and Leech Lakes.

Bullheads, like the brown bullhead pictured here, are abundant in most of Minnesota. It grows to nearly three pounds.

Rock bass are found in most lakes and streams all over Minnesota. In some lakes they grow to several pounds.

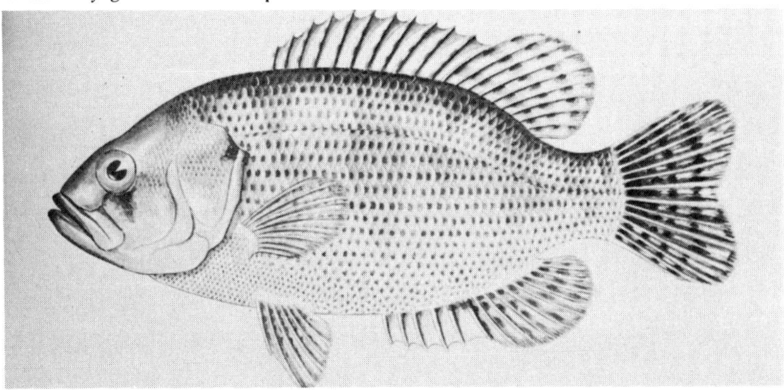

eggs.* But they might not be so abundant if fishermen realized just how good they are to eat. If I were going to choose between walleye and perch fillets, I'd take the perch! They have light sweet meat, delicate in flavor—yet few anglers consider taking them home to eat. Perch are easier to clean and eat than bony northerns and are a lot better tasting than muddy bass. Perch are fat-free and keep better under refrigeration than all other species. More than once I've returned gamefish to the water and kept the more desirable perch for the table. If you want good eating, you'll never find better than the common, over abundant, bothersome yellow perch that most anglers ignore and throw away while often going home skunked!

Perch eat anything you feed them. They gobble minnows, worms of any kind, crickets, crayfish and larva of various insects. They'll hit an artificial fly or spoon, a strip of chamois or bacon rind—anything!

The slow-witted bullhead shows no more sense. This ugly character that looks like he came from a hole in the bottom of the lake will seldom hit an artificial. On occasion he'll get ambitious and take a whack at a spoon or a jig but not very often. He likes to take his food with deliberation. Bullheads eat a variety of food and can be caught on anything from shrimp to meatballs. Some swear by raw beef.

Roy Fox, owner of "30" resort on Lake George is a man of the raw beef school. "Got to use beef," Roy told me when I fished bullheads with him a year ago.

"Nothing else works near as well as beef." A block

*Surber and Eddy in Northern Fishes.

from his dock, just outside the weed beds he convinced me he could be right.

It was nearly dark when we dropped anchor and began to fish. I rigged my spinning tackle as Roy did the butchering. He sawed at a chunk of meat, cutting off cubes that a pike would think about twice before tackling. We baited our hooks and waited, both watching Roy's bobber as it drifted against the boat. Suddenly his float twitched and ran out from the shadow of the hull, bounced lightly a few times and went under. Roy set his weight against the unsuspecting fish and missed. Then I felt a tug and waited for the fish to clamp down and start away. In response to my wishes, the bullhead knocked on the weeded lake floor. The beefsteak was working and the light of conviction shone on Roy's face.

"I'm convinced, Roy," I said, as I played the fish in the increasing light of a full moon.

"Beef steak seems to be the answer," I added as I lifted a two-pound bullhead into the boat.

Try fishing for bullheads just outside the weed beds in lakes. In rivers try for them below spillways where food is carried into the eddies on the side, at stream mouths and river backwaters. All of Minnesota's southern lakes have bullheads. They're the only fish tough enough to withstand oxygen depletion and freeze-out conditions that occur in shallow lakes. Bullheads are gregarious fish, usually moving in schools. Where you find one there are sure to be others nearby. Of the three distinct species present in the state only the brown bullhead grows to a weight exceeding three pounds.

Yellow and black bullheads are somewhat smaller and a big one will go a shade under two pounds.

If you want a clue to fishing fun, watch the native anglers of southern Minnesota. Watch the country boy fishing a farm pond or creek, the small-town grocer or businessman relaxed beside the river or the retired farmer in his flat-bottomed boat and you'll see that part of the appeal of fishing perch and bullheads lies in the simple equipment required. An inexpensive cane pole can be rigged for practically nothing and requires very little skill or effort to operate. No fancy equipment is needed for this relaxing and rewarding way to fish. Try it when all your game fish plans have gone awry. When the wind is blowing out of the east and a full moon is shining at night, when the barometer says fishing is lousy, try fishing perch or bullheads and find out for yourself why so many natives and tourists spend their time cane-pole fishing. Fishermen are passing up a lot of good, easy-to-get-at fishing because they turn up their noses at "rough fish."

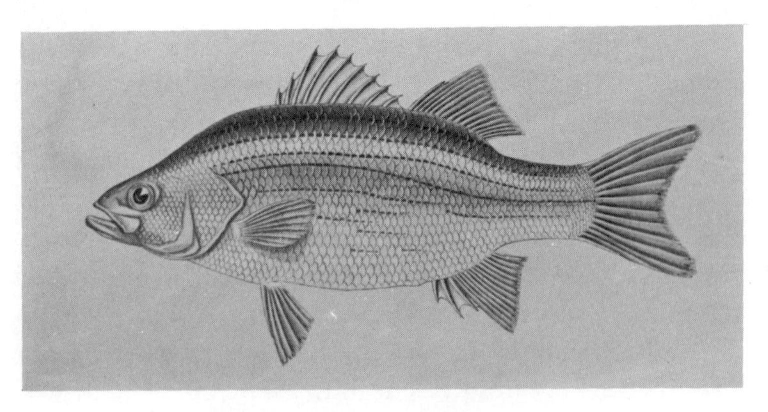

A popular, hard fighting river fish, the silver bass.

Often rough fishing has some unusual rewards. While you're fishing carp, whitefish or bullheads you'll occasionally catch some odd-balls. These uncommon species are almost the exclusive prerogative of relaxed bait fishermen. Some day you might hook a useless but thrilling dogfish, an ugly prehistoric gar or an unbelievably powerful hackleback sturgeon. You could, out of even greater chance, tie into an equally ancient paddlefish, a great harmless fish that looks like a shark and has a sword-like paddle which he uses to stir up the bottom in search of food.

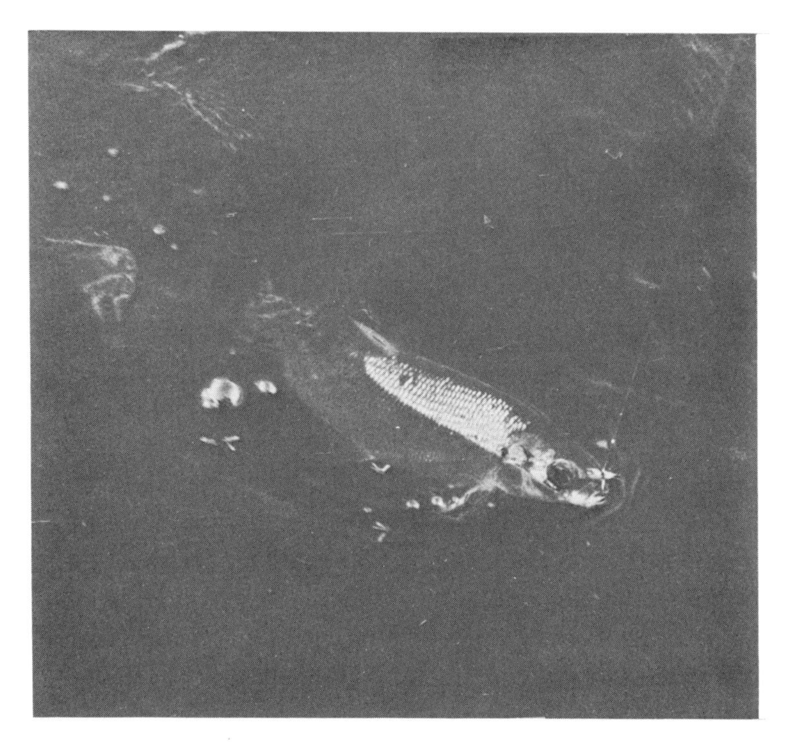

Few anglers are aware that tullibees will take flies. Here the author brings one up to the boat with fly clearly visible in its mouth.

Tom McCutchan grins over large carp that he took on bucktail jig from Prior Lake.

A parting suggestion. For greater fishing fun and increased catches use light tackle. Spinning will add a lot to your fight with a 10-pound carp and will make a big yellow bullhead seem a lot stronger than he really is. Of course, if you're going after heavy-weight sturgeon or are fishing where you might hook other big fish equip yourself accordingly. But remember that all fish have a natural wariness and you will do better if you present your bait as naturally as possible.

CHAPTER XIII

Lake and River Fishing

Every prejudiced opinion, including those held by fishermen, is based on experience or lack of it. Whether you hate or love martinis, TV Westerns or fat politicians, hinges on what you know or don't know about the subject. This chapter on river and lakes is considered necessary for that very reason. Because if you've done a great deal of fishing in both you know that one is not always best for all kinds of fishing, and that fishing will vary from lake to lake and river to river as well. But if you don't have fishing experience and success to back your thinking, you can get false and lopsided ideas concerning one phase or another.

What makes this difference in lake and river fishing? Mainly this. Most Minnesota rivers are free-flowing bodies of water where currents and water levels are subject to greater and more sudden changes than those in lakes. As a result of a constantly moving current, no thermicline or temperature stratification of water develops in rivers. Lakes on the other hand form temperature layers, some suitable, others unsuitable to the needs of fish. Then, too, some species need certain requirements found only in river environment while other fish thrive in habitat characteristic to lakes and rivers as well.

River fishing is urgent, but often more exciting. You never know what you may catch.

Lake fishing is more relaxing unless heavy water catches you in an inadequate boat.

A majority of anglers might already know that lakes in Minnesota, most of them somewhat isolated from the river systems, have characteristic fish life. Bass, panfish, walleyes, northern pike, perch, bullheads and suckers are commonly present in the bulk of our inland unconnected lakes. In addition to these fish, whitefish and tullibees occur in some northern lakes while carp are present in the southern waters. Some of these species are found in the big rivers also but are usually thought of as lake fish. These as well as certain minnows generally comprise most of the lake fish population.

River and lake fish of the same species live somewhat different lives. Lake fish, for example, have no currents to buck, except perhaps in spring during their annual spawning runs. As a result they are harder for anglers to locate than stream fish. As a rule, lake weed beds which harbor the schools of small forage fish, are naturally attractive to the predators and they can be found during feeding periods at the edge of these areas.

Oxygen requirements of different species play an important role in the location of fish. Fish must stay in water that has enough oxygen and where food is available as well. In some lakes, the deeper ones, a thermicline develops in late June when the water begins to warm on top. Then fish seek out this insulated thermicline below the warmer top water and spend the summer there. Occasionally they'll leave this desirable zone at night or during rainy or windy days to feed in newly oxygenated surface or inshore waters. When the cold nights of fall bring temperatures down on the surface, fish move into the upper waters again in and around the weed beds, onto shallow bars and flats. All lake fish . . . bass, walleyes, lake trout . . . all of them will be near the surface again in the spring and will move as deep as their needs indicate. Lake trout which may have hit your flies at ice-out will perhaps be in a hundred to two hundred feet depth by July.

River fish are less often confronted with an oxygen problem. For one thing moving water picks up oxygen and carries it constantly to the fish. Besides, most rivers are fed by coldwater springs and have spring holes where sensitive species congregate during warm water conditions. So, while you can see both lake and river fish are found in specific locations on the basis of their requirements, these places aren't always the same.

For example, if I were looking for river walleyes during a July day I'd fish below a stream mouth or the lower end of the rip-rap foundation of a channel buoy. (Don't anchor to the buoy though because the Coast Guard frowns on the practice.) In the evening I'd look for them on bars where the water was moving moderately fast or cast the lip of a pool below a rapids. On the other hand, I'd fish for river walleyes on shallow bars and right at the stream mouths in spring and fall.

These techniques don't hold true of lake fishing for walleyes. To catch lake walleyes consistently in mid-summer you should begin fishing on a bar out from a weed bed and begin by casting off the edge of the bar into deeper water. Keep moving into still deeper water a little at a time until you locate some fish. You won't have telltale river eddies to guide you to a likely spot but you should be able to tell something about the bottom of the lake by the feel of your lure as it comes up on the bar or by the count required to sink the lure to the bottom. These are just little differences but details compounded add up to a successful technique.

Naturally it also helps to know what you're fishing for. You won't find lake trout in the Mississippi or carp in Bowstring Lake. There are no speckled trout in Red Lake or sturgeon in Lake Osakis. But you'll find specks in Helwig creek and carp in Lake Marion or the Crow River. Generally in addition to most game species, Minnesota rivers harbor some weird fish, fish that never or rarely bite on a baited hook or take a fly or spoon. The sucker-mouthed quillback, the heavy scaled buffalo-fish, the paddlefish, gars, mooneyes, gizzard shad, and the biggest of them all—the lake sturgeon which grows in excess of a hundred pounds! Minnesota rivers, then, offer a conglomeration of species to fish for and this is perhaps the real fascination of river fishing. Lakes on the other hand have less variety, each lake being made up of a typical population of one sort or another.

Basically there are four types of lakes in Minnesota. It's impossible to fit every pond in these categories but it will certainly serve as a useful yardstick to the angler who yearns for a specific kind of fishing. There are the roughfish-crappie lakes of the southwestern section of Minnesota. Shallow, silted, highly fertile waters that offer carp, crappies and bullheads between winter kills. Under improved management these lakes promise to offer better fishing in the future. On the hardwood fringe of the prairies, in lakes engineered by melting ice-blocks at the terminal edge of the ice shields last advance, lie the bass-panfish lakes. They lie in a westerly arch which starts near the Twin Cities and peters out in the vicinity of Fergus Falls. Most of these lakes are weedy, with timber shorelines, and constitute an average area of around 600 acres. In addition to bass and panfish many of them have good pike populations. Walleyes are seldom present except where the practice of stocking is applied. The walleye lakes—larger in size than the panfish lakes—are a third, and possibly the most important class. These lakes lie in the infertile coniferous-covered sandplains where little or no agriculture has been practiced. Here walleyes, burbot, northern pike, tullibees, suckers and perch make up the population. But walleyes are the prime gamefish in this area. The large lakes of Becker, Hubbard, Itasca, Crow Wing and Aitkin Counties make up the greatest array of walleye waters found anywhere!

Last, but of increasing importance, are the rock-bottom, basalt and granite-shored lakes of the north eastern counties. Soft-water trout lakes, where fishermen claim that anyone dropping a bar of Ivory over the side of the boat would be lost in his own suds for a week! This is nearly all trout water although some of these lakes are two-level propositions where walleyes and northern pike often frequent the upper waters and trout inhabit the deeper holes.

There are all sorts of shades between, of course, but a guide that might list each lake and its populations would provide very little more information of likely value to the reader. These groupings, however, serve to show clearly how different Minnesota's lake populations are from her rivers with their transient-migrant fish populations made up of a Duke's mixture of odd-shaped many-sized varieties. Except for trout streams, river fishing in Minnesota is often a grab-bag operation where you might catch one species or you may get a mixed bag of a dozen varieties.

One strange factor related to the subject of lakes and rivers concerns food preference and food supply differences of a species found in both habitats. There must be in rivers, for example, an abundance of small forage minnows—just the size that delight crappies—because crappies seldom bite well in rivers except during extremely high water when baitfish are scattered. There are many thousands of crappies in the big rivers of Minnesota, yet few anglers even know they are there, much less catch them. I recall one summer five years ago when the Minnesota River was at flood stage until mid-June when every stream mouth that emptied into the river was choked with hungry crappies. But ask an average river fisherman if there are crappies in the Minnesota River and he'll tell you to get your head examined. But actually crappies are plentiful in the

A quillback seldom bites on hook and line. As a result few anglers have ever seen one.

The Mooneye is little known to Minnesota anglers. Found in the Mississippi draînage they bite on flies and streamers.

Minnesota as well as the St. Croix and Mississippi Rivers. In fact, the state's record crappie, a five-pounder, came from the Vermillion River, which joins the Mississippi near Hastings.

On the other hand lake crappies bite steadily throughout the summer. For lakes have no renewable source of food, and as the always hungry crappies cut an ever-widening swath in their food supply an angler's tethered minnow becomes more of an easy target. As a result you'll always have much better crappie fishing success in the bass-panfish lakes than you could hope to have with hog-fat river fish.

Unfortunately Minnesota doesn't have the launching facilities it should have, a disadvantage to the trailering fishermen. This problem is more pronounced on various stretches of Minnesota rivers than on lakes. It seems to be the main reason so little is known about river fishing in the middle west, and Minnesota in particular. It looks like interest in access procurement has been stimulated by a recent bill passed by the state legislature that in essence provides for future management only on lakes that provide public, free access. Since great stretches of our rivers are inaccessible and river fish change their feeding grounds according to the stage of the water, a large part of our major rivers seldom if ever see a fisherman. Fish move into channels and backwaters during highwater but abandon them as the water recedes, and as a rule anglers can't get at them most of the time.

Perhaps I can better illustrate this by relating an incident of two summers ago. My home town river, the Minnesota, had been above normal well into the summer, overflowing the bottom floodplains. Tributary streams were just beginning to drop when we discovered an unbelievable northern pike concentration in a small lake a hundred yards upstream from the mouth of Nine Mile Creek where the stream cuts through the steep bluffs of Bloomington to meet the Minnesota River. Northerns were in the little lake by the hundreds, concentrated in a deep hole where the stream emptied in. The rest of the lake, a shallow muddy flat, willed us by the army engineers, was nowhere more than two feet deep and the water level was dropping fast. While spinning from a canoe at the point where the creek joins the lake, Tom McCutchan and I caught and released, sixty-four northerns in two and a half hours, losing many more and sacrificing nearly a dozen lures apiece to fish we couldn't hold or that cut our leaderless lines with their sharp teeth!

Two days later when I took my son and two out-of-town friends there to enjoy some easy fishing, we fished several hours and caught only a half dozen small pike. The water had dropped only a few inches—just enough to make conditions intolerable for the fish. Minnows were still present in great swarms so feed was no problem if they had stayed. But, as the river dropped they moved on to new feeding grounds. Without a boat and a place to launch it, when the fish decide to move, fishermen are unable to follow. Fortunately for the anglers wanting to fish this stretch of the Minnesota there's a place to put a boat in just below the old highway bridge on US 65.

A fisherman trying river angling for the first time will catch more fish if he can learn to distinguish

Three slim, river fish. Sturgeon, short and long nose gars.

A good big water boat like this 16-foot Model K Aluma Craft will take a 35-horse motor and get you in fast if you're fishing a long way from home base.

Fishing at night off Stillwater river bridge, these anglers landed this sturgeon which was under legal size and had to be returned.

between high water fishing and low water fishing. During periods of high water the best fishing is at and IN the mouths of tributary creeks. As spring's high water recedes, fish like walleyes, for example, hang around the streams but will be found in the deep hole downstream from the stream mouth and below springbanks or in the deep pools below rapids. Crappies will be timidly hiding in the shadows of bridge pilings and icebreakers. River northerns will be in the pools, backwaters and at stream mouths. Sturgeon and catfish stay in the deeper channels throughout the year.

What I like best about river fishing is the endless possibilities of catching some unrecognizable, exotic-looking species. Fat little miller's thumbs, strikingly silver mooneyes—rapacious gars and ragged-tooth muskies. Undoubtedly this is why each season sees more anglers turning to the river that runs past the farm and to fishing the spillways and stream mouths a few miles from the heart of the Twin Cities.

If you don't like the grab-bag rivers and you have the time to travel, Minnesota's lakes will yield more consistent catches of panfish and equal results on walleyes during early summer. I'm sure fishermen who have never fished Minnesota before will catch northerns with greater consistency in the lakes of upper Minnesota than in the hard-to-get-to river spots. The native who has learned to read his local river might take exception to what I'm saying, but his hue and cry will go unheard because his favorite spot is already too crowded to suit him anyway.

Where you fish and what you intend to catch can perhaps help too in selecting a boat that best suits your requirements. A few anglers have more than one boat, a large one for big water and a smaller boat or canoe for small trout lakes and sheltered waters. Walleye anglers are going to deeper wider craft, boats capable of riding out heavy weather on the bigger lakes and able to withstand the wakes of river barges and tugs. New, deep-bowed boats aren't nearly as cumbersome and heavy as they were in the old days. Modern trailers and a new drive for access has made loading and unloading a boat a relatively simple matter for two men. With newly introduced powerful outboards anglers are fishing farther from camp, thus increasing their chances of having to face rough weather or of riding out a storm. As a result boats in the 16-foot class are becoming increasingly popular on big water. However, for fishing on most lakes a twelve-footer like Aluma Craft's Model E with a 54-inch beam is just right. Modern 14-foot boats will handle up to a twenty-horse motor, and provide room enough for three men and all their gear.

You're going to find that Minnesota lakes and streams offer the visiting fishermen unlimited oppor-

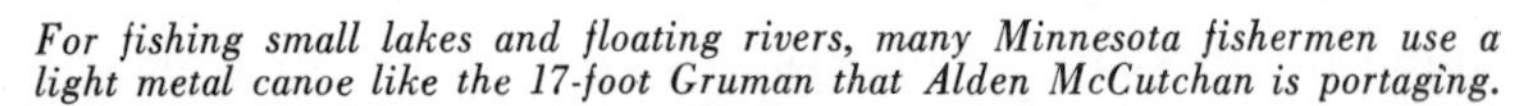

For fishing small lakes and floating rivers, many Minnesota fishermen use a light metal canoe like the 17-foot Gruman that Alden McCutchan is portaging.

tunity and variety of fishing and surroundings. An angler can troll down the Vermilion River south of Hastings and be surrounded by jungle scenery. As long-legged herons and egrets fly up ahead of his boat he'll be reminded of a Brazilian piranha fishing expedition. He will sense the stillness of a mountain wilderness while fishing Bogus Lake, high in the range of hills above Lake Superior. He'll get the discoverer's feeling of endless waterways as he travels the island-studded reaches of Rainy lake—the exhilarating view of an ocean as he fishes the swells of the Big-Sea-Water of Superior.

One last thing. You as an angler can help perpetuate this fishing valhalla by taking a little time to inspect the minnows you have left after a day's fishing before you release them. Minnesota has been able to control the spread of carp to her northern lakes by carp control dams but eventually, unless we continue to exercise caution, they can easily spread further. State law prohibits the transport of carp minnows but now and then a stray will get mixed with your shiners. So if you can't identify a carp minnow perhaps you can learn to know them and remember to look for them among your bait minnows. Destroy your minnows rather than chance introducing this nuisance fish to uncontaminated waters. Their rough character and undesirable habits make them highly undesirable where they don't yet exist.

Possibly this chapter has helped you find your niche in the vast circulatory system of Minnesota's lakes and rivers. Now just settle down to some of the best fishing you can hope to find anywhere.

CHAPTER XIV

The Fishing Picture

Before Minnesota residents were required to carry a fishing license there were actually more than three lakes for every out-of-state angler. At the turn of the century it was possible to fish for weeks and not see another fisherman. By 1927, the first year a resident was required to buy a 50c permit 42,000 nonresidents and 331,000 residents bought tickets. Nineteen years later in 1956, Minnesota sold a total of well over a million licenses. With the increase in licensed anglers it was imperative that management of sport fishing resources keep pace.

Management was no problem at first. Lakes were better balanced than they are today and no one worried about the depletion of desirable balance species. In most cases there were no limits. Gradually over the years as fishing pressure increased, smaller, but still liberal limits were imposed. The effects of license revenue were the beginnings of pioneering research in fisheries work. In fact, Minnesota was managing walleyes to a very limited degree, as early as 1910, holding fish and taking spawn for restocking long before other states were doing so. Because Minnesota has been supplied by nature with more top-notch walleye habitat than any other section of the country* the foundation research on walleye management is still paying off. Walleye egg stripping and rearing pond techniques developed by Minnesota's early fisheries men in the school of trial and error, and the nature of Minnesota's walleyes lakes guarantees good fishing for this species for years to come. Lakeshore development, both legal and illegal spearing, drainage and road building have spoiled our best northern pike habitat and decimated our pike population but have had very little effect on our walleye population. This is because walleyes spawn in the lake itself or a tributary river while northerns must spawn in adjacent swamp areas. Most of the best walleye range is in the timbered part of the state and these lakes haven't suffered much from silting except in the southernmost fringe where careless farming practices have caused considerable damage. The result is that walleyes are still producing naturally at a high rate and fish are almost as large on an average, as they were when fishing was said to be at its peak. It's doubtful that the lakes yielded more fish in 1858, the year Minnesota became a state, than they do today. Discounting lakes lost through drainage and siltation the walleye lakes of Minnesota number well into the thousands. Even as industry and farming continue to work the land and channel the rivers, habitat changes, except for pollution of certain areas of the Mississippi River, have been few. We still catch walleyes in the Mississippi River below the Ford dam in Minneapolis. Lakes rimmed by classy resorts and private cabins continue to be walleye factories. The big windswept stretches of Red, Leech,

*Cobbs, Trans. American Fish. Soc. 53:95-105.

Winnie, Rainy, Lake of the Woods and Mille Lacs Lakes still have fabulous and nearly inexhaustible walleye populations! Minnesota has taken good care of its walleye waters since it has recognized the increasing importance of water resources to the state's financial security. Financially, Minnesota's walleye-northern pike lakes mean more to her than all the rest of her waters combined.

But if walleyes have taken on increased importance so have other species. Native trout which inhabited many streams and a few smaller lakes are beginning to create a new stir and are becoming increasingly important in the fishing picture of the future. Fish species introduced into Minnesota waters; brown trout, wise in the ways of man and temperamental rainbows, have given trout fishing new impetus. Fishermen are refining their fishing style and are becoming increasingly interested in hard-to-catch fish. The end result will be improved trout fishing in many areas. Variety and wider distribution of trout has given many more fishermen an opportunity to practice the subtle art of matching their fishing maturity with a deserving adversary.

Present-day trout management in Minnesota includes "put and take" stocking, stream improvement and the stocking of "wintering streams" where trout are able to survive the rigors of the winter months. Lake reclamation also has been successful. So successful in fact that Minnesota has currently expanded its program and has created trout populations where game fish did not exist. Small lakes on the backbone of the Superior watershed and deep little pools in central Minnesota provide trout fishing that is equal or better than many trout states. Not content to rest on their laurels, always interested in providing new angling thrills, lake reclamation men are reaching into new fields. Minnesota, as a result of this, is the only state east of the Rockies that has a grayling population. These exotic fighters were introduced from Saskatchewan in 1955 and the first grayling season opened for nine days in September, 1957. The results of that season were so amazing that Montana grayling may well be a permanent addition to the already imposing list of Minnesota game fish species.

If you're a bass fisherman, take heed! Presently the land of lakes has a terrific bass population and in spite of the howl raised by pressure groups for earlier seasons, they probably will continue to have one. Fisheries' people have learned to go slowly, feeling possibly that our bass population is a resource of the future, one to be used but not exploited. Even now as fishing competition for some kinds of fish becomes keener anglers are gradually turning to bass fishing and finding for the first time that bass fishing in Minnesota is good—in fact, very good! With management in step with increased bass fishing popularity future generations are assured of the same good fishing you can enjoy.*

Unfortunately the history of the northern pike presents a different story. Pike have suffered from name calling (snake, jackfish), lack of a size limit, legal and illegal spearing, drainage, real estate development of

*While refuting pond rearing as an effective bass management tool, Minnesota fisheries research men are not sure that an early bass opener in northern counties is in the best interest of the sport.

Alan Maxson displays purple grayling before returning it to the water. Minnesota is first state east of the Rockies to have grayling season in 60 years.

Grayling were introduced into Twin Lakes in 1955.

lakeshore and road building. These things have directly or indirectly caused the loss of many pike and pike-spawning areas. Once they get the protection they need and spawn grounds become secure from destruction, fishing for other species will improve. In waters where out of the lake spawning grounds cannot hope to be achieved thought is being given to introducing muskies. Since muskies spawn in the lake much as walleyes do, biologists have considered the possibility that stocking them in suitable waters might return some lakes to their former productive capacity.*[1] Work, of course, is being done to eliminate the evils that affect the northern pike, Minnesota's No. 1 predator fish. With the aid of Dingle-Johnson funds (fishing tackle tax), a number of spawning improvement sights have been acquired. In the past five years sixty spawning beds have been improved. Bad publicity is slowly driving the spear wielder against the spiked wall of criticism and no doubt the days of legal spearing are numbered.*[2] Even more damaging than dark house spearers are those who selfishly and thoughtlessly spear northern pike during the cold nights in April when fish are traveling into

[1]*Many lakes which need predatory species suffer severely from northern pike spearing. Unless spearing is permanently curtailed on any waters where muskies are introduced there is little real hope that their presence would improve fishing. Sadly enough our present musky waters are being speared to death under legislative sponsorship! Spearers admit they cannot tell a musky from a northern until after it's been speared! Until we take the right to set seasons away from the vote-seeking legislators on Minnesota's game and fish committees and follow the example of states like Vermont by giving that job to our fisheries experts, our fishing will continue to pay the price of political expediency. Minnesota is a hundred years old this year—how much longer will it take us to learn constituent-conscious legislators are bent on destroying our most important recreation and third largest industry?

[2]*Anglers are becoming more aroused every day about a means of taking fish which discriminates against the non-resident, affords selection of only large fish and takes them in a method which could never be defined as sporting.

Stripping eggs from ripe female musky at Shoepac Lake fisheries station in northern St. Louis county.

Young muskies like these have little chance of survival in lakes where young-of-the-year northern wait to eat them as they hatch.

marshes to spawn. During this annual run pike are vulnerable to predation and each spring thousands are taken. Education is beginning to support the long arm of the law. Wanton violations are less common than even a few years ago. Minnesota is far short on warden man power, but what men they have are stressing education and assistance. By fairness and by encouraging sportsmanship, they're slowly convincing fishermen that violations only serve to spoil their fun and the sport of others.

While the presence of man is bound to affect fish life to some degree, a large part of Minnesota—from sprawling Rainy Lake in the west to the shores of Lake Superior—is an endless network of lakes which still lie practically virgin and almost completely unspoiled. Much of this area is accessible only by canoe or portageable boat. The lakes on the fringe of this mass of water support no more than a scattering of resorts. This is primitive Minnesota—a land unchanged from the days when *engage's* of the great fur companies trapped and traded for beaver with the native Crees and Chippewas. Where fishing camps do exist on the margin of this wide area, good boats are available to fishermen. Some resorters accommodate fishermen with boats located on more than one lake where different kinds of fishing can be had. But to fish the lakes within this canoe country you need to carry or portage in your own craft. There are some good outfitters in the major towns in the Superior National forest area where canoes can be rented for about $2.00 per day and a complete camping outfit and guide service are available. You'll discover some wonderful smallmouth bass fishing in this

State fisheries workers have "poisoned out" many small lakes before stocking them with trout and other desirable species.

Fish removal crew pulls rough fish nets from Reed Lake, Waseca County. Carp and tullibees make up most of rough fish crop.

region. Rainy Lake, Basswood and Knife produce smallmouth bass in the 6-pound class every season. These are not the native stomping grounds of bass of any description but recent smallmouth introductions have already made these lakes famous for their bass fishing. In this same wild country you will find the majority of this country's lake trout waters and some of the best walleye and northern pike fishing you can hope to find anywhere. This whole section, north of US highway 53 and state highway No. 1, is world known for freshwater fishing of almost every kind—and the beauty of the country is something you will have to witness to believe!

Even in the settled areas of Minnesota there are hundreds of lakes that are seldom fished at all, or by no more than a few parties a year. Unnamed, back-woods lakes exist almost everywhere in the state. When you vacation in Minnesota you'll learn that local resorters know of a lake or two off the beaten path where you can stand on the shore and catch bass or northerns or paddle out beyond the weed beds and catch big sunfish and crappies.

One of the portages on the Knife Lake chain in the wilderness—roadless area of northeastern Minnesota.

Lake reclamation has provided some excellent trout waters. This rainbow was caught from the shore of Echo Lake near Finland by Rod Bell.

And here's good news for anglers that tote their own boat trailers. An access law passed by the 1957 state legislature, providing for management of only those Minnesota lakes that offer free public access, is already making it easier for the trailering fisherman to get his craft afloat. No access, no rough fish removal or restocking. One potential access that is overlooked, however, is the access to fishing from bridges. Some states like Florida have recognized the wisdom in providing for a wide fishing walkway on bridges crossing fishable waters. Except in marked navigation channels fishing should be allowed from Minnesota bridges. Older anglers and visiting fishermen could make use of such facilities and it would encourage new business as well as making some of the best fishing spots available to the casual, and economically important, fisherman.

You don't have to stay at a plush resort or motel if your family prefers to camp out. A dollar sticker will get you into all and any of Minnesota's state parks, many of them on good fishing lakes. However, if launching fees and camping charges in addition to the dollar permit discourage you, or you prefer a more natural wilderness setting, you can have that too. Campers who use the delightful national forest campsites, which have no bothersome caretakers nor modern conveniences which most campers prefer to do without, might find them much more fun. There are several of these primitive camps in the north and north central parts of Minnesota.

In Minnesota you can pick tourist accommodations according to your pocket book. The amount of cabbage you spend for a roof over your head won't necessarily mean good fishing. Accommodations by the week range from $45.00 to $80.00, or higher, depending on how plush a layout you require. This includes a boat in most cases, swimming privileges and inside plumbing in well-furnished cottages. Many of these places have guide service available for around $12.00 per day. For the fishermen that's dropped a pile of money for tackle, traveling expenses and a place to stay, a day with a good guide is a sensible investment. I've been on lakes where no one caught fish except those who were either with a guide or who had learned the hot spots from someone else.

Launches like this one on Mille Lacs will take you out on the big lake for a few dollars per passenger.

The fisherman who is crossing Minnesota on his way west or north will often find it hard to resist all the fishable water he sees along the way and he will quite often break down and spend a few bucks for a license and go fishing. You can rent a good boat for as little as $1.00 a day or two bits an hour if you get the urge to wet a line for a few hours. Maximum boat rental is never over $2.50 per day. Bait will cost from 35c a dozen for good crappie minnows to 20 cents each for big sucker minnows used for catching muskies and northern pike.

You can't avoid it—if you want to go fishing anywhere these days you have to have license. But this is a fairly inexpensive item—the lowest priced nonresident ticket in the midwest. The four dollars you pay for a fishing license is the biggest fishing bargain you can get anywhere! Many states charge that much for a ten-day permit. If you're a resident, you can buy either an individual angling license for $1.50 or a combination, man and wife permit for $2.00. Members of your family under sixteen years of age may fish without a license. Members of a non-resident fishing party under sixteen may fish without a license also provided they are accompanied by a licensed parent or legal guardian. Any one in the armed forces who is a resident may fish during a furlough or leave without a license and non-residents in military service officially stationed in Minnesota may fish after procuring a $1.50 resident tag. Citizens of Minnesota receiving Old Age Assistance or who are blind will, upon application, be issued a fishing license without cost.

You are allowed to fish with two lines in boundary waters between the states of Minnesota and Wisconsin, Iowa and South Dakota and two lines are also permitted when taking panfish and rough fish from any waters of the state except trout water. Only one line is allowed, however, for bass, walleyes and other game fish. Three flies may be used while fly-fishing at any time. Plugs and other artificial lures may have more than a single hook. If you seine your own bait, you are allowed to keep for your personal use no more than twelve dozen minnows. Be sure you're not seining them from a designated trout stream, however. Minnows don't keep too well in warm weather so it's a good idea not to take more than you can use. Limits on game fish change from time to time. So before you go fishing, pick up a copy of the synopsis of fishing laws. You can get them where you buy your license or write to the Division of Game and Fish, Minnesota Department of Conservation, State Office Building, St. Paul.

Minnesota is fully aware at last of the boundless recreational value of her lakes and rivers. Fishing here is big business—a multi-million dollar industry! Therefore, fishing will continue to get a lot of attention and present efforts to keep abreast of latest management practices will be stepped up.

If you have never visited Minnesota before, you could become confused with so much fishing water at your command. Minnesota has over 2,000,000 acres of water not counting the maze of border lakes and Lake Superior. If you have an idea of the kind of fishing you prefer and you want specific information on just where to start, drop a line to Tourist Information, State Office Building, St. Paul. They can help you get started and once on your way the momentum of fishing fun will keep you going. Whether you spend a day on a launch deep trolling for lakers out of Hovland or cast for bigmouth bass in the Crow Wing chain, from a rowboat, you'll get the feeling that you're fishing the best waters in the country. You're right!

Minnesota, long called the land of 10,000 lakes, has been selling itself short. On the basis of national standardization of lake sizes, Minnesota has OVER 16,000 lakes, more than any other two inland states combined!

While exploring this water wonderland I hope your casting hours will be fruitful. And it's my wish that this book will give you added insight and confidence as you fish in the top fresh-water fishing state in the country. And here's hoping you'll run into a lunker now and then that will leave you talking to yourself.

Typical winter ice fishing contest. Such get-togethers attract hundreds of winter anglers each year.

Appendix

Sport Fishes of Minnesota

This listing gives the standard common names of Minnesota sport fishes taken from a list formulated jointly by the Outdoor Writers Association of America and the American Fisheries Society, as well as denoting local names that might otherwise confuse anglers unfamiliar with them. For instance, Northern Pike are known in some sections of the state as northerns while anglers in another area may call them pickerel or jacks. Scientific names have been avoided since they are seldom or never used by practicing fishermen. While record weights listed are accurate so far as known, there have been no official state records kept. These weights are taken from prominent state fishing derbies and represent the most complete unofficial catch record currently available.

Range of fish refers to general distribution. For example, some lakes will not have bass or bluegills even though these fish are found in all sections of Minnesota.

Because Minnesota is almost completely bounded by water on three sides, seasons and limits are set co-operatively by Minnesota and the adjoining states or provinces of Canada. Seasons and limits for Ontario-Minnesota border water, for example, are always different from those for Minnesota-South Dakota boundary waters.

NAME	MINN. RECORD	RANGE	SEASON*	ABUNDANCE	BEST PLACES TO FIND THEM
Muskellunge, Musky	58 lbs.	North Central	May-Feb.	Uncommon	Wabado, Little Boy, Leech Lakes. Big Fork River, Mississippi R. above Anoka.
Northern Pike, Northern, Pickerel, Snake, Jackfish	41 lbs.	Statewide	May-Feb.	Abundant	Over weedbeds in all northcentral waters except trout water. Lake of the Woods, Lac La Croix, Red Lake, Lake Vermillion, Leech Lake.
Largemouth Bass, Black Bass	10 lbs.	Statewide	June-Feb.	Very Common	Annandale, Detroit Lakes, Alexandria areas. Inshore waters among pads and rushes.
Northern Smallmouth Bass, Gray Bass	8 lbs.	Scattered Lakes and Rivers	June-Feb.	Fairly Common	Rocky lakes. Basswood, Hungry Jack, White Bear, Miltona, St. Croix, Mississippi and Rum Rivers. Eddies, pools and streammouths.
Walleye, Walleyed Pike, Pike	18½ lbs.	Statewide	May-Mar.†	Abundant	Bars and mud flats of cold, clear lakes. Mille Lacs, Big Winnie, Leech, Lake of the Woods, also smaller deep lakes and most rivers. Especially Mississippi, Minnesota and St. Croix.
Sauger, Sand Pike	None	Spotty	May-Mar.†	Uncommon	Found with walleyes.
White Bass, Silver Bass, Silver	5 lbs.	Southeast	Continuous	Abundant in Range	Mississippi R. below St. Paul, St. Croix R. and Minnesota R. Some lakes south of Twin Cities.

NAME	MINN. RECORD	RANGE	SEASON*	ABUNDANCE	BEST PLACES TO FIND THEM
Lake Trout,*** Laker, Landlocked Salmon, Salmon Trout	42 lbs.	Northeast and Northcentral	Jan-Sept.	Common in Range	Lake Superior. Deep lakes of Cook, St. Louis and Itasca counties. Mouth of Superior streams.
Steelhead Trout, Coaster	13½ lbs.	Lake Superior Watershed	April-Oct.	Common in Range	Lake Superior streams. The Knife, Sucker, Lester, Stewart, Split Rock river.
Grayling, Montana Grayling	None	A Few Small Lakes	Special Season	Rare	Lakes opened only by commissioners order. Twin Lakes, Lake County. Species introduced from Saskatchawan and Montana in 1955.
Eastern Brook Trout, Speckled Trout, Brookie, Speck or Native	4 lbs.	N.E. and Central Counties	May-Sept.	Fairly Common	Small lakes, streams and beaver ponds in Gunflint Trail and Two Harbors areas. Streams of Park Rapids and Sandstone regions.
Brown Trout, Brown, German Brown	14 lbs.	Scattered Statewide	May-Sept.	Quite Common	Whitewater, Straight and Blackhoof Rivers. A few small lakes and streams. Lake Superior stream mouths.
Rainbow Trout, 'Bow	8½ lbs.	N.E., Central and S.E. Counties	May-Sept.	Common	Ram, Trout, Echo, Grindstone Lakes. Streams near Red Wing.
Rock Bass	None	Statewide	May-Feb.	Abundant	Around docks, pilings and rushes in many lakes and rivers in the state.
Bluegill, Sunnie, Sunfish	3 lbs.	Statewide	Continuous	Over Abundant	Almost any lake, out from weedbeds in 6 to 25 feet deep. Lakes in Park Rapids, Detroit Lakes area.

NAME	MINN. RECORD	RANGE	SEASON*	ABUNDANCE	BEST PLACES TO FIND THEM
Crappie, (Black and White)	5 lbs.	Statewide	Continuous	Over Abundant	Pelican, Miltona, Dead and Crane Lakes. Outside of weed-beds and near drop offs. At the edge of rushes and over weed-beds.
Channel Catfish, Cat, Fiddler	None	Scattered Rivers	May-Feb.	Common in Range	St. Croix, Minnesota, St. Louis and Mississippi Rivers. Lake Pokegama and Cross lakes near Pine City. Embarrass, Esquaga-ma and Ceder Lake near Vir-ginia.
Shovelhead Catfish, Mississippi Bullhead, Mud Cat	62 lbs.	Scattered Rivers	May-Feb.	Common in Range	Approximately same range as channel cat.
Bullhead	None	Statewide	Continuous	Over Abundant	Farm ponds, muddy streams and rivers and most lakes.
Hackleback** Sturgeon, Shovelnose or Sand Sturgeon	236	St. Croix and Miss. drainage	May-Oct.	Fairly Common	St. Croix, Minnesota, Mississippi and St. Louis Rivers. Pokegama and Cross Lakes, near Pine City.
Tullibee, Herring, Cisco	10	Northhalf	Continuous	Over Abundant	Feeding on surface in bays, Keb-atogama, Gunflint Lakes.

*Seasons are subject to legislative changes.
**Sturgeon legal only in St. Croix drainage.
***Separate trout regulations for Lake Superior.
†Walleyes seasons differ on various state boundaries. See annual synopsis of fishing laws issued by the Minn. department of conservation.

Minnesota largemouth takes to the air; bass are underfished in most Minnesota lakes.

FISHING MAP FOR MINNESOTA

To locate fish species you prefer simply refer to list of keyed species below and locate number on fishing map. Towns listed below are keyed to the latest official highway map of Minnesota to help anglers locate fishing areas described on this map—See pp. 310-311.

1. Muskelleunge
2. Northern Pike
3. Largemouth Bass
4. Smallmouth Bass
5. Walleye
6. Sauger
7. White or Silver Bass
8. Lake Trout
9. Steelhead
10. Rainbow Trout
11. Grayling
12. Brook Trout
13. Brown Trout
14. Rock Bass
15. Bluegills
16. Crappies
17. Catfish
18. Bullhead
19. Sturgeon (hackleback)
20. Perch
21. Tullibees and Whitefish
22. Carp

Towns

Virginia	M7
Hallock	B2
Baudette	G3
International Falls	K3
Ely	N5
Grand Marais	R6
Two Harbors	O9
Duluth	N10
Grand Rapids	J7
Bemidji	F7
Park Rapids	F9
Detroit Lakes	D9
Wheaton	B13
Montevideo	D16
Windom	E19
Alexandria	E12
Willmar	F15
Mankato	H18
Faribault	K18
Rochester	M19
Minneapolis	K15
St. Paul	K15
Red Wing	M17
St. Cloud	H13
Sandstone	L12
Brainerd	H11

Lakes and Rivers Key

Red Lake	F5
Mille Lacs	J11
Lake of the Woods	F2
Leech	G8
Winnibigoshish	H7
Cass	H7
Lake Itasca	E8
Rainy	L3
Vermilion	M6
Dead, Ottertail	D11
Minnetonka	J16
Saganaga	P5
Miltona	E13
Traverse	B13
Big Stone	B14
Snowbank	O5
Turtle Lake	F7
Clearwater	Q5
Pelican	L5
Basswood	O5
Hungry Jack	Q5
Mellissa	D9
Kabetogama	K4
Big Sandy	K10
Crane	M4
Farm Island	J11
Rush	L13
Shetec	D18
Waconia	J16
Green	F15
Geneva	E12
L'Homme Dieu	E12
Clearwater	H14
Crow Wing Chain	F9
Wabado	H9
Trout Lake	R6
Grindstone	K11
Lac La Croix	N4
Whitewater R.	N18
Blackhoof R.	M10
Straight R.	F9
Manitou R.	P7
Big Fork R.	J5
Rum R.	K14
Rainy R.	J3
Bois de Sioux R.	B12
St. Louis R.	N10
Pigeon R.	S5
St. Croix R.	L16-M12
Knife R.	N8

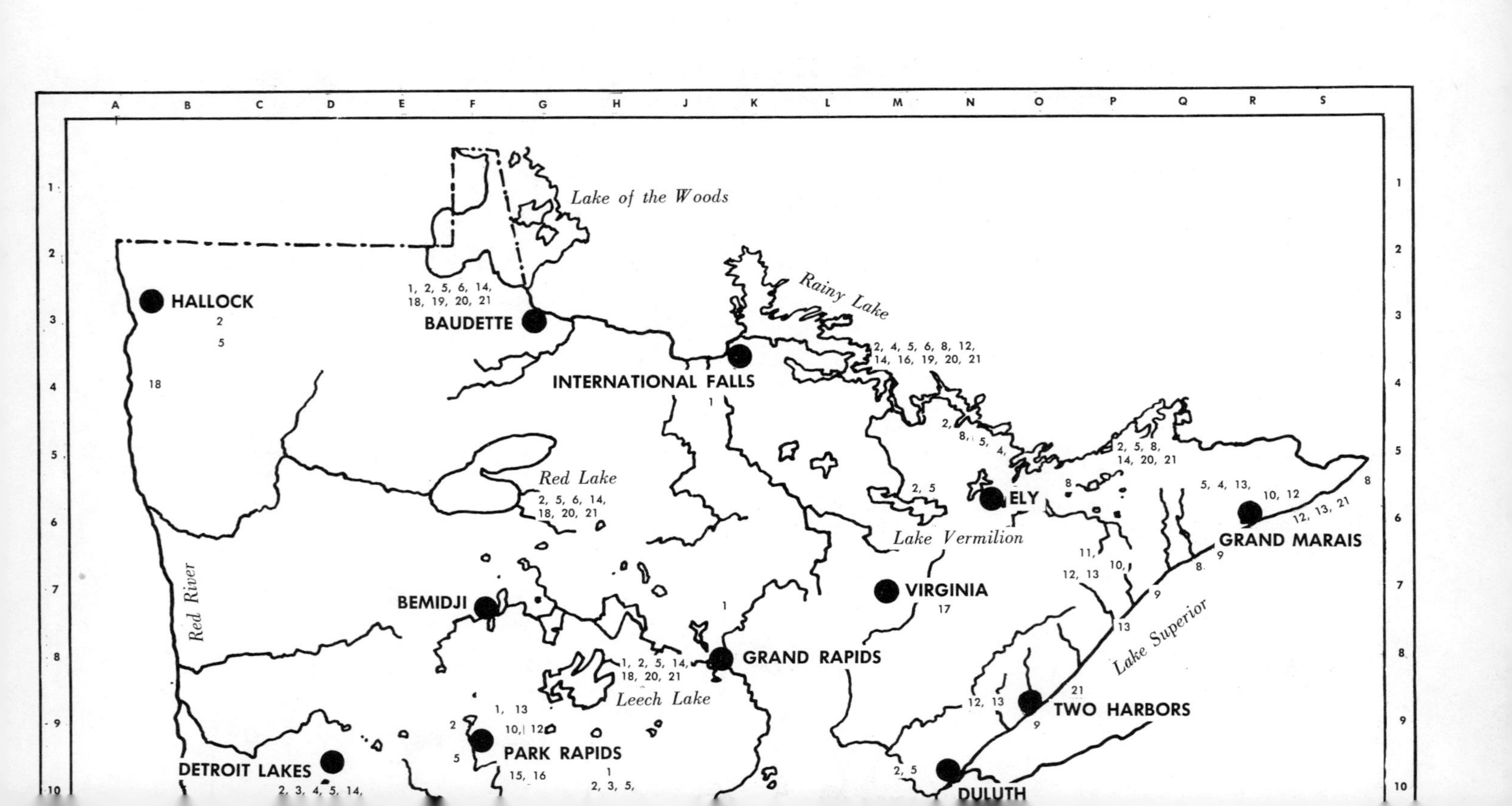
A
B
C
D
E
F
G
H
J
K
L
M
N
O
P
Q
R
S
1
2
3
4
5
6
7
8
9
10
Lake of the Woods
HALLOCK
2
5
18
1, 2, 5, 6, 14,
18, 19, 20, 21
BAUDETTE
Rainy Lake
INTERNATIONAL FALLS
1
2, 4, 5, 6, 8, 12,
14, 16, 19, 20, 21
Red Lake
2, 5, 6, 14,
18, 20, 21
2, 8, 5, 4,
2, 5, 8,
14, 20, 21
2, 5
ELY
8
5, 4, 13,
10, 12
12, 13, 21
8
GRAND MARAIS
Lake Vermilion
11,
12, 13
10,
8
9
Red River
BEMIDJI
1
VIRGINIA
17
9
13
Lake Superior
1, 2, 5, 14,
18, 20, 21
GRAND RAPIDS
Leech Lake
21
12, 13
TWO HARBORS
9
1, 13
2
10, 12
PARK RAPIDS
5
15, 16
1
2, 3, 5,
DETROIT LAKES
2, 3, 4, 5, 14,
2, 5
DULUTH

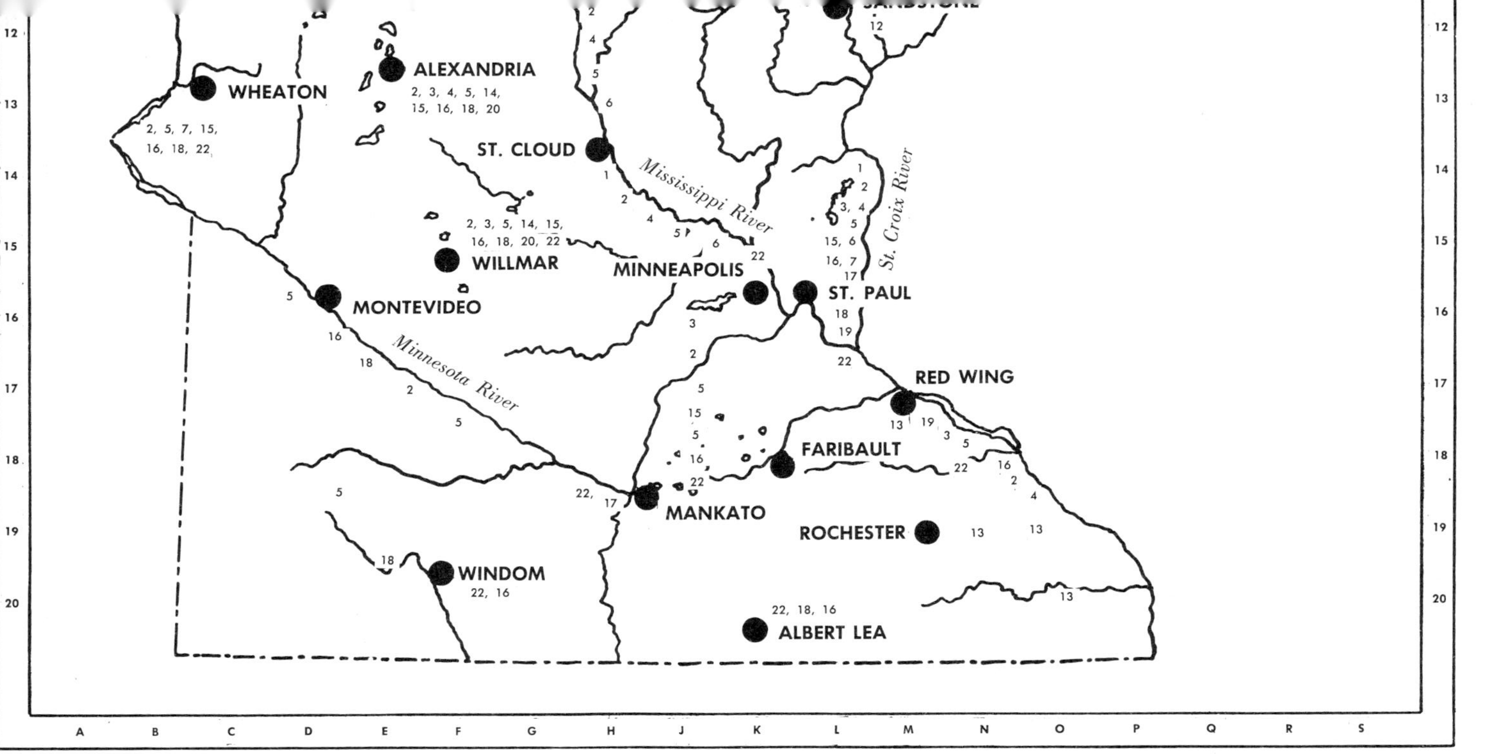

FISHING MAP OF MINNESOTA

See key on page 309

PHOTO CREDITS

Bronson Reel Co.,
Division of Higbie Mfg. Co.
Bronson, Mich.

Creek Chub Bait Co.
Garrett, Ind.

National Expert Bait Co.
Minneapolis, Minn.

John Dobie,
Minnesota Dept. of Conservation

Umpco Corporation
1717 - 4th Ave. South
Minneapolis, Minn.

Louis Johnson Company
1547 Deerfield Rd.
Highland Park, Ill.

Kautzky Lazy Ike Co.
Fort Dodge, Iowa

R-Jay Industries, Inc.
Box 204
Cayahoga Falls, O.

Wallster Tackle Co.
5343 Diversey Ave.
Chicago 39, Ill.

South Bend Tackle Co.
South Bend, Ind.

James Heddon's Sons
Dowagiac, Mich.

The Author

Bureau of Business Development

Irwin Norling,
Bloomington Sun

Langley Corporation
310 Euclid Ave.
San Diego 14, Calif.

Sila-flex
1919 Placentia Ave.
Costa Mesa, Calif.

Ted Williams Co., Inc.
4026 N.W. 25th St.
Miami 48, Fla.

Thommen, Inc.
28 E. 22nd St.
New York 10, N. Y.

Courtland Lure Co., Inc.
Courtland, N. Y.

Garcia Corporation
368 Fourth Ave.
New York 10, N. Y.

Seneca Tackle Co., Inc.
56 Cooper Square
New York 3, N. Y.

Jim Peterson,
Minneapolis Tribune

Aluma Craft Boat Co.
1515 Central Ave.
Minneapolis, Minn.

Continental Arms Corporation
New York, N. Y.

Minnesota Dept. of Conservation

Alan Maxson

Western Fishing Line Co.,
Glendale 4, Calif.

Index